Donald Trump and the Branding of the American Presidency

Kenneth M. Cosgrove

Donald Trump and the Branding of the American Presidency

The President of Segments

palgrave
macmillan

Kenneth M. Cosgrove
Department of Government
Suffolk University
Boston, MA, USA

ISBN 978-3-030-30495-9   ISBN 978-3-030-30496-6   (eBook)
https://doi.org/10.1007/978-3-030-30496-6

Cover image: © Harvey Loake

This Palgrave Pivot imprint is published by the registered company Springer Nature
Switzerland AG
The registered company address is: Gewerbestrasse 11, 6330 Cham, Switzerland

For LaDonna, Jerry, Amy and Paul Sullivan.

Acknowledgments

This project was pushed along by several different people. Most notably Michelle Chen who thought this was an excellent fit for Palgrave-MacMillan. As in wouldn't take no for an answer. Thank you, Michelle. Richard Nimijean (Carlton University Ottawa, Ontario, Canada) was someone who I bounced a lot of ideas off and was a constant judge of what worked and what I should move on from. Elizabeth Eves likewise was someone who had an excellent sense of what made sense, what did not and had a quite distinct perspective on Trump and my project than did I. This was most useful. Darren Lilkiker, Utta Russmann, Milos Gregor, and Otto Eibl were excellent co-panelists who gave me things to think about regarding this project. The same is true of Jennifer Lees-Marshment, Phil Harris, Jaime Gilles, Vincent Raynauld, Andre Turcotte, Alex Marland, and Edward Elder.

Suffolk University funded the travel to three conferences in which research that formed the genesis of the idea was honed. Suffolk students in the American Presidency class during the Fall of 2018 learned more about Donald Trump than they ever wanted to, but their feedback made the idea behind this manuscript so much clearer. Parts of this work have been presented in Cardiff, Wales, Montreal, Quebec, Philadelphia, PA, Auckland, NZ, and in Boston, MA.

The staff at the Hampton Falls, NH Free Library both helped me locate materials and let me bounce ideas off them. Thank you.

Erin Cosgrove had to live with this as much as I did. I got to write about it, and she got something like a news program entitled "Today in Trump" in which she had to listen to what her husband found out today and why it mattered. She made several timely suggestions that improved the quality of the work. Our companion animals helped a lot. Our cat, Joise, stationed herself on my desk behind my monitor while I was writing every day but left in the end. Fionn Mac Cumhail came and very much lived up to his name. Our dogs Tony, Reddzo, Declan, Eoin, Kiera, Maire, Kayla, and Nolan were a constant source of peaceful reassurance and contentment. And lastly my horses, Officer Toby and Mr. Chocolate were like a regular vacation from this because there is one thing you can think about but staying on the trail, the horse and right-side up while riding. Ronald Reagan once famously said "there's nothing better for the inside of a man than the outside of a horse." And he was right.

Hampton Falls New Hampshire   Ken Cosgrove

INTRODUCTION

This book argues that the way in which Donald Trump used branding, social media, targeting, and customer data to win show how one marketer with an excellent brand story and understanding of social media took on the political establishment, won and turned American politics on its ear in the process. Trump used sticky branding to build a brand that connected with the target audience and seemed to be everywhere, all the time. He is an accomplished marketer and brand builder who has sold everything from real estate to wine and a celebrity who has starred in his own reality tv show as well as appearing as himself on the World Wrestling Entertainment broadcasts. Trump built a political brand and excelled at the use of social media to build a sticky, omnipresent brand, something that his predecessor Barack Obama did not do. Trump is a marketer first and a politician second. He is always selling but his proclivity to improvise rather than following rules and norms is significantly different than what Americans had seen from recent Presidents. He is not somebody who has tried to unite the country but has instead focused relentlessly on delivering on his brand promises and keeping his customers happy. This book will look at the ways in which Donald Trump built a sticky brand and pursued brand omnipresence to win the Presidency and then try to govern in the social media age. We've never had a President like him before but the techniques that he used to win could work for a wide variety of candidates thus Donald Trump's election doesn't signal the end of our democracy as his critics have claimed, it really signals that the dominance of elite gatekeepers have waned and the chance for more ideological diversity in the political system has appeared. The Trump era will be remembered as a time in which branding, targeting, segmentation, and political marketing were dominant meaning social consensus and unity proved to be elusive thus showing the limits of political marketing to achieve domestic tranquility.

CONTENTS

CHAPTER 1

Donald Trump and the Branding of the American Presidency

Abstract This introduces the book Donald Trump and the Branding of the American Presidency. It discusses the Trump brand value proposition, targeted audiences, the types of segmentation Trump has used during his campaign and in office, and introduces the concepts of brand omnipresence and sticky branding. Donald Trump represents something different in American politics: a politician who developed a multi-platform commercial and celebrity brand and then applied it to politics. Trump shows how a modern political branding and marketing campaign works in the social media age and how to achieve brand omnipresence. By generating continual attention brand omnipresence can be achieved even in an overcrowded political marketplace. Trump gained a tactical advantage because most of his contemporaries in both parties were not using branding in a fashion similar to the way in which Trump was using it.

Keyword Donald Trump · Hillary Clinton · Ronald Reagan · Republican Party · Presidency · Branding · Presidential Election of 2016 · Presidential Election of 2020 · Political branding

© The Author(s), under exclusive license to Springer Nature Switzerland AG 2022
K. M. Cosgrove, *Donald Trump and the Branding of the American Presidency*, https://doi.org/10.1007/978-3-030-30496-6_1

Donald Trump's election and administration showed the strengths of branding.

The Trump era shows the importance of keeping brand promises. Trump rode emotional, personal, and sticky branding to electoral success in 2016. Trump's strategy of being everywhere, all the time kept audiences across the political spectrum engaged. The Trump era showed how a political brand can become omnipresent and build deep loyalty using direct-to-consumer marketing. The Trump campaign succeeded in 2016 by aiming its brand at specific audiences in just the right number of places. President Trump continued marketing by remaining active on Twitter, by appearing in targeted conservative media, and by regularly engaging with the White House Press Corps. These activities helped make the Trump brand omnipresent and remind voters that brand promises made by candidate Trump were being kept by President Trump. While Trump lost in 2020, he did so despite attracting more votes than he had gotten in 2016. This is evidence that the brand strategy Trump adopted builds deep loyalty and elevated levels of customer engagement.

Political branding offers considerable benefits to politicians who use it effectively but considerable risk to those who do not. Trump ran on the promise of being a strong manager and promised meaningful systemic change yet when the worst public health crisis in a century appeared and set off a series of other crises, Trump's management abilities did not seem to live up to his brand promise. The brand's potency can vary by the user's strategic situation, customer experiences with the branded products, and market conditions. Donald Trump's brand was very potent in 2016. He ran in an open-seat election held at the end of eight years of Democratic control of the White House. He faced an opponent in Hillary Clinton whom Republicans had spent years branding negatively. His brand was less potent in 2020 because he was running as an incumbent meaning the voters had tried the Trump political product once and now, he was trying to get them to buy it again. Incumbent President Trump now had a record to defend and was charged with leading the country's response to COVID. He was faced with a different kind of candidate in Joe Biden than he had faced in Hillary Clinton. Biden could present himself as a working-class hero in a way Hillary Clinton could not have and Biden could stress his empathetic personal traits as a contrast to Donald Trump's more acerbic persona. Despite changed strategic and market conditions, Trump stuck to his core brand, brand emotions, and products. That it almost worked shows the upside of political branding and that he lost shows its downsides. Trump generated significant repeat business and attracted new customers to the party in a time of economic and social upheaval. Trump's 2020 difficulties show how important it is for political brands to be nimble and reposition in response to the emergence of a crisis that changes customer concerns. The world changed in the Spring of 2020, but Donald Trump did not. Had he made a few emotive and substantive adjustments, he well might have won reelection.

The Trump brand attracted new constituencies to the GOP but also repelled many of its established supporters. Trump alienated a host of public figures, public and private institutions and keep his political opponents engaged throughout his time on the national stage. Trump lost voters that Republicans often win in bigger numbers than the working-class supporters he attracted. He faced unstinting opposition from a host of prominent institutions and individuals, many of which had traditionally been apolitical or less overtly political and kept his opponents engaged throughout his term. This produced a continual sense of disquiet and, eventually, exhaustion in the electorate. It meant that his opponents were willing to turn to a candidate who was much older and perceived to be more moderate than they to defeat him, Joe Biden.

The Trump era shows that branding, brand style, segmentation, and policy choices combine to shape the behavior and public perceptions of a Presidency. This period shows how branding turns complex policy discussions into emotional stories around which political identities are built. This era shows that the marketing imperative of building a brand in which promises made must be kept and the product must work as advertised poses significant problems for the functioning of the political system and the health of the democracy. The Trump experience further shows that the pursuit of brand omnipresence comes with the downside risk that the audience might grow tired of the brand. The Trump experience shows that the ethics of the marketer matter a great deal. An emotive sticky brand that is omnipresent when combined with segmented media might lead to things like a candidate's supporters refusing to accept the legitimate outcome of an election or, as we saw, storming the US Capitol on behalf of their candidate.

The branding imperative encourages partisan polarization in government and in the country. Branding's incentives make policymaking through the traditional process based on compromise and consensus building more difficult. The brand's imperatives have ushered in an era in which policy has come to be made through executive orders, agency rulemaking processes, interesting legislative devices like reconciliation, and judicial rulings. Americans have learned more about the rules of the Senate filibuster and legislative process in general than prior generations had felt the need to know because of the imperative parties have to stand by their brands. All this results from the need for brand promises made to be kept for the marketer to keep credibility with their customers. Trump's brand promises differentiated from his primary challengers in 2016, from other Republicans, and from the Washington Establishment during his time on the national stage. His branding made him stand out in a crowded marketplace, built deep customer loyalty and also made both him and his opponents dig in thus precluding compromise and consensus policies. His frequent out-of-the-mainstream statements were part of his brand. Trump said and did things that positioned him as being a disruptive insurgent in Washington and in a country that he argued, did too many things for elites but too little for average Americans. He sold himself as an outsider who entered politics to save the country from an incestuous elite that had led it to the brink of ruin. The relentless opposition he faced from Democrats and some Republicans, some federal bureaucrats and judges, academics, and other members of the elite helped Trump prove the truth in his brand promise to his target audiences even if a lot of the rest of the country found them to be unconvincing.

Donald Trump is a branded individual because of his long years of commercial and celebrity activity. He was vulnerable to attacks because he was proposing meaningful change to a considerable number of policies that many people supported, because they threatened a liberal policy regime and narrative history that no Republican had really made much of a dent in and because Trump's brand values lacked empathy and compassion. President Trump was easy to attack because of his own traits and behaviors because he had no experience in elective office at any level never mind the national level meaning he had a long learning curve once in office about the ways in which Washington worked and what the public expected of a President. His decisions and behavior were things that more seasoned politicians would have either engaged in privately or not at all. His frequent direct-to-consumer communication, his use of social media, and his sparring with journalists and political opponents reduced the majesty of the Presidency but kept himself in the public eye thus achieving brand omnipresence. Other administrations might have sought to communicate directly with the public via radio or television, shaped the media narrative, or dominated news cycles.

This country had never had a President who was always trying to sell and close or whose thoughts were as accessible to the average citizen, while he was in the White House, before Donald Trump arrived there. Building the Trump brand depended on this kind of omnipresence regardless of what impact this had on the institution of the Presidency. Trump's strategy of building an omnipresent, sticky, brand meant that he had to be at the center of everything all the time. The strategy was a social media age attempt to make Trump stand out in a crowded marketplace, show how brand promises made were being kept and make sure his followers knew what he was up to daily. The result was to deepen the relationship between them and the Trump brand. Trump's supporters loved to hear his thoughts and his examples of how he was trying to deliver. Those who were not his supporters either grew wearier or angrier and more engaged as the Trump era unfolded. Trump did not fit the traditional image of the President and did not always use the full power of the office to promote his Presidency. Instead, he stuck to his personalist, nationalist sticky branding. His failure to adjust did not redound to his benefit when he ran for reelection because, after four years in office, the problems facing the country were his in a way that they had not been when he was a challenger.

Trump stayed true to his brand emotions, sticky brand, and omnipresence strategy during the COVID crisis. In some ways, this was a missed opportunity for him to have built social consensus. Trump's strategy led to him being overexposed, unable to leverage the kinds of marketing opportunities that the Presidency usually offers to its occupant and turned him into the face of a bungled response to a pandemic. Trump inadvertently made himself into the face of the crisis by holding regular press briefings while remaining in the White House. It was a strategy like the one Jimmy Carter had used to manage the Iranian hostage crisis and it produced similarly negative results. Unlike Carter, Trump intended to make himself the center of everything. Thus, a major problem with the omnipresence strategy is that it can depend on events beyond the user's control as happened when COVID appeared in the United States. The American Government would have struggled to respond to COVID because of the structure of the system and the population's values. Structurally, the national government and the President do not have the kinds of power that a lot of Americans think they do or that leaders in more unitary systems of government really have. Trump could not have taken some of the actions that were being urged on him like implementing a universal mask mandate and a nationwide lockdown because America's federalist system limited his ability to do so but his branding said he could do otherwise. His promise of strong, effective management was called into question by his erratic media appearances, by his Administration's decision to defund the White House Office of Pandemic Preparedness, and his seeming lack of understanding that the national government would be well served to cooperate with instead of competing with state governments in managing the crisis. Donald Trump was not responsible for the structure of the US Government, how it can limit Presidential power, or the important powers it reserves to the states. Donald Trump was not the only American President who decided to invest in the military to the exclusion of other priorities like public health infrastructure. Generations of American politicians had defined security in military terms and Trump was stuck with the results during the pandemic. The United States lacked the public health infrastructure to mount the immediate response to COVID-19 that countries that had recent severe experiences with viruses could mount. The political system's structure made it impossible to mount the kind of response that a unitary system like the United Kingdom or New Zealand could mount. Instead, he could do some things, governors could do others and Trump's interest in coordinating with any of them seemed to vary over time. Trump did not have the resources or the system that would have allowed him to resolve the pandemic himself, but his branding put him squarely at the center of it meaning that it set him up to fail. Donald Trump's omnipresent sticky branding strategy helped him get attention as an insurgent candidate. Once in office, he and the brand strategy ran headlong into the symbolic realities of holding the office of President and the substantive constraints that exist on that office's power.[1]

These strategies can build loyalty for the politician's brand with the target audience and awareness of it among potential targets. They also are a way to keep the brand at the center of a crowded marketplace and show progress on a regular basis. The way in which Trump used them meant that they built deep loyalty in a few segments not broad social consensus. Despite being impeached twice, refusing to accept the results of the 2020 election, likely costing the GOP a Senate majority by telling his supporters in Georgia that the election process was so corrupt that their votes wouldn't count in two post-2020 general election runoff contests, running a marketing campaign for weeks in advance of and speaking at a rally that likely contributed to civil unrest on January 6, 2021, then not attending the inauguration of his successor, Donald Trump's brand is so strong that he is considered a contender to run again in 2024 or play a major role in deciding who will be the GOP standard bearer in that contest and many Republicans consider the Biden Presidency to be illegitimate because of Trump's baseless electoral fraud claims. This is a testament to the power of the techniques that he used to build his political brand.

Despite his marketing and branding chops, Trump had a steep learning curve in the White House. He struggled to organize White House and opted for a lean management approach that, while common in the corporate world, had not really been tried in government before. He had little sense of how to deal with Congress or how to manage the bureaucracy as Schier and Eberly (2017) note. Trump's Administration had been hobbled from the get-go because he left many people who had served in the Obama Administration temporarily in positions of power and they caused him no end of grief. As Trump aide David Bossie put it: "This is the one regret of the president, and I agree with him. That if the president had come in and fired all the Obama holdovers, every single one of them, President Trump's job would be a lot easier to do."[2] He seemed to care more about marketing his brand than governing the country. Beyond his core campaign promises that could be dealt with via executive orders, his Administration outsourced a lot of the things to Congress and lobbyists who epitomized the swamp his campaign promised to drain.[3] These tendencies were on full display during the COVID-19 pandemic. While Trump held regular and long news briefings for marketing purposes, the actual American response was outsourced to a task force headed by the Vice-President and state governors.

Like Ronald Reagan, Donald Trump was a marketer in the White House. He emphasized different personal traits and skills than Americans normally expected from Presidents. One of the key traits that Americans should consider in electing a marketer in chief is the brand personality that person brings to the Oval Office. Reagan and Trump had significant policy differences. Reagan was a fiscal conservative while Trump did not seem to care about the national balance sheet. Reagan was a foreign policy globalist while Trump was a nationalist. They shared a view that federal programs benefitted the few at the expense of the many. The difference was that Ronald Reagan was a professed admirer of Franklin Roosevelt and presented his program as a corrective to those of subsequent liberal Democrats. These liberals had spent too much money, raised taxes too much, and gave too much power to the federal government. Trump was running against the entire system and elites in both parties.

Trump and Reagan shared a critique of Democrats yet did so using different brand personalities and emotions. Reagan presented himself as optimistic and forward-looking while Trump presented himself as angry and yearning for a great lost past America. Reagan, whose Make America Great Again, branding Donald Trump directly copied presented himself as the restoration of American values, economics, and strength as Donald Trump tried to do.[4] Further, Ronald Reagan had a more traditional White House media and marketing operation something Donald Trump absolutely eschewed in favor of a more hands-on approach. Reagan was an outsider and an insurgent but was also an experienced politician having governed California and, as a result, had a sense of what could be done in office. Reagan did not overpromise as wildly as Trump did in some key areas like getting Mexico to pay for his wall. Emotively, Reagan's brand values were more optimistic than angry and more humorous than sarcastic. Where Reagan, like Barack Obama, would use humor, a regretful tone, or a sense that nobody in their right mind could argue with his point, Trump bombastically argued that his opponents were stupid, subversive, or both for opposing his ideas. Trump told much more of a charged emotive story than did Reagan because in the age of Trump there is much more environmental noise and a clearer ability to segment the audience than existed in the Reagan years.

Trump differed from Reagan in that he had been directly involved in his marketing and media relations operations. Trump had no experience in office and took pride in speaking his mind. As he told CPAC in 2019, "I'm not on script."[5] The Trump White House was, outside of its first flurries of executive orders, unable to take advantage of the communicative strategies Presidents usually use to build Congressional and public support for their ideas. Instead, it stuck to its core brand and audiences. Trump lacked message discipline around building a theme of the day or week but instead bounced from topic to topic but always selling the Trump brand story. This was a strategy for building brand omnipresence not passing specific legislation or promoting specific policies. Trump's constant activity and pugnacity helped to build brand awareness, omnipresence, and loyalty in the target audiences even if it did not lead to a lot of legislative successes. The emphasis on brand meant it focused on keeping promises, telling emotionally engaging stories, and visually showing people what is being done on their behalf. Omnipresence demands constant motion to generate attention hence the constant flurry of activity to keep up with the relentless pace and noise of the social media world. Trump did so and created an environment in which there was no escaping the Trump brand. The goal of creating omnipresence meant that the Trump brand was everywhere all the time and the country revolved around it. Trump, like Bill Clinton, has an aura of scandal and immoral behavior around him and like the Clintons in office, Trump has pushed forward rather than giving in to critics.[6] Given that Trump saw Clinton as his role model for managing a scandal, it should not be surprising that during the House Impeachment proceedings his Administration fought requests for documents, witnesses, and subpoenas at every turn. Unlike Clinton, there would be no apology for most of his behavior, instead, Trump hit back at his opponents. In the one case he did apologize, Trump launched an effective attack the same weekend against his opponent.

Trump often pointed out the number of brand promises that he kept during his term. At press events and rallies he would stand behind a podium or in front of signage that read "Promises Made, Promises Kept." Trump's focus on appealing to his targeted segments exemplifies the sticky branding strategy that Miller, 2015, outlines. Miller's sticky branding strategy has 12.5 principles including positioning to win by developing a simple, clear selling proposition, a focus on niche markets in which the marketer can win over time, being authentically different in terms of the visuals of the brand and the experiences provided by it, brand omnipresence, an emphasis on big goals and bold actions and pride in being able to serve (Miller 2015). Donald Trump's campaigns and administration followed these principles. One place the sticky branding strategy is implemented is in the way in which Trump used language (Adams 2017). Another was in the way he identified underserved audiences in the political marketplace and turned it out including in states that most observers had counted in the pro-Clinton category (Pollack and Schweikart 2017).

Trump, like most marketers, focused on his best customers and still has high approval ratings with them. Trump said and did things that deviated from the civility Americans expect their Presidents to display in the office. As the 2018 midterm election and 2020 Presidential results showed, adopting such a focused strategy has downsides. First, Trump's working-class brand personality only resonates favorably within a few segments. Second, the power of the Trump brand is directly proportional to the situations in which it is placed. Trump and his advisors struggled with how to approach a contest with Bernie Sanders because Sanders is also emotive, talks about issues of concern to average Americans, and has a highly authentic brand persona[7] Sanders, as Adams (2017) notes, used many of the same persuasive and pre-persuasive strategies in his campaigns that Trump employed in his. Trump opined that running against a different candidate, like Michael Bloomberg might be easier: "Frankly, I would rather run against Bloomberg than Bernie Sanders, because Sanders has real followers, whether you like them or not, whether you agree with them or not," Trump said. "I happen to think it's terrible what says. But he has followers."[8] Like Trump, Bernie had built an emotive brand and deep loyalty to it among a sizable number of Americans. Trump's brand might not have been as effective in a direct contest against Sanders because this head-to-head matchup would not have provided the direct contrast between Trump and the establishment that worked so well for him with his target audiences. Trump's analysis is seen through the lens of marketing and the number of customers a given competitor or policy alternative might have and this is in keeping with the way he approached his campaign and administration.[9]

What Trump did not count on was running against a candidate who could pitch working-class voters like Sanders could while appealing to a cross-section of upper-income voters and could credibly claim that he was in no way like Donald Trump: Joe Biden. Biden's campaign message amounted to saying that he was a decent, civil, and empathetic person—the embodiment of the anti-Donald Trump. A case in point is provided by their public approaches to COVID. Biden promised to "follow the science" around the virus, personally wore a mask, downsized his campaign events, and regularly practiced social distancing. Donald Trump did none of these things. Biden's appeal worked because Trump had repelled so many opponents but also because Biden's offering of more empathy and competence fit changed market conditions better than Trump's offering.[10]

Donald Trump was not a unifying figure. A steady drizzle of accusations about his business and personal behavior served to produce a political death of a thousand cuts. Trump was the stationary target and became the subject of a steady stream of opposition attacks that negatively redefine the target's public image.[11] The impact of this constant trickle of negativity is clearly shown in a December 2019 Suffolk University poll that found an eleven point gender gap in terms of Trump's favorability along gender lines with men being much more positive about him than women, a yawning partisan gap of eighty two points in terms of favorability between Democrats and Republicans, a nine-point difference in regional support between Trump's best performing area (the South—the only region in which Trump had a positive ratio of favorable to unfavorable evaluations) and his worst (the Northeast where he was underwater by seventeen points), a stark racial divided with Trump enjoying a slight majority of white support (51 points) while performing in the single digits with African Americans (8 points) and a huge skew toward older audiences with Trump's best performing segment being people in the 50–64-year-old age range (53% favorable) and his worst-performing segment being those between ages 18 and 34 (31% favorable)[12].

The voters knew more about Donald Trump by 2020 than they did in 2016 and they had seen his performance during the pandemic up close and personally because the omnipresence strategy kept Trump on TV regularly for extended periods of time. The voters had a much clearer picture of who he was than they might have had in 2016. Prior to COVID, President Trump often pointed to the findings of the Russia investigation, claimed there was a deep state conspiracy against him, railed against his impeachment, called out jurists with whom he disagreed, and demonized his opponents in both parties and in Congress to explain why there had been so much disquiet during his first term. He crowed about his tax cut policy, the way in which the economy was performing, and the amount of money he spent on a border wall. By 2020, the problems of the country and the world were Trump's meaning that his solutions and results were the central issues of the election. Thus, Trump started 2020 in a more difficult strategic position than he faced as a challenger in many respects. That COVID dramatically changed the political marketplace in a few short weeks did him no favors.

Trump seemed most interested in showing he had kept brand promises on the economy and trying to run for reelection by using media availabilities as surrogate rallies rather than coordinating an Executive Branch response himself. As Brad Parscale noted after the election, Trump could have adopted a more empathetic tone as Americans suffered through 2020 but his tone instead remained constant.[13] Trump ran on his core brand in the Fall campaign. He added in the promise of a miracle vaccine rollout that would end the pandemic quicker than was thought at the time. While the miracle vaccine did appear, it did so after the election. Trump was promising something to the voters they could not see and that many experts thought could not be delivered as fast as it eventually was. The 2020 Biden campaign wisely used Trump's omnipresence strategy against him by practicing the political equivalent of the rope a dope boxing strategy in which it stayed out of the way while Trump flailed away against the crises besetting the country.

In addition to playing up his accomplishments, the Trump campaign tried to make his opponents into the unacceptable alternative just as Barack Obama had done to Mitt Romney.[14] The Democratic primary field was filled with progressive candidates, most of whom were positioned left of the general population on many issues, meaning it looked like Trump would have a lot of material to work with once they finished beating each other up. For example, half of the independent voters at the time thought that the Democrats have gone too far to the left and these are the voters that often decide elections.[15] Trump tried to build fellowship between Biden and the progressives once Biden clinched the Democratic nomination by highlighting what a Biden win would mean for the economy especially around 401 (k) performance, taxes, and spending.

Trump was not afraid to use issues of class, race, and ideology as part of his marketing efforts. He would sometimes use all three at once. For example, during July 2019, he attempted to make four leftist first-term female members of Congress of color into the face of the Democratic Party. By doing this, Trump attempted to differentiate between his nationalistic branding, his traditional values pitch, and his free market economic focus from socialism with a visible minority face. Creating a contrast between Democrats and Republicans around socialism and capitalism plus another between traditional values and liberalism has worked for Republicans for several decades, Trump's injection of race and national origin might have fit with his brand and pleased his core audiences, but it also allowed his opponents to present him as a racist thus raising the discomfort level with him the key swing voters blocks had about him.[16]

The strength of Trump's brand raised questions in both parties about what their products, brands, and target audiences should be. Trump's direct-to-consumer marketing campaign showed how social media has weakened the party as an organization and elite media's ability to screen out candidates and ideas. The weakening of the gatekeepers as the expansion of the diversity of candidates indicates that, far from indicating the death of American democracy, Donald Trump's election indicates its revitalization is underway. Like most of his predecessors, Donald Trump used the media as a foil. He went further by accusing them of being "fake news" instead of simply complaining about their bias against Republicans as his recent predecessors had done. This was an effort to delegitimate the media to clear the field to allow Trump to disseminate an unmediated brand narrative to his customers. Not surprisingly, his media coverage has been negative outside of conservative circles even though he regularly schmoozed with the journalists he complained about.[17] His fights with the media were a way to show that he was keeping his promise of disruption because he was taking on Washington elite journalists himself. They were also key to the omnipresence strategy because the media just could not stop covering him. People might have loved or hated him, but they could not stop watching him. The Trump White House did not run the White House media and marketing operation that Americans have grown accustomed to over the last century. Instead, he was his own unscripted marketing operation meaning that he said and did things that fit his brand well but were not factually accurate. He regularly got into one-on-one fights with journalists. His stories and confrontations were intended to attract attention for his brand and help it to stand out in a crowded, overstimulated, marketplace. Trump's White House media operation was all about keeping attention to his brand and selling its wares. That Trump was impeached was probable given the way in which he sought to change so many things and the way in which he continuously activated his opponents.

Not surprisingly, more ideological, and more intellectually and racially diverse candidates are seeking office and ideas once dismissed out of hand are gaining thoughtful consideration as the gatekeepers have lost some of their control over the nomination and election processes. Trump showed that there are significant numbers of people who feel disengaged from politics and if they can be engaged by a candidate that could be a path to victory. Two examples from the 2018 electoral cycle are Democratic Members of Congress Ayanna Pressley and Alexandria Ocasio-Cortez both of whom similarly targeted intermittent and new voters, used niche media and door knocks to reach them, presented them with emotionally branded appeals, turned them out, and won elections that most observers thought they would have difficulty winning.[18] Bernie Sanders used similar rhetoric in the 2020 Democratic primaries as Sullivan (2020) notes Senator Sanders picks: "his target group, demonizes it, and relentlessly attacks. Sound familiar? Replace billionaires with illegal immigrants and throw in a huge helping of the 'mainstream media is unfair to me,' and you have a perfect match."[19]

Like Trump, these candidates told emotionally engaging stories to specific audiences that might not have been targeted by earlier campaigns. These stories contain attractive propositions that are simple on their face. They present voters with commonsense solutions to national problems. In fact, these solutions would usually be difficult to pass into law and then be complicated to implement as policy or they have other impacts that are not contained in the story. Just as was the case for the Wall in the 2016 Trump campaign, it is easy to float ideas for free college, tax reform, Medicare for all, or a Green New Deal as aspirational stories or brands. It is harder to present them in terms of policies when one must present the total cost, how it is paid for, who pays for it and through what mechanisms, what effects it might have that were not intended, and what kinds of cost control mechanisms will have to be put into place to make them work. All of this was shown by the public reaction to the detailed Medicare for All Plan that Senator Elizabeth Warren floated in the Fall of 2019. It went from being a centerpiece of her campaign in November 2019 to something she barely spoke about by January 2020.[20] Emotional branding tells people a much simpler, clearer story than the murky world of politics and policy ever could. It does so without producing winners or losers and costs or benefits that the actual policymaking process produces. Emotional branding says that a candidate's proposal will be better for most people, someone else will pay for it and there will be no unintended consequences or cost containment mechanisms while the real political world produces a starkly different reality. Candidates can get elected doing what Donald Trump did but unless they are better prepared for life in government and develop an ability to present their brand aspects and policy proposals in a way that produces unity, they will face the same struggles that Donald Trump encountered in office and in seeking reelection.

Trump's success with an emotive omnipresent sticky brand as a challenger and failure as an incumbent show that people might be willing to try something once, but a politically branded product has to deliver like any other product delivers. If it does not, it will not generate repeat business. In 2016, Trump's disruptive branding was effective because he was a challenger offering a break from the status quo. In 2020, Trump represented a status quo that was facing major challenges. Once in office, Trump seldom reached out to any but his loyal customers an approach that as a governing philosophy was not conducive to dealing with Congress, managing the bureaucracy, or producing domestic tranquility. It has worked to retain brand loyalty among his customers but also kept his opponents activated.

Donald Trump hardly followed the dictates that Richard Neustadt outlined in the Presidential Power (1991). He was not always strategic in the use of his power to make the system work. He was quite strategic in a marketing sense about getting in fights with Congress, the bureaucracy, and the media then using these battles as part of his effort to show that brand promises made have been kept and to explain away his Administration's shortcomings. Trump was more akin to being a First Marketer than either the clerk or leader model with which Neustadt analyzed the Presidency. In office, Trump was more of an outsider than an established politician, as Schier and Eberly (2017) note. He made strategic and ethical errors that more experienced politicians would have avoided. As they note, Trump's prior professional career consisted of running a small family-owned business meaning that the size, scope, public and media scrutiny plus the legalities of running that entity differed utterly from running the Executive Branch. To say that Donald Trump had a long learning curve would be an understatement.

Trump's performance in office raised the question of if it is possible for anyone to meet these images and the associated expectations that Americans hold about the Presidency in such a fragmented country. As Suri (2017) notes, Americans have invested increasing amounts of faith in the office of the Presidency to deal with all problems and Presidents have tried to meet their expectations but have often fallen short. Like Barack Obama before him, Trump too had a pen and a phone. Unlike Obama who wanted to use the phone to negotiate with Congress but threatened to use the pen to issue executive orders in case such negotiations failed to bear fruit, Trump used the pen to sign executive orders and then got on his phone to tweet about them as examples of brand promises having been kept. During the Trump years, working with Congress in the way that Presidents traditionally did appear to have been far down his to-do list. Even when his orders were challenged and sometimes blocked by federal courts, this also provided an opportunity for Trump to tweet and generate positive brand impressions among his followers. The weakness of Trump's strategy in a policy sense was obvious when Joe Biden issued a flurry of Executive Orders, undoing most of what Trump had done by fiat, during his first weeks in office.

Donald Trump's election raised questions about who has the standing to govern the country and the relationship of classes to each other that are at least as old as the Industrial Revolution and in some ways as old as the Republic itself. These questions emerged in the twentieth century as the government began to become more specialized in function and as the media set a specific image in the public mind of what a President should be like. The paradigm for this began to be set when the former President of Princeton University, Woodrow Wilson became President, gained speed with the election of Franklin D. Roosevelt but was cemented by the election of John F. Kennedy. Most of the people at the highest levels of American politics and the people covering American politics were products of the same institutions (something C. Wright Mills noted the onset of in his 1956 work, The Power Elite). Trump's election was a challenge to that classes' dominance of government even though Trump himself was a product of an Ivy League institution and was by most accounts, strongly oriented toward hiring Ivy League graduates in his White House. His brand persona and presentation of self are anti-elite right down to his choice of brand heritage: President Andrew Jackson, the first American President who was not born on the East Coast and whose image the Obama Administration had sought to remove from the twenty-dollar bill in favor of freed slave Harriet Tubman.[21] Trump presented himself as a populist, stood up for tradition, and it could be argued white identity, and positioned himself as being different from the Republican and media establishments in one fell swoop.

Donald Trump showed that candidates can present their descriptive traits as part of the brand and that can be used to engage specific subsets of the population. Donald Trump presented himself as a wealthy businessperson and as a working-class guy from Queens. His brand was aimed at working-class audiences, and he spoke in a language that resonated with working-class people. His cultural references and assumptions were those to which older working class and especially older working-class white married people would respond. He presented social institutions in a way that reflected the values of his target audiences. Given that presentation of self has traditionally been a key brand attribute for politicians, it should not be surprising that building a brand with which people can identify is an important undertaking. It should be equally not surprising that the brand can include matters like race, ethnicity, gender, religion, regional origin, or ideological positioning.

Given the significant underrepresentation of working-class people and working-class interests in government that Matthew Carnes (2013) documented, Donald Trump's choice of brand persona, positioning, and issue platform spoke to people who did not see people like them, or their concerns being represented in government. Even though Trump was not actually a working-class person he had sold enough things to working-class people and been around enough of them during his formative years in the real estate business, that he spoke their language, articulated their concerns, and did so in a way that resonated with them. Trump was the second recent Republican to have success pushing a working-class outsider persona: Vice Presidential candidate Sarah Palin showed that such a persona could resonate with many Americans in 2008.[22] Like Palin before him, Trump took on the establishment and was, in turn, mocked by it.[23] Palin has been described by former Fox News anchor Megyn Kelly as: "almost a pre-Trump" who generated unprecedented excitement among Republicans.[24] Palin's turn on the national stage was akin to a test market for Donald Trump because she showed that a more populist persona could resonate with a large audience and that an emphasis on facts might not matter as much as did the ability to tell a good story.[25]

One of the things that disadvantaged Trump in 2020 was the great amount of emphasis media organizations put into fact-checking and the way in which social media companies shifted their terms of service to advantage specific facts over brand narratives. Not surprisingly, some of the people behind these efforts while working for tech companies and social media platforms later ended up working in the Biden Administration.[26] Thus, the fact checks can be seen as an activity intended to shift the public discussion of issues in the direction of specific communicative styles and toward the fashion preferred by particular social classes and occupational categories. As the electorate and communications platforms diversify and as even more detailed databases come online, it will not be a surprise to see more candidates doing what Donald Trump did by adopting brand personas and issuing platforms that appeal to specific communities while pushing others away. The Trump strategy fit the current environment because he built an omnipresent brand and tried to use it in all situations. In an environment in which people are bombarded with too much information every day, Trump's brand strategy made him stand out for years and that is no small accomplishment.

Donald Trump the President was more like a first marketer who identified and tried to serve his best customers rather than a national leader.

Trump held the public's attention but did not build the kind of consensus other Presidents have managed to create because he was so focused on his core audiences. Even during COVID, Donald Trump continually opted to serve his best customers by doing and saying things that would appeal to them instead of seeking common themes and values that would resonate with all Americans as Presidents have historically tried to do during national crises. Donald Trump's successes and struggles show that while it is good to have a market focus and do market research to understand one's customers and how to reach them along with a well-articulated brand story, these things do not produce domestic tranquility or positive results because it takes a selling orientation, understanding the customer and how to reach the said customer, a strong brand story and constant effort to win in the current environment. Trump's 2020 loss provides a cautionary tale about the current moment because the political marketplace can shift quickly and dramatically meaning a marketing campaign that worked in the past might fall short in the present.

Trump focused on building an emotive brand that appealed to his target audiences and received favorable treatment in conservative media outlets.[27] Trump was the first American President to try to govern using an emotive, sticky brand. He saw a market receptive to his wares. Trump, despite his calls for more unity, took advantage of the country's diversity to build a tightly targeted brand that resonated deeply with a few audiences. He and his team worked relentlessly to make that brand omnipresent. While social sorting was an important part of Trump's success, he did not create the current environment in the United States, he just tapped into it.[28] Our national disquiet is being caused by targeted emotive branding and Donald Trump is one of the prime movers in its use.

Trump articulated a sharp vision of what he wanted to accomplish in office. He served as a visible symbol of a lost America to some of his supporters. He spoke to Americans who remember an industrial economy in which a single culture was stressed, a common language was spoken, Christianity was more publicly expressed, and one in which whites were both the dominant and referent group. He speaks to the part of the country that seeks more uniformity than diversity. Trump's brand stressed commonality and a single culture not multiculturalism. Much like Margaret Thatcher's overt statements, Trump's "Make America Safe Again" branding argues we will have order by which he means the police will be respected, traditional cultural institutions like the church will have primacy and gender roles will be respected.[29] The appeal to order was clear in Trump's response to unrest in American cities in the wake of a series of incidents involving African Americans killed by police officers. After several nights of disorder around the White House in June 2020, Trump walked across Lafayette Square to St. John's Church. The Church had suffered some damage in the disorder. Trump stood in front of it holding a bible in an obvious pitch to two of his target audiences: people concerned about order and his religious base. Trump's branding argued that globally America should flex its muscles while acting in its own interest. Trump's vision of immigration was more based on the need for economic development rather than humanitarian relief or refugee admissions. Further, Trump latched onto the idea that speaking English is important. As Peter Beinart has argued Trump figured out that a lot of people wanted more emphasis on the common cultural elements that make a nation including speaking English.[30]

Trump spoke in cultural terms to working-class voters in a way that the Democrats did not during the Obama years. Trump told his audiences a story in which the college-educated urbane elite internationalists looked down on them and their country. He tapped into cultural angst about race and ethnicity, the way the economy had changed to advantage intellectual over physical work and the nation's role in the world that existed in the country. In part, he accomplished this by using one of the standard themes of American politics: the political leader seeking to help the virtuous everyday people, who do most of the country's difficult and dirty jobs, take their country back from an elite that had sold them out. He stressed the theme that the forgotten men and women who fought the nation's battles were mostly drawn from the working class and from communities that had not benefitted from neo-liberalism as elites had. These patriotic Americans were sent off to war and then were abandoned in their time of need by an uncaring government bureaucracy: the Veterans Administration. In this tale, their sacrifice was unshared or rewarded, their arduous work was taken for granted and their culture was devalued. Trump tapped into their sense that they, their culture, and their country were under attack from elites promoting the values of another America. Trump's brand story fell on the conservative side of the culture wars by arguing for order, tradition, nationalism, patriotism, the value of work, and respect for authority. While Trump might not have been anything of these things personally, he told a memorable story that positioned him as the defender of these values and people faced with a liberal onslaught.

While Trump played a working-class guy in his branding, his policies were closer to those that the Republican Party has sold since the Reagan years than they were anything new. Trump's policies, management style, and personality played differently when he was an incumbent versus when he was a challenger. As an incumbent, he was responsible for the problems facing the country and the results that his Administration had produced. In seeking reelection, Trump had to defend a record that people were familiar with meaning that he had to do more than simply attack the elite status quo that he had attacked as a challenger. The problems of the country and the world were his in 2020 meaning his solutions and their results were things to be defended. He had a tougher sales job as an incumbent than he had as an insurgent challenger. The Trump campaign and administration tried to make his opponents into the unacceptable alternatives into which Barack Obama had turned Mitt Romney Trump had a lot to work with given that about half of the independent voters thought the Democrats have gone too far to the left and these are the voters that often decide elections.[12] He pointed to the findings of the Russia investigation, claimed that his impeachment was a fake, and slammed obstructionist Obama judges and disloyal Republicans and Democrats sitting in a do-nothing Congress to explain the blemishes on his record until COVID came along. Trump's performance during COVID was devastating for his brand story and it raised questions about how well his product offering worked. Joe Biden, not being perceived as a wild-eyed liberal and with a long record of competent public service was ideally positioned to give Trump a run for his money in 2020.

Trump's 2016 victory, his Administration, and the 2020 campaign scrambled the partisan landscape. Both parties have had to rethink what their products are, who their target audiences should be and what their brands should represent. If Trump challenged the establishment Republicans then the Bernie Sanders campaigns in 2016 and 2020, as well as Michael Bloomberg's 2020 campaign, challenged the establishment Democrats in two ways. First, Sanders' campaigns raise the question of who should be in the party and what its policies should be given that Sanders is a self-described Democratic socialist. Second, Bloomberg tried to use marketing and branding to run an entire campaign something that Donald Trump succeeded at in 2016. The difference was that Trump used the branding strategies described herein to succeed while Bloomberg did not and failed.

Trump's support raised questions about why people vote as they do and raised the possibility that, what Norris and Inglehart (2019) describe is driving contemporary American political behavior. It is possible that post-materialist and identity issues have surpassed economic issues as the most important thing for many voters. For these authors, Trump's emphasis on restoring traditional values (and some would argue traditional racial and cultural alignments) put him on the authoritarian side of a post-materialist values split that positioned him differently from most of his opponents in both parties who were more libertarian on these matters. Most of the things Trump said had been standard GOP talking points in decades past. Trump's overt class message was straight out of the 1970s when and Republicans regularly talked about "limousine liberals" happy to force people to do things that they did not have to do themselves and oblivious to the cost impact their regulations had on small businesses and the economy because they have never run a business themselves and a complaint about taxation.[31]

The success of the Trump brand demonstrates the importance of class in American politics. Class matters in political branding and segmentation; it can be one way to segment the electorate for political marketers and the class divisions have significant implications for American politics moving forward.[32] Trump's public persona was that of a traditional working-class white guy. Trump has called himself "white trash" just like he thinks his audience is only a lot richer.[33] He espouses traditional attitudes toward women and evinces a surface traditional masculinity. He is blunt and could be accused credibly of being uncouth, unsophisticated, and at a minimum unconsciously racist (others would argue that he is overtly so). Trump is a huge fan of fast food in general and McDonalds something that average working Americans eat. He is a huge fan of the musician Elton John and other mainstream musical acts popular with his audiences.[34] This persona is authentic, and it supported Trump's political brand. Trump channeled this persona and these sentiments closely in his campaign marketing. Candidate Trump was the older working-class white voter personified. He differentiated himself from the Washington establishment in both parties and by doing so from a lot of the middle and upper-class knowledge workers.

Trump built a class-based brand around notions of commonality, social order, restoration of lost glory, patriotism, and a sense that the status quo served narrow interests.[35] He pointed out that many of the policies elites favored came with costs for average Americans while most of the benefits went elsewhere. Trump told a tale of a lost America in which there was much more commonality, stronger institutions, more order, and more respect for authority than is the case now. Trump's brand story appealed to specific portions of the United States because it promoted an idealized version of America in which most people are white, speak English, are married to a member of the opposite sex, have children, and work at middle management or blue-collar job. This was made clear by Trump's musing on suburbanites during the 2020 campaign when he tried promoting the idea that Joe Biden's proposed housing policy would dramatically change their lives and living situations.

Trump was also the candidate for those who did not win during the Obama years. Trump criticized the Obama Administration's economic policies and argued that Trump would do better. As his Administration went on and the Democrats drifted to the ideological left, Trump has positioned himself as the defender of American values and the free market against socialists and people who hated the country. This is clear in the previously noted controversial tweets of mid-July 2019. Trump argued that if four Democratic first-term House members, all of whom were women of color, were not happy in the USA then they should return to where they came from and fix the problems there. This produced a firestorm of a response in which Trump was widely accused of being a racist. He certainly was using nationalist themes in these tweets, but they can be seen as being a way for Trump to switch the subject from bad polling numbers, a capitulation on adding a citizenship question to the census that angered some of his base and many conservative legal activists, and immigration raids that were much less dramatic than he had advertised in order to instigate a fight designed to make the left and the visible minority female left at that, the image of the Democratic Party in the 2020 election. The members of Congress he went after were all unpopular with his base and two of them (Reps. Omar and Ocasio-Cortez) were much lower rated than was Donald Trump. This what could be seen as a racist theme could also be seen as an omnipresent brand being positioned for its next marketing campaign as Trump's tweets show:

> We will never be a Socialist or Communist Country. IF YOU ARE NOT HAPPY HERE, YOU CAN LEAVE! It is your choice, and your choice alone. This is about love for America. Certain people HATE our Country.[36]
> So sad to see the Democrats sticking up for people who speak so badly of our Country and who, in addition, hate Israel with a true and unbridled passion. Whenever confronted, they call their adversaries, including Nancy Pelosi, "RACIST." Their disgusting language.[37]
> ....and the many terrible things they say about the United States must not be allowed to go unchallenged. If the Democrat Party wants to continue to condone such disgraceful behavior, then we look even more forward to seeing you at the ballot box in 2020![38]

In these tweets, Trump positioned himself as defending those who love America and arguing that his opponents hate the country and Israel (a strategic initiative to encourage more American Jews to vote Republican) and working with an "America: Love It or Leave It" theme that came straight from the tumult of the 1960s.

He then criticized his four opponents in a comparable way that the Chair of the Congressional Black Caucus had also done regarding their frequent cries of racism, took a swipe a Nancy Pelosi for tweeting that "When @realDonaldTrump tells four American Congresswomen to go back to their countries, he reaffirms his plan to 'Make America Great Again' has always been about making America white again. Our diversity is our strength and our unity is our power"[39] before closing with a positioning statement about the 2020 elections. This typified the way in which Trump built an omnipresent sticky brand, the way he drove the media narrative, and catered to his best customers. The media, his opponents, and some members of the GOP spent hours discussing these tweets but all the problems that he was trying to hide from the public mind because they were damaging to the Trump brand disappeared as if by magic. Instead, he initiated the kind of fight over race, nationalism, and identity that helped him win in 2016. Social media let Trump control the pace of the discourse and shape much of the daily information content news outlets and social media platforms presented to the public.[40]

While the real Donald Trump might not have been more of a flawed individual than many of the other people who have held the Presidency, his flaws were more on display than any of the other people who had held the office because of his brand omnipresence strategy. He won and narrowly lost because people felt familiar with him because his brand built a relationship with them but did not wear well over time with some of them. Trump had two advantages: (1) he was well-known and (2) he could point to his wealth as a sign of his acumen and his selflessness in taking on the Presidency. These differentiation points helped him to assert that he knew the game was rigged because he had played it himself and this, in turn, allowed him to present himself as a latter-day Cincinnatus come to save the Republic. Thus, part of why Donald Trump was reluctant to dole out the kinds of personal information political candidates always have is because his personal history is so at odds with the normal stories of those who have been President and could muddle his brand persona. Trump would not give his opponents any help on the finance part because he refused to release his tax returns. While Trump argued that the rationale for not doing so was that he was under audit, it is likely that these could have been a treasure trove of information for opposition researchers and undermine Trump's claims about the extent of his wealth thus undermining his brand story. Even when information got out about him that was unfavorable, he knew how to use social media to shift the focus away from the unflattering. While this produced an onslaught of fact checks and contrary examples in the media and his political opponents, Trump's brand, and the way he used social media to build it to omnipresence limited their impact. In some ways, Donald Trump was an easy target for his opponents. He had not served in the military or held elected office. He was only the second person to hold the office who has been divorced, had a reputation for infidelity and shady business practices. Most interestingly Trump started his political life as a rich guy from New York in a country that does not really love either thing. During his Presidency he changed his residency to Florida, something that fits the Republican brand better, and took his final flight as President home to a state he was not a resident of when his campaign began. In a sign of the power of emotional branding, he campaigned as a specific rejection of the East Coast Establishment and the rich even though he was based securely in the headquarters of both then moved to be part of the rising Republican Sunbelt.

Trump's election and Presidency raised basic questions about the durability of the liberal order that came out of the late 1960s and the more recent Democratic strategy of arguing for multiculturalism and diversity instead of a common American identity. By 2016, a lot of the country considered their membership in specific racial, cultural, or lifestyle group to be of paramount importance and the Democrats built campaigns around that but, as a Democratic consultant Krystal Ball wrote shortly after the 2016 election of working-class Midwestern white voters after the election: "They said they were facing an economic apocalypse, we offered 'retraining' and complained about their white privilege. Is it any wonder we lost?"[41] Trump's brand of economic and cultural nationalism was a sharp contrast to that of the Democrats. Given this, it should not be surprising that Trump's story of a common American identity resonated with some people, especially people who cared a lot about their own status in a diversifying America. In 2020, Joe Biden offered Americans a combination of material and post-material slogan in "Build Back Better" and sometimes discussed specific economic policies he would implement that would benefit the audiences that Donald Trump had targeted.

Much of Donald Trump's platform and policy choices as President were standard Republican offerings but there were a few notable exceptions. Tariffs were not a conservative favorite. Increased border security and tighter immigration policy have been in and out of favor in both parties as has the idea of adopting a more nationalistic foreign policy. The emotive Trump brand continually showed how he was different from the Republicans and Democrats his audiences usually had to pick from. His emotional sticky branding made these sentiments more vivid than any Republican that had run a successful national-level campaign had previously. He connected with people who felt they had long been ignored and his product contained just enough to hold many conservatives on board. At the same time, Trump's brand persona disgusted others in the GOP and set off a never-Trump movement. It terrorized his opponents into a scorched earth resistance against him. Trump marketed himself differently from his GOP predecessors because it is now possible to execute a niche narrowcasting campaign and win an election in a way that it was not previously. The databases, social media platforms, and the World Wide Web that fueled the Trump campaign did not exist in Reagan's day. Trump's brand touched on the conservative themes prominent in the nation's long-running culture wars thus it has a deeper brand heritage than just Trump himself. Trump's election reinvigorated battles over race, rights, and taxes that Edsall and Edsall (1992) argued have been instrumental to the success of the Conservative movement during the period leading to the Reagan years. Given how many in both parties thought the culture

wars were over and the liberals won, Trump's reinvigoration was an acti-
vation and differentiation strategy designed to turn out those alienated by
the moderation some in the GOP were expressing as necessary to secure
the party's future.[42] Further, Trump articulates a cultural nationalism
that is in stark contrast to what the last several administrations expressed.
Trump's brand produced a strong reaction from those who benefitted
from the previous policies, feel threatened by the monocultural nationalist
ideas of Trump, or preferred the brand emotions, value proposition, and
styles of other recent Presidents (especially Barack Obama). For people
who either benefitted from the established immigration and trade policies
of recent decades, cared about the environment more than the economy,
believed that the world was in a post-national era that emphasized diplo-
macy and multilateral agreements over military battles, Donald Trump's
election was a rude awakening and a direct threat. If one was a member of
the LGBTQ2+ community that secured the right to marry in the former
case and access to Medicare benefits in the latter case because of court
rulings and bureaucratic rule-making processes, then Donald Trump's
election presented a threat to either personal status or things one believed
in.

Trump's brand promoted a vision of a single American culture in
which there were clear norms and values that have implicit class and
racial appeals within them. Trump could or would not control the white
affinity groups that were attracted to his campaign, but he could control
his responses to current events, the behavior of his staff, or some of his
personal history. People affiliated with his campaign sometimes sent out
tweets with a white nationalist symbol (Pepe the Frog) in them, Trump
added to these concerns because he has been slow to condemn violence
against people or communities of color while in office, has a long history
of making statements like questioning President Obama's birthplace or
calling for the death penalty in the Central Park Five jogger case that
could be seen as at a minimum racially orientated and at a maximum
racist and has negatively tweeted about African American athletes like
NFL players to build up his own brand. Trump might have been signaling
some audiences about his brand with these statements but, in doing
so, he repelled other audiences. Even though Trump had reached out
to working-class African Americans during the campaign, he had done
more in a way that encouraged them to disparage the results of four
decades of policy than it was to make them feel like the Republican Party
valued their concerns and encouraging them to try something different, a

common product marketing strategy. In the age of segmented emotional branding, gaining just enough support from an audience one has no hope of winning a majority from can be one way to win an overall majority.

Trump has struggled with women voters because of his personal traits and his adoption of traditional conservative positions on social issues. His campaign did an expert job of dealing with a leaked recording of Trump admitting to sexual assaults that he could get away with because he was a celebrity by pointing out to whom his opponent was married and what they had both done to weather similar assaults in their own past. Trump was, as he said he would be, disrespectful to the Democratic nominee who in this case was female. While his development of the "Crooked Hillary" brand was expert, it was not welcoming to women who might have ever been picked on themselves by a powerful man and pro-feminist groups made much of the idea that Donald Trump was like the sexual harassers that many women had faced in their own lives and the discriminatory men that they had dealt with themselves.

One of the great paradoxes of Trump's political brand is that it has been propelled using social media tools of which Trump's target audiences are not heavy users. Trump figured out that he could use these tools to generate earned media and, using the unfiltered statements that he made on them, to position his brand differently from those of his competitors. The earned media portion was a good insight because of the number of journalists who are represented on social media in general and especially Twitter. Trump could use Twitter to get his own message out in his own words without having to answer questions from the press or being reliant on third parties or overwhelming amounts of paid advertising to get his message out. The Trump Administration mostly discontinued press briefings until COVID reduced their ability to travel during the campaign because those brought the kind of contentiousness that has marked the period on social media into the mainstream. While Trump himself often talked directly with the media, the long-standing tradition of the daily or at least periodic press briefing disappeared for much of his Administration returning only when the Biden Administration revived it. While Trump can get his message out directly on Twitter, there are no rules regarding journalistic objectivity on Twitter especially not when one is simply opining rather than reporting. Trump can get his message out, but it is also subject to real-time rebuttal, editorializing and fact checking from the media. Journalistic social media presences have sped up what the RAND Corporation described as "truth decay" in jour-nalism.[43] Since 2000, RAND's study found that the news had become more about personality and conflict than facts with the trend being more pronounced on television than in print.[44] Donald Trump was tailor-made to take advantage of social media given that he stressed his personal traits and did not shy away from confronting his opponents. Trump specif-ically sought out intermittent voters meaning it was necessary for him to develop an emotionally charged narrative to get their attention. The emphasis on narrative over facts is reflective of the noise generated by social media and the way in which a coherent, emotive narrative helps the marketer cut through the increased amount of clutter extant in the social media age.

The Trump brand style is ideally suited for the social media age. Trump's brand style is an important way that Trump differentiates himself from his opponents and critics. Aside from media professionals, social media's audience demography differs significantly from that of Trump's target audiences meaning that his preferred platform is full of people recasting his message negatively.[45] These audiences object to Trump because of his specific policy proposals in part but many disliked his brand style or personal traits. Trump as a marketer probably does not care because his social media opponents are not his targets. To these audiences, Trump is objectionable because he is the anti-Obama personally, in terms of credentials and preparation to hold office, policies, and the emotions within his brand. His election disrupted what many had predicted to be an era of Democratic dominance. On the other hand, his election united the Democrats and papered over a series of important debates and divi-sions about what the Democratic product and positioning that emerged again during the first year of the Biden Administration. The party is split between a centrist and a progressive wing neither of which holds a clear majority as the 2020 nominating contest showed. A lot of Democrats and independents might dislike Trump, but they might not be enamored of a shift to socialism either. Trump and the GOP tried to do something like what Stephen Harper did in Canada as an incumbent: run as the person that the times called for and point out that even though people might not like Donald Trump's personal traits? They cannot argue with the job that he has done on the economy or in trying to keep his promises. Support for this idea is buttressed by the ad the Trump team ran during game 7 of the 2019 World Series that said "he's no mister nice guy but sometimes it takes a Donald Trump to change Washington.[46]"

Trump aggressively promoted the powers of the Executive Branch just as all his recent predecessors have. Trump, rather than undermining the rule of law, has replicated, and attempted to advance the behaviors of recent Presidents and his successor. His underlings were not the first recent executive branch officials to get into fights with Congress about subpoenas, they were hardly the first to run afoul of government ethics requirements (most of which did not exist prior to Watergate), he was not the only President we have ever had who won the Electoral College but lost the popular vote nor is he the first President to try to steer government contracts and plum positions to supporters. What he did was violate a series of norms that are not laws but are reflective of the class that created them. Thus, when one gets into how Trump is undermining either the rule of law or American Democracy what one finds is a complaint about institutional infighting and Trump vigorously promoting the interests of the Executive Branch or complaints about things undone that are not legally required but are norms reflective of the class that created them.

All these things rested at the center of the Impeachment tussle that took place in the Fall of 2019. After a disastrous appearance by Trump campaign staffer and conservative activist Corey Lewandowski on September 17th during which Mr. Lewandowski gave as good as he got from the Democrats on the House Judiciary Committee, the House moved forward with impeachment proceedings based on a whistle-blower complaint around Trump's dealings with Ukraine. The Democrats promised to show that there had been a quid pro quo in which Trump sought to cut off aid to Ukraine unless that government dug up dirt on one of his more difficult Democratic opponents, Joe Biden, centered around Biden's son's business dealings in that country. After three months, the Impeachment process convinced nobody of anything. If one liked Donald Trump, the whole thing was just more of the same scorched earth resistance from the Democrats. If one did not like Donald Trump, the episode showed he was corrupt and unfit to serve. The articles of impeachment, which were approved mostly along partisan lines argued that Trump's dealings with Ukraine amounted to an abuse of power centered on his actions involving Ukraine and contempt of Congress because of his refusal to cooperate with Congress. The day after these articles were passed, Senate Majority Leader Mitch McConnell dismissed them as unserious and argued that he would be working closely with the Trump Administration to coordinate a defense during a Senate trial.

This episode can be seen as a Democratic effort to counter Trump's omnipresent branding. As Trump's defenders pointed out, there is a long history of Presidents doing things in the foreign policy arena that might not be open and many of them were quick to raise Barack Obama's comment to then-Russian President Dimitry Medvedev that after his reelection campaign against Mitt Romney he would have more flexibility to deal with Russia. The process itself provided hours of live television coverage and millions of impressions for the Democrats negative branding around Donald Trump that amounted to him being unfit to be President. The weeks of hearings acted like an infomercial through which the Democrats could build loyalty among their target audiences while trying to attract swing voters. Conversely, Trump's defenders had a counter narrative that could point to some Democrats arguing just hours after the 2016 election that Trump should be impeached and a slew of statements by Democratic members of Congress that this had been their intent all along and that Trump was only in trouble because his policy preferences differed from those held by a group of unelected bureaucrats thus showing that Trump, far from doing anything wrong, was actually keeping his brand promise to drain the swamp. These assertions were buttressed by the way in which the Democrats had invested heavily in the Mueller Investigation and Report only to see that fizzle. Some critics of this kind of investment, like journalist Matt Taibbi, argued that the basis for the whistleblower complaint that triggered impeachment was equivalent to the basis for the Mueller Investigation because it had been triggered by the same people.[47] The Democrats refusal to produce the whistleblower in person to testify before Congress, until the actual impeachment hearings, did little to buttress the credibility of their argument with independents or Republicans but it was not necessary to build support among their target audiences who had been invested in the narrative of getting Donald Trump out of office since minutes after his election. Conservative media was happy to present this entire affair as an exercise in political marketing and branding, especially after Democrats changed the words that they used in describing the alleged offenses from "quid pro quo" to "bribery." *The Washington Post* reported that the Democrats changed their terms in response to focus group testing in battleground states in which bribery was found to be the most potent term in going after Donald Trump.[48] Thus, the Democrats gained the ability to run the kind of campaign that Donald Trump ran based on targeted messaging and strong emotional appeals against his omnipresent brand. Trump's task would have been simpler absent the pandemic: use his brand to convince people that his opponents are unacceptable, that the charges against him are simply politics by another means, and that based on his performance in office, he deserves to be reelected.

Donald Trump and the reaction to him raise important questions about the traits Americans look for in a President and about the job that they expect the President to do. Is it possible that Americans want a leader who can hold their attention as an entertainer even if that leader is deeply flawed personally or is our system driven by the same kind of brand loyalty that sports fans have in which we minimize the transgressions and maximize the performance of our favorites while doing the opposite to those whom we root against? If this is so then, like sports fans, we will be permanently locked in a single brand story, have difficulty appreciating the commonality we have with others instead, and will be doomed to being each other's opponents instead of fellow citizens.

This work will show that in contemporary American politics, branding a simple and clear brand proposition and understanding of the customer base being targeted are vital to success. Donald Trump developed an omnipresent sticky brand that resonated with just enough people in just enough places to win. While this worked to barely get him elected in 2016, it produced a narrow defeat in 2020. Trump consistently appealed to his key audiences but few other people thus his reelection strategy is premised on the idea of turning out at least as many of the same audiences as in 2016 and, as some analysts argue because of demographic change he had to turn out even more to get the same result.[49] Because of the way in which he has consistently appealed to his key segments and few other people, his best hope for future success is that the Democrats nominate someone who can be positioned as being beyond the pale for swing voters and who makes him look reasonable in the side-by-side product comparison that is a general election. It should not be surprising that Donald Trump's Ukraine misadventure was fueled by a concern about a centrist Democrat who can speak to the working class convincingly yet has the Obama brand heritage as a potential 2020 general election opponent.

Trump raised questions about the way in which the Executive Branch is organized, how it functions, how many people it takes to staff it, and if it is responsible to either of the other two branches or not. Further, his actions and the response to them raised basic questions of federalism regarding the extent to which the federal government can make states and municipalities bend to its will and the amount of flexibility subnational jurisdictions have in implementing federal policies. During the Trump years, the Democrats rediscovered federalism, and the key role subnational jurisdictions can play in shaping public policy in this country. A question is if this is a sea change in structural orientation or an artifact of having someone in office they simply do not like? Donald Trump's hostile takeover of the Republican Party and the challenges to the Democratic leadership in the House that we have seen in recent years raise an important question about the viability of the political party as organizing principle in the social media age. Donald Trump and "The Squad" in the Democratic Party show that it is possible to build strong brands and emotionally engage people in policy and politics continually. On the other hand, the way in which the system is constructed makes delivery much more difficult than would be the case in a parliamentary system. We saw fights between Trump and members of the House and Senate in both parties. During the early phase of the Biden Administration, we have seen fights within and between members of both houses of Congress in the same party. All of them show that one of branding's limitations is that its users cannot quite deliver the goods as commercial marketers can because the system is specifically set up to limit its ability to do so. On the other hand, this kind of intra-partisan battling shows that the key role that a small elite that functioned as gatekeepers once played in screening out the acceptable from the unacceptable has weakened in the social media age. An obvious question that emerges considering the Trump case is if anyone in either party has the marketing chops to focus on building brand omnipresence at the same level that Donald Trump has or if doing so is even desirable given Trump's struggles in office. These kinds of battles are likely to become common in both parties because the barriers to mass participation that once allowed elites to dominate political parties and government have collapsed.

Neither Trump nor his opponents had any interest in or incentive to bring the bulk of the population together. Political marketing in a narrow-casted social media-driven country produces an incentive to focus on a target audience, emotionally engage and turn them out via branding and win narrowly. The way in which segmentation encourages targeted appeals and the way in which branding requires its users to keep their promises make this so. Politicians are incentivized to build brands that position them distinctly from their competitors and deeply engage their audience targets. Given the ubiquity of branding, the need to stand by the brand and keep promises, no matter how polarizing, are of paramount importance. While emotional branding, targeting, and segmentation have significant upsides in terms of engagement, they have significant downsides in terms of building social consensus and the distance between those things and the reality of the era was accentuated by a candidate seeking to build an omnipresent brand from which there is no respite or escape.

To understand the differences between the way in which Donald Trump used political branding versus the ways in which traditional politicians use it consider the omnipresent sticky emotive branding that Donald Trump used in contrast to the more traditional corporate consumer marketing approach with its many layers that the Biden Administration has adopted. Biden sits at the head of a large communicative apparatus. His public appearances are limited and scripted. He sometimes speaks from a set that was purpose-built for his appearances that looks like the White House but is a soundstage and he seldom takes unscripted questions from the press. Trump would engage all comers, but Biden hardly ever will do so and hardly ever does interviews. Biden has deemphasized high-profile public appearances in favor of more targeted afternoon availabilities and daily briefings by the White House press operation. This is as much of a strategy as the one Trump employed. The difference is that Trump was the front man for his Administration while Biden occupies a symbolic role that outsources the substantive marketing role to others. Trump's approach produced a focus on him while Biden's approach produced a focus on others.

NOTES

1. Schier and Eberly (2017).
2. Ian Schwartz. "Former Trump Aide David Bossie: 'If Trump Fired Obama Holdovers, His Job Would Be a Lot Easier, Deep State Is Real.'" Real Clear Politics. February 13, 2020. https://www.realclearpolitics.com/video/2020/02/13/former_trump_aide_david_bossie_if_trump_fired_obama_holdovers_his_job_would_be_a_lot_easier_deep_state_is_real.html, accessed February 18, 2020.
3. See for example David Mora. "Update: We Found a Staggering 281 Lobbyists Who've Worked in the Trump Administration." ProPublica. October 15, 2019. https://www.propublica.org/article/we-found-a-staggering-281-lobbyists-whove-worked-in-the-trump-administration, accessed February 18, 2020.
4. Michael D'Antonio. "When Donald Trump Hated Ronald Reagan: The GOP Frontrunner Praises the Conservative Icon Now But in

1987 Trump Blasted Reagan and His Team." Politico. October 25, 2015. https://www.politico.com/magazine/story/2015/10/don ald-trump-ronald-reagan-213288, accessed January 2, 2020.

5. "Remarks by President Trump at the 2019 Conservative Political Action Conference." March 3, 2019. https://www.whitehouse.gov/briefings-sta tements/remarks-president-trump-2019-conservative-political-action-con ference/, accessed July 30, 2019.

6. Wolff (2018, p. 233).

7. Alex Isenstadt. "Trumpworld Torn over Running Against Sanders." Politico. January 20, 2020 https://www.politico.com/news/2020/01/ 28/trump-aides-torn-bernie-sanders-2020-108226, accessed February 18, 2020.

8. Ian Schwartz. "Trump: I'd Rather Run Against Bloomberg than Bernie Because He Has Real Followers, Bloomberg Is Just Buying His Way in." Real Clear Politics. February 12, 2020. https://www.realclearpolitics. com/video/2020/02/12/trump_id_rather_run_against_bloomberg_ than_bernie_because_he_has_real_followers_bloomberg_is_buying_his_ way_in.html, accessed February 18, 2020.

9. See for example Gabriel Schonder. "Interview with Stephen K. Bannon." for PBS Frontline for an example of how Donald Trump's thinking was shaped on immigration policy by his marketing background. Interview conducted September 19, 2019. https://www.pbs.org/wgbh/frontline/ interview/steve-bannon-4/.

10. For an indepth description of why Biden provided such a difficult contrast for Trump see Ken Cosgrove and Nathan Shrader. "Political Branding in the USA Election of 2020." in Mona Moufahim (ed). *Political Branding in Turbulent Times*. Palgrave-Macmillan, 2021.

11. Jarol b. Mannheim the Death of a Thousand Cuts, 2001.

12. Suffolk University Poll with "USA Today". December 19, 2019. https:// www.suffolk.edu/-/media/suffolk/documents/academics/research-at-suf folk/suprc/polls/national/2019/12_18_2019_tables_pdftxt.pdf?la=en& hash=83C1809042F439DFD1E15292C0D5A87975DF3EAE, accessed January 2, 2020.

13. Ted Johnson. "Brad Parscale Said Donald Trump Erred in Not Expressing Empathy." Yahoo News. December 1, 2020. https://www.yahoo.com/ entertainment/brad-parscale-says-donald-trump-010813572.html.

14. Michael Bender. "Trump Rests His 2020 Hopes on Some Old Tactics." *Wall Street Journal*. July 17, 2019. https://www.wsj.com/articles/ trump-rests-his-2020-hopes-on-some-old-tactics-11563376363, accessed July 17, 2019.

15. Tess Bonn. "Nearly Half of Independents Say Democratic Party Leans Too Far Left." *The Hill*. July 31, 2019.

16. See for example Ronald Brownstein. "Trump's Base Isn't Enough." *The Atlantic*. July 19, 2019. https://thehill.com/hilltv/what-americas-thi nking/455574-nearly-half-of-independents-say-democratic-party-is-too-far-left, accessed August 5, 2019.
17. Amy Mitchell, Jeffery Gottfried, Galen Stocking, Katerina Eva Matsa and Elizabeth Grieco. "Covering President Trump in a Polarized Media Environment." *Pew Research Center: Journalism and Media*. October 2, 2017. https://www.journalism.org/2017/10/02/covering-president-trump-in-a-polarized-media-environment/, accessed January 2, 2020.
18. Maeve Duggan. "24 Percent of 7th District Primary Voters Had Not Voted in Previous 5 Primaries." WBUR News. January 4, 2019. https://www.wbur.org/news/2019/01/04/ayanna-pressley-first-time-voter-file-analysis, accessed August 4, 2019.
19. Terry Sullivan. "Sanders Isn't So Much Trump's Challenger as He Is His Sequel." *Wall Street Journal*. February 23, 2020. https://www.wsj.com/articles/sanders-isnt-trumps-challenger-so-much-as-his-sequel-11582477250?emailToken=fdc0d8bde88f9df81abddc5459e5f5548yV5/uswAUQW8EclGPh67CC9OvhsHP50W1a6GUKKPVX05pNjVUy+azi kVxMYkjYzmlg29P/txpIUx98qC5co6kGJ8m14qGaMJ005W01Gapb EKHtrzVoxNdExQkqXdeXJ&reflink=article_copyURL_share,   accessed February 24, 2020.
20. See Astead W. Herndon. "Elizabeth Warren Isn't Talking Much About Medicare for All Anymore." *New York Times*, January 1, 2020. https://www.nytimes.com/2020/01/01/us/politics/elizabeth-warren-medicare-for-all.html, accessed January 2, 2020.
21. United States Department of the Treasury Press Release. "Treasury Secretary Lew Announces Front of New $20 to Feature Harriet Tubman, Lays Out Plans for New $20, $10 and $5." https://www.treasury.gov/press-center/press-releases/Pages/jl0436.aspx, accessed February 19, 2020.
22. Pollack and Schweikart (2017, p. 116).
23. Ibid.
24. Patrice Taddonio.'A Serial Liar: How Sarah Palin Ushered in the Post-Truth Political Era in which Trump Has Thrived." PBS Frontline. January 10, 2020. https://www.pbs.org/wgbh/frontline/article/a-ser ial-liar-how-sarah-palin-ushered-in-the-post-truth-political-era-in-which-trump-has-thrived/, accessed February 19, 2020.
25. ibid.
26. Chuck Ross. "Biden Has Ties to Five Major Tech Companies." Daily Caller. January 10, 2021. https://dailycaller.com/2021/01/10/biden-big-tech-apple-facebook-trump-parler/
27. for example, see "interview with Stephen Bannon" from the PBS Frontline Documentary Zero Tolerance". The interviews were conducted by Michael Kirk and Gabrielle Schonder respectively on March 17 and

September 19, 2019. https://www.pbs.org/wgbh/frontline/interview/steve-bannon-2/, accessed February 19, 2020.

28. Mason (2018) and Bishop (2009) both present book length treatments of social sorting.

29. See Green (2017) for a discussion of the importance of order and traditional institutions to the Trump campaign and its lead strategist Steven Bannon especially Chapter 10.

30. Xvii Peter Beinart. "How The Democrats Lost Their Way on Immigration: In the Past Decade Liberals Have Avoided Inconvenient Truths About the Issue." https://www.theatlantic.com/magazine/archive/2017/07/the-democrats-immigration-mistake/528678/, accessed July 15, 2019.

31. For an overview see Thomas Edsall and Mary Byrne Edsall Chain Reaction (1992).

32. For a book length treatment on class and class divergence among whites in America see Murray (2012).

33. Wolff (2018, p. 23).

34. As Lewandowski and Bossie (2017) note Trump loves to crank up the Elton John on his plane, pp. 91–92.

35. see for example Pollack and Schweikart, p. xvii.

36. @realdonaldtrump tweet July 14, 2019, accessed July 16, 2019.

37. @realdonaldtrump July 14th, 2019, accessed July 16, 2019.

38. @realdonaldtrump July 14th, 2019, accessed July 16, 2019.

39. @speakerpelosi, tweet July 14, 2019, accessed July 16, 2019.

40. By Matt Flegenheimer (December 30, 2017, Saturday). The Year the Traditional News Cycle Accelerated to Trump Speed. *The New York Times*. Retrieved from https://advance-lexis-com.ezproxysuf.flo.org/api/document?collection=news&id=urn:contentItem:5R95-PMY1-JBG3-6525-00000-00&context=1516831. And Kalev Leetaru."Numbers Show How Trump's Tweets Drive the News Cycle." Real Clear Politics. September 11, 2019.
    https://www.realclearpolitics.com/articles/2019/09/11/numbers_s how_how_trumps_tweets_drive_the_news_cycle_141217.html.

41. Krystal Ball. "The Democratic Party Deserves to Die." Huffington Post. November 9, 2016 https://www.huffpost.com/entry/the-democratic-party-deserves-to-die_b_58236ad5e4b0aac62488cde5, accessed November 9, 2016.

42. See for example the PBS Frontline documentary "Zero Tolerance" for an examination of how Trump's reinvigoration of the conservative position in the culture wars energized supporters.

43. Jennifer Kavanagh, William Marcellino, Jonathan S. Blake, Shawn Smith, Steven Davenport, Mahlet G. Tebek. News in a Digital Age Comparing the Presentation of News Information over Time and

Across Media Platforms. https://www.rand.org/pubs/research_reports/RR2960.html.
44. Ibid.
45. Adam Hughes and Stefan Wojick. "10 Facts About Americans and Twitter." *Pew Research*. August 2, 2019. https://www.pewresearch.org/fact-tank/2019/08/02/10-facts-about-americans-and-twitter/.
46. Will Steaken and John Santucci. "Trump Campaign Runs a Surprise World Series Ad: It Takes a Donald Trump to Change Washington. ABC News. October 31, 2019. https://abcnews.go.com/Politics/trump-campaign-runs-surprise-world-series-ad-takes/story?id=66670804, accessed January 3, 2020.
47. Matt Taibbi. "The Whistleblower Probably Isn't." *Rolling Stone*. October 6, 2019. https://www.rollingstone.com/politics/political-commentary/whistleblower-ukraine-trump-impeach-cia-spying-895529/, accessed February 22, 2019.
48. Mike DeBonis and Toulse Olorrunnipa. "Democrats Sharpen Impeachment Case, Decrying 'Bribery' as Another Potential Witness Emerges Linking Trump to Ukraine Scandal." *Washington Post*. November 14, 2019. https://www.washingtonpost.com/politics/pelosi-calls-trumps-actions-bribery-as-democrats-sharpen-case-for-impeachment/2019/11/14/0ee9a202-0702-11ea-b17d-8b867891d39d_story.html, accessed January 3, 2019.
49. For an example of this kind of analysis see Aaron Zitner and Dante Chinni. "Demographic Shift Poised to Test Trump's 2020 Strategy." *The Wall Street Journal*. January 3, 2020. https://www.wsj.com/articles/demographic-shift-poised-to-test-trumps-2020-strategy-11578047402?mod=hp_lead_pos9, accessed January 3, 2020.

REFERENCES

Adams, Scott. *Win Bigly: Persuasion in a World Where Facts Don't Matter.* Penguin, 2017.
Bishop, Bill. *The Big Sort* Mariner Books, 2009.
Carnes, Nicholas. *White Collar Government.* University of Chicago Press, 2013.
Edsall, Thomas and Mary Byrne Edsall. *Chain Reaction: The Impact of Race, Rights and Taxes on American Politcs.* W.W. Norton, 1991.
Green, Joshua. *Devil's Bargain: Steve Bannon, Donald Trump and the Storming of the US Presidency.* Penguin, 2017.
Lewandowski, Corey R. and David N. Bossie. *Let Trump Be Trump: The Inside Story of His Rise to the Presidency.* Center Street, 2017.
Mason, Liliana. *Uncivil Agreement: How Politics Became Our Identity.* Chicago. University of Chicago Press, 2018.

Miller, Jeremy. *Sticky Branding: 12.5 Principles To Stand Out, Attract Customers and Grow an Incredible Brand*. Page Two Books, 2015.

Murray, Charles. *Coming Apart; The State of White America*. Crown Forum, 2012.

Neustadt, Richard. *The Presidential Power: The Politics of Leadership from Roosevelt to Reagan*. Free Press, 1991.

Norris, Pippa and Ronald Inglehart. *Cultural Backlash: Trump, Brexit and Authoritarian Populism*. Cambridge University Press, 2019.

Pollack, Joel B. and Larry Schweikart. *How Trump Won: The Inside Story of A Revolution*. Regnery Publishing, 2017.

Schier, Steven E. and Todd E. Eberly. *The Trump Presidency: Outsider in the Oval Office*. Rowman and Littlefield, 2017.

Suri, Jermi. *The Impossible Presidency*. Hachette Book Group, 2017.

Wolff, Michael. *Fire and Fury: Inside the Trump White House*. Henry Holt and Company, 2018.

CHAPTER 2

The Old Order and Its Discontents

Abstract Donald Trump's omnipresent political brand disrupted the ways in which American politics work and threaten to displace the nation's political gatekeepers. Cosgrove argues that Trump's class-based politics, brand persona, and policies are upending the status quo by expanding the backgrounds that political leaders come from and the political products on offer to Americans. Just like Colin Kaepernick and Nike's ad campaigns show, the omnipresent Trump brand shows that there is much to be gained by segmenting the political marketplace and targeting a few segments of it instead of trying to appeal to all of it. Such techniques, Cosgrove concludes do not assure social harmony but might lead to more ideological, issue, and candidate diversity. Cosgrove notes that Donald Trump's political brand combines populism and nationalism. Trump targeted and expanded the participation of underperforming segments to build a favorable electorate. Trump has designed his political brand persona to be that of a celebrity Cincinnatus entering politics to restore the lost greatness of the country. Trump's brand story presented him as a patriotic nationalist battling the forces of globalism, secularism and elitism that had harmed his target audiences to restore the country to its lost glory. The closest comparisons to Trump's branding are found among very progressive Democrats like Bernie Sanders, Alexandria Ocasio-Cortez, and her fellow members of "The Squad." They and Donald Trump are using branding, segmentation, and targeting to broaden the voices represented in the public square.

K. M. Cosgrove, *Donald Trump and the Branding of the American Presidency*, https://doi.org/10.1007/978-3-030-30496-6_2

Keyword Sticky branding · Populism · Nationalism · Make America Great Again · Washington establishment · Social sorting · Political parties

Donald Trump is many things: a performer, a promoter, a real estate developer, and an expert marketer. He is also a disrupter who promised to shake up a political system many Americans felt did not respond to their concerns while it kept billing them for a string of policy failures.[1] Trump was elected in the wake of a terrorist attack on US soil, two wars thereafter, an economic crisis that lowered living standards and for which nobody who benefitted from these excesses was punished.[2] Trump, like Reagan and Clinton, got elected on a platform of dramatically changing Washington. Trump had extensive non-political work experience that allowed him to credibly claim that he was an outsider, not an insider participating in a Washington culture that appeared to many Americans to be insulated from life in the bulk of the country.[3] He won the Presidency because he took advantage of a series of policy failures but also from a sense of bipartisan tone-deafness among the country's political elite.[4]

Any Republican nominee in 2016 would have had an excellent chance of winning the White House given the reluctance Americans have historically shown to vote for the same party three times in a row. Conservatives were energized because Barack Obama implemented policies that alienated them thus meaning a generic Republican nominee could also have tapped into the power that negative partisanship can give a brand.[5] Trump was advantaged because President Obama represented a cultural and racial challenge to the world view that many of Trump's target voters held.[6] Trump's brand fused cultural and racial concerns with traditional Republican positions on taxes, regulation, immigration, patriotism, and morality. He added a distinct nationalist element to the Republican brand. In a bid to attract working-class voters, it included a significant deviation from Conservative orthodoxy on trade. This brand produced a win in 2016. Trump's incumbent status and a series of crises roiling the country in 2020 meant that the voters had different concerns and more knowledge of Donald Trump than they had in 2016. Thus, Trump's failure to appear to live up to his brand promise during the pandemic and failure to adjust to the realities of an election conducted in a changed environment led to his defeat in 2020.

As Adams (2017) notes, Trump's political brand used the sticky brand strategy articulated by Miller (2015). It focused on winning niche audiences, being authentic, being active building omnipresence, and creating a real community of supporters. The Trump campaign figured out that niche selling could win the Electoral College and that it, not the popular vote, was the metric than won the contest as Jared Kushner noted. Thus, it allocated resources in ways that helped it win the Electoral College instead because that is what the contest really was.[7] Consistent with the sticky branding strategy, Trump willingly alienated some audiences to build deep loyalty within others. Trump's product kept just enough traditional Republicans onside, and his class-based brand personality mobilized enough intermittent voters to win in 2016 but just enough to lose in 2020 even though he increased his vote share in defeat.

As an insurgent Donald Trump promoted a brand style that resonated with working-class voters. His offering also included policies that many traditional Republicans could support. Trump promoted political, economic, strategic, and cultural nationalism in a country in which these things had been widely thought to be antiquated notions. Trump's rhetoric spoke of a return to the America that existed before the social and economic revolutions that have occurred since the 1950s. In this, he mirrored the ideas of Ronald Reagan and can be seen as a disjunctive leader trying to hold a fraying coalition together (Skowronek 1997). The Reagan coalition, policies, and worldview have dominated the United States for a little over forty years and the problems Reagan was elected to solve have been, but these solutions produced recent problems that the Reagan worldview could not solve. The electorate is comprised of different people with different life experiences than when Reagan was first elected.[8] The paradigm of a politically marketed politics that Ronald Reagan brought to the national stage has reached full flower but has been radically changed by the rise of social media from a top-down, mass activity into a co-creative niche activity. It was during the Obama campaigns that social media came on the scene in American politics and during the second Obama campaign that both candidates ran many niche campaigns meaning that segmentation was beginning to take over politics.[9]

Much of what Donald Trump sold as a candidate and implemented in office represents standard Republican fare packed into a sticky brand. Even his musings about toughening up the border and reforming immigration policy resembled proposals both parties had flirted with since the last major immigration reform in 1986. The ways in which Trump expressed these ideas and the venues in which he did so differentiated him from his predecessors. Trump's pitches generated potent responses from friends and foes alike. Trump's brand persona was the opposite of his immediate three predecessors and as David Axelrod argued he was a viable candidate because he was the anti-Obama in policy and brand personality.[10] Trump could credibly claim that he had nothing to do with the policies that led to 9/11, two wars, or the financial crisis. He had a list of actions that the Obama Administration had taken during its eight years that could be used to engage latent conservative voters and those disappointed with the moderation Obama showed in office. Trump reached out to voters who had different demographic and psychographic profiles from those voters Barack Obama engaged so adopting such a radically different brand personality, even if a lot of the substantive policies were standard Republican fare, was an intentional choice. The Trump brand was aimed at the non-college educated, those who did physical labor, ran their own businesses and were middle class. As Trump famously said: "I love the poorly educated" in response to a powerful performance among lesser educated voters during the 2016 Nevada caucuses.[11] His audiences were older, whiter, and more male than it seemed possible to win with in contemporary America.[12] Trump's voters were either terrified by what Obama's Presidency represented in racial and cultural terms and angry at his Administration's policies or disappointed that he was more pragmatic than radical. As Zito and Todd note, in 2016, a subset of voters picked Obama twice and then voted for Trump. Trump, like their other choice Senator Bernie Sanders, promised to upend the status quo. Further Ekins (2017) found five distinct types of Trump voters: Conservatives, Free Marketers, Anti-Elites, the Disengaged, and American Preservationists (who are economically progressive but nativist in terms of cultural and immigration issues).[13] The two biggest groups were Staunch Conservatives and Free Marketers accounting for 56% of the sample but two other big groups of voters (around 20% each) were responded to anti-elite or cultural preservation messaging.[14] These were important votes for Trump to attract because they were not people who would normally vote for a Republican. Additionally, five percent of the Trump vote came from people who did not normally vote and were not loyal Republicans. Thus, Trump attracted people because of his personal and political brands, not the GOP brand.[15] This meant that he attracted a lot of business by offering a new, different product from those people usually saw but that he would face the challenge of attracting repeat business in 2020.

Trump presented himself as a working-class outsider made good who became interested in politics after seeing the suffering of the average American at the hands of the elite. In this, he echoed American populists like Huey Long, George Wallace, Richard Nixon, Ross Perot, and Pat Buchanan, all of whom presented themselves as fighting for the average American against the self-interested elite. Like his populist predecessors, Trump appealed to working-class people in their own language thus producing the same derision from the educated class and its representatives as they had. This elite questioned Trump's intelligence, as they had questioned his populist predecessors' intelligence because Trump spoke in terms that his audience targets could understand. This was a wise marketing strategy. Trump's rallies and his verbal style were in keeping with his brand personality. They were large raucous events in support of a raucous candidate.

The downside to Trump's branding was that it repelled some traditional Republicans and better-educated voters. This seemed to be a smart trade-off because, while these audiences are likely to vote, they are also much smaller than other audiences that might potentially vote for Trump. As the 2020 result showed, one of the problems with this model was the geographic distribution of each category of voters. The audiences Trump pushed away lived in big numbers in suburban areas in swing states. His party suffered big losses in the 2018 Congressional elections and Trump was defeated in 2020 partly because of the geographic distribution of his desired and fired audiences.

Trump's 2016 election victory was a rare defeat for the narrow bipartisan elite who have dominated modern American politics. From 1980 through 2008, there had been a Bush or a Clinton on one ticket or the other in every Presidential year. The streak was ended by Barack Obama in 2008. Obama in terms of educational background and a personal brand was very much of said elites. Like the Bushes and Clintons was part of the long winning streak for Harvard and Yale graduates at the Presidential level. Trump too was an Ivy Leaguer, but his brand persona did not trade upon this credential. Trump could sell himself as an outsider because he had only dabbled with politics and political statements before 2016. Instead, he had spent his time building a successful brand. In addition to his real estate business, Trump shilled for all kinds of products. He had been a TV star and even a World Wrestling Entertainment character.

Although he had run for President previously as a Libertarian and had mused about doing so as far back as the 1980s, Trump had no prior experience in office when he launched his 2016 campaign. Trump's success ignited a moral panic among the elite gatekeepers and leaders of both parties. His ability to win the election in the face of their prognostications and efforts to derail him marked a direct threat to their power and positions. Something similar happened in the 2020 Democratic Primary as Bernie Sanders was building momentum in the early contests. The Democratic elite showed its muscle in its 2020 primary process. Once Joe Biden won the South Carolina primary, the party elite consolidated behind him thus stopping the insurgent Bernie Sanders and avoiding a protracted ideological battle.[16] The Biden victory represents a triumph for Democrats but also for a variety of other elites who spent four years trying to put the populist genie Trump unleashed back in its bottle.

Trump used branding and direct-to-consumer marketing to circumvent the elaborate screening system that had developed in the second half of the twentieth century. Trump upended a set of informal arrangements in which elite journalists and Washington wise folks had a great deal of say in who was taken seriously as a potential President and which ideas merited consideration in the public square. Many of the loudest voices that complained about his brand persona, policies, and personal traits would have never voted for him. Trump represented a different social class, culture, or policies than they would have supported. Trump and the reaction to him show the ways in which politics has become about branding, brand style segmentation, and differentiation more than it is about issues and policy. Trump's sticky branding, direct-to-consumer marketing, and small donor fundraising showed how an outsider could overcome the expertise and funding advantages that political professionals enjoy. Trump's strategy was a challenge to both political parties, Washington-based interest groups, consulting firms, political action committees, and media gatekeepers. Trump incited a moral panic among these groups that really represented a battle for control of the levers of power and the public agenda. Given the professionalization of politics in the wake of the advocacy explosion, the rise of think tanks, and the proliferation of media it was also a battle over what government was going to fund and who was going to pay for those things. On the right, Trump threatened to displace an extensive number of conservative entrepreneurs who had built their own brands and businesses. Trump's success kicked off a battle over prestige, market share, and affluence in Conservative circles.

Something similar took place in the battles Trump waged against the bureaucracy. As Bachner and Ginsburg (2016) argue, civil servants often take their own policy preferences to be identical to what the public wanted. Donald Trump's election showed that this might not be so thus igniting another battle for power. As Skowronek et al. (2021) note the federal bureaucracy has its own interests, agencies have their own cultures and individual bureaucrats have their own political preferences. As they further observe, when Trump talked about the "Deep State" his language might have been imprecise, but he was pointing to a phenomenon that had grown over time: the ability of the unelected portions of the American Government to block the preferences of some in the elected part of the government. This battle has taken place across all sorts of policy areas. It even led to the first Trump impeachment in 2019. Trump's success ignited a moral panic among the elite, a power struggle with the bureaucracy, and broad concerns that society was entering a much more fractious era in which voices once thought to be too extreme became prominent.[17] While this could be so, quietude produced through elite mediation is not a requirement for or necessarily an indicator of a healthy democracy. One can argue that the domestic tranquility that Americans enjoyed for so long was more a reflection of the levers of power being held by a narrow elite than it was reflective of public opinion. Given the vast changes in the country economically, regionally, demographically, and culturally, why would it follow that the same class of people from the same institutions concentrated in a few places in the Northeast would continue to dominate politics? The rise of Trump and his progressive counterparts, most of whom do not have Ivy League degrees, show that their continued dominance is not a given. Joe Biden's success shows that neither is their defeat assured.

The broadening of voices in the public square indicates that American democracy is revitalizing itself. Political marketing techniques like branding, segmentation, and direct-to-consumer marketing are leading the way as the success of candidate Trump showed. It is now possible for candidates representing communities and voices that had previously been excluded from the public square to achieve levels of public awareness and support that were not previously possible. Mr. Trump's election, far from indicating the onset of an authoritarian period, was a sign that a new

American politics, driven by tightly targeted brand narratives and heightened emotions, is developing and offered the potential to engage more Americans than had been engaged in recent decades. Trump offered one version of disruption, but other versions exist especially among Democratic progressives. Trump, as some of his progressive counterparts are doing, built a brand that distinguished him from his competitors, aimed it at specific audiences, and used earned and social media to distribute it. His success showed that a well-crafted, tightly targeted brand can win elections on the cheap if the candidate uses market research to find and understand an audience that it tries to engage through social media and target marketing.[18] His subsequent failure to win reelection shows that the amount of money a campaign raises doesn't necessarily correlate with success, that market conditions matter and that running as an incumbent is a different strategic undertaking than running as an insurgent challenger meaning that politicians in that situation would be wise to adjust their brand to reflect that reality.

Mr. Trump's brand was class-conscious as are those with which progressive Democrats work. Even the 2020 Biden campaign made some class references. The resurgence of class-consciousness in the United States and its appearance in political marketing should not be surprising given how the country has been socially sorted in recent decades as Bishop (2009) and Mason (2018) have independently noted. The rapid change happening here and elsewhere has produced a fight over values as Norris and Inglehart (2019) show. Trump and his progressive rivals have created an emotive brand battle over what it means to be an American. They have built deep brand loyalty among some audiences and deep brand antipathy among others as emotional brands are wont to do. Trump's brand combined class-consciousness with concern about a series of other trends in American life. One was the increasing amount of racial, ethnic, religious, and cultural diversity of the population driven by the Immigration Act of 1965 and its successors.[19] A second was the various philosophical and rights revolutions that have taken place here in recent decades have produced fights over values and policies that split the country demographically and psychographically. A third as Norris and Inglehart (2019), argue is that issues of identity and post-materialist values have come to dominate over all other concerns. Mason (2018) took this further to argue that Americans have developed deep meta-identities around political parties and movements. Donald Trump caused none of these things, but he understood that the conditions were ripe for an emotionally branded candidate to succeed when he ran in 2016.

While Donald Trump won by building a sticky brand that capitalized on economic dislocation caused by globalization and the Great Recession plus the rising importance of identity and social issues, he was not the only disruptive candidate who could have succeeded. Such success is now possible because technological changes have made it so. Database marketing exists and has been applied to politics, the internet has changed the way Americans live and social media has become ubiquitous. Political branding has become more of a co-creative, activity as a result. While the extent to which it really is co-creative can be debated, there is no question that Trump's sticky branding strategy represented an effort to build a sense of community among his customers. In 2016, Trump was aided by recent history because Americans have been unwilling to vote for the same party three times in a row for President. Once Trump won the nomination, he had a good shot of winning the general election just because he was not a Democrat. Given that, it is less surprising that he won the general election than he won the nomination. In addition to his deviation from the traditional Republican economic plan and his personal flaws, candidate Trump had tenuous ties to the party. His branding and voter targeting were effective because they helped him reach enough primary voters to overcome these obstacles to win the nomination.

The Trump campaign built a social media optimized brand around its candidate and his opponents in both the primary and general elections. Trump's sticky social media brand was more emotive, more targeted, and more distinct than anything else in the marketplace. It helped him to stand out and continually capture attention in a crowded marketplace. His effort was aided by the unique nature of the 2016 campaign and the well-defined opponent that he faced. Trump benefitted from a series of leaks and conspiracy theories about Secretary Clinton that amounted to an assertion that she was not like the average American voter something that Republicans had long been saying. Her long tenure in high-profile positions on the national stage meant that she was a well-known commodity making it easy for Trump to build fellowship with prior anti-Clinton marketing campaigns. Trump tried to negatively brand Joe Biden in 2020 but the effort failed because Biden had a different personality than did Hillary Clinton, because Trump was running as an incumbent and had a record in office to defend and because COVID changed the political marketplace in ways that were unfavorable to the kind of brand that Donald Trump had built.

If brands in the current age of content overload must always be with us to be effective, then this explains why the branded Trump became the omnipresent President. Trump was everywhere, all the time and everything ended up being about him. The Trump political brand was omnipresent in ways that other political brands, including that of Joe Biden, have not been. Trump was at the head of a gushing fountain of information and noise daily thus his message, his story, and his brand personality were always in the public eye. This was a major accomplishment in an era of fractured media, fragmented audiences, and short attention spans that only ended because Trump was banned from Facebook and Twitter after the events of January 6th, 2021. Until that point, the Trump brand and brand story appeared on every available platform all the time. In this, Donald Trump practiced state-of-the-art branding. When combined with the use of machine learning and bots, this means a brand can always be available to its target audience.[20] Even in a world of overwhelming content, Trump's sticky and brand omnipresence strategy set him apart and helped him to deeply engage his customers. Trump's brand was omnipresent because it dominated the discourse across platforms. As a performer, Donald Trump was disciplined. He repeatedly told his basic brand story and reiterated his brand values. He often applied these things to new subjects or situations as they presented themselves. He was not afraid to say bold things because by doing so, he gained attention and stood out from his rivals. A good indicator that his strategy was effective is provided by the relentless attention and criticism he attracted.[21] A good indicator that his strategy had big downside costs include his becoming the face of a bungled pandemic response and the overall weariness toward him that many voters eventually developed.

Trump's brand was omnipresent because it defined the way in which people considered situations and events that might not be political and because it was universally recognized. He was seen as being authoritative among his supporters.[22] His omnipresence strategy built deep brand loyalty and antipathy. On the other hand, people know who he is, what he is about, and if they like him or not. People thought about him all the time because he was at the center of everything for years. Like Howard Stern whose radio show Mr. Trump has appeared on, the people who disliked him still pay attention to everything he says and does. Trump, like Stern, captured attention because both added elements of shock and sensation to their presentations to stand out in a crowded marketplace. Trump has achieved political brand omnipresence meaning that we could not easily escape the messages he and his critics aimed at us. Thus, Trump's brand drove the news cycle and the topics on most people's minds for years.

Trump's tagline "Make America Great Again" was first used by Ronald Reagan. Trump's use of it was a clear effort to tap into the Republican Party's heritage brand. Like Reagan, Trump tried to position himself as the person who could restore the country to the lost glory that years of Democratic alleged mismanagement had stolen away. Trump's brand personality and emotions were much angrier than those of Ronald Reagan. The way in which Trump presented his policy proposals did not resemble the ways in which the Gipper presented his. Trump adopted a more working-class persona and brand style. Trump's approach gave the Republican Party the marketing problem of having to incorporate the new audiences that he attracted while trying to keep its other well-performing audience segments. The result of the 2018 midterm election showed that, without Trump on the ballot, the GOP would struggle to turn out his audience but with him on the ballot other audiences would defect to the Democrats. Trump ended up being a mixed blessing at the ballot box. Trump succeeded in 2016, as Michael Moore argued, by speaking to the concerns of working-class white Americans and working-class white men in a way that nobody had recently and because of Democratic candidate problems.[23] By 2020, he had driven away enough other audiences that, even though he did very well with working-class voters, he did not have enough overall support to win the election.

Because branding means keeping promises meaning that politicians who use a brand strategy are incentivized to stand by their brand rather than compromising to get things done in government. This disjunction has important implications for governance because the separated American system usually functions best when those in its institutions find ways to compromise. This disjunction is amplified in the United States because a divided government is a frequent occurrence at the federal level. The political brand exists to support political products and to be most effective requires politicians to unstintingly stand behind its promises. How can compromise occur if it means undermining the integrity of the political brand and the politicians and parties that build said brand? While this problem exists for all political marketers, it is exacerbated in the United

States because of the way in which power is divided between the federal and state governments, as well as, between the national and state governments. The brand promises that the product will work as promised but how could the political consumer believe it did if politicians compromised on its promises to get things done?

Governing, rather than becoming something in which everyone works together to reach mutually agreeable solutions, has become a zero-sum brand battle. Trump sought and achieved brand omnipresence for himself and his Administration's undertakings. These accomplishments were not sufficient to win reelection because this brand was too targeted at its best performing segments. This was different from what other Presidents, including Presidents who have tried to use branding, have done. Presidents usually try to strike a balance between marketing and governing in the office while attempting to be a unifying national figure. Donald Trump concentrated on serving his best customers and on continuously selling to them rather than trying to be a unifying Presidential figure. His approach to being President reinforced the segments into which people had sorted rather than the society of which he was officially the leader.

Trump did for political branding what Nike had done for consumer goods branding. Trump and Nike changed the focus of brand-based marketing from seeking to gain broad popularity to seeking to popularity from the right audiences. Nike has run an ad featuring controversial former San Francisco 49rs quarterback Colin Kaepernick doing the voiceover and appearing in some of the shots along with other athletes. Kaepernick's presence made the ad controversial but as Nike CEO Phil Knight told a Stanford University business school audience "It doesn't matter how many people hate your brand as long as enough people love it. And as long as you have that attitude, you cannot be afraid of offending people. You can't try and go down the middle of the road. You have to take a stand on something, which is ultimately I think why the Kaepernick ad worked."[24] Nike doubled down on its position by withdrawing a pair of sneakers that displayed the thirteen-star Betsy Ross flag on their back from the market at Mr. Kaepernick's suggestion and even though this decision generated an immediate backlash, it was just a continuation of the strategy Mr. Knight outlined above.[25] Given that Nike's sales had gone up after the first ad, this was a good business decision despite all the opposition it had generated.[26] Nobody would ever accuse Donald Trump of being afraid of offending people or "going down the middle" rather he used branding to tell his core supporters a story that they liked regardless of what anyone else thought of it just as Nike had done.

Trump's words and deeds exemplified state-of-the-art targeted branding in the narrow-casted social media age. Trump's approach to immigration, asylum, and border policy is a case in point. He tried to build a wall, put a citizenship question on the census, and tighten the asylum policy. He presided over a series of detention facilities in which migrants were held in grueling conditions. Trump's retort to his critics' complaints about the detention facilities in general and the treatment of migrant children specifically might have infuriated his critics but resonated with his core audiences: "If Illegal Immigrants are unhappy with the conditions in the quickly built or refitted detentions centers, just tell them not to come. All problems solved!"[27] Trump had preceded this missive with a Twitter broadside against his Democratic opponents who had criticized his policies: "Mexico is doing a far better job than the Democrats on the Border. Thank you, Mexico!"[28] Statements like these helped Trump brand the Democrats as the party of open borders and illegal immigration. He pounded away on this theme, defended the quality of the detention facilities, and supported the work of the ICE and CBP in the same set of tweets by saying: "Our Border Patrol people are not hospital workers, doctors or nurses. The Democrats bad Immigration Laws, which could be easily fixed, are the problem. Great job by Border Patrol, above and beyond. Many of these illegal aliens are living far better now than where they ...[29] came from, and in far safer conditions. No matter how good things look, even if perfect, look visitors will act shocked & aghast at how terrible things are. Just Pols. If they really want to fix them, change the Immigration Laws and Loopholes. So easy to do!"[30] In his third tweet in the thread, Trump offers a way out of the issue by saying: "Now, if you really want to fix the Crisis at the Southern Border, both humanitarian and otherwise, tell migrants not to come into our country unless they are willing to do so legally, and hopefully through a system based on Merit. This way we have no problems at all!"[31] Trump had introduced an immigration reform bill that moved the focus of the system from reuniting families toward attracting immigrants with skills that were in short supply in the United States weeks earlier. Trump used sticky language to explain the situation at the border in a way sure to reassure his supporters, infuriate his critics and promote his policies. This is consistent with one of the core Trump brand elements because it presents the Democrats as willing participants in the destruction of America's national identity in service of their political goal of building a durable electoral majority. Overall, this was a similar approach to the one that Nike took in selling shoes. Unlike Nike, Trump had to win enough voters in enough states to win the Electoral College to be reelected and this proved to be too tall of an order in 2020. Donald Trump became the omnipresent branded President. He showed Americans that the President could become an inescapable brand that some loved, some hated but all paid attention to and by whom many felt exhausted.

Trump's efforts to expand the audience for his products were hardly unprecedented even if the ways in which he accomplished his goals were. He identified an underserved audience and tried to serve its needs. In this, he was like some of the more successful progressive candidates who have a dedicated focus on expanding the marketplace for their products. Trump's brand was aimed at some people who had only been minor voter targets previously. Their mutual goal of expanding participation points more toward the revitalization rather than the decline of representative democracy. While the traditional mediating institutions and gatekeepers might be seeing their influence decline, the Trump message tapped into a long-standing anti-elite streak in America. Trump consciously made the first version of the anti-elite candidate, Andrew Jackson, a part of his brand heritage. Jackson because he was the first American President whose political career had not been spent on the Atlantic seaboard. He was a rough-hewn military man much like his fellow inhabitants of what was then frontier Tennessee. Jackson brought a streak of everyman populism into national politics and combined it with the kind of regionalism that has periodically reappeared in our national life. The most recent example of the phenomenon was Ronald Reagan who claimed to speak for an alienated West in the face of a national government serving more Eastern interests.

Trump was hardly the first American politician to make very targeted appeals aimed at well-defined audiences. Like Barack Obama before him, who focused on increasing the number of youth and visible minority voters in the electorate, Donald Trump found an underserved audience, engaged it, and mobilized it: white voters having a high school diploma or less.[32] He added this to several other GOP segments to win in 2016. His victory caused Democrats to put heroic effort into voter registration drives and mobilization campaigns in 2020 to defeat Trump. The Trump phenomenon is the culmination of an increasingly public-mediated and marketed Presidency. The Presidency was advantaged during the last century as the number of communicative channels at the disposal of Presidents and their staffs increased.[33] From the early days of Theodore Roosevelt and Woodrow Wilson meeting with a few chosen reporters to Edward Bernays's efforts to make Calvin Coolidge more popular with the American public to FDR's fireside chats, Kennedy and Nixon's slick advertisements and jingles to Ronald Reagan's introduction of a full marketing and branding model, the Presidency has become the omnipresent American political institution. Presidents are expected to deal with all problems at a moment's notice and the people occupying it have been expected to be both brilliant and of high moral character. Presidents and the Presidency began to be packaged like many other consumer products because doing so was a straightforward way to reach a large audience quickly.[34] The Presidency became this kind of institution because the technology came into existence that made it possible. Presidents started using new communicative technologies and marketing techniques to cut through the ever-increasing noise of a crowded American consciousness to build relationships with the public that could then be used to sell their personalities and policies. The politicians changed the way in which they communicated with the public because the way the public was reachable and the concerns the public had were more precisely knowable than they had been in the past. Trump's innovation was to brand the institution in a memorable, personalized way.

Donald Trump took account of the fact that Americans were highly sorted by the time he ran for President.[35] While they had once largely lived in rural areas or worked in industrial jobs that put them into union membership and close-knit neighborhoods that in turn put them into civil organizations but moved to cities, suburbs, and professional occupations during the twentieth century.[36] The net result was to make modern Americans ripe targets for marketed politics in ways earlier generations had not been. One of the biggest drivers of social sorting is higher education. It is difficult to understate the importance of college in promoting the social sorting and individualization that first leads to political marketing and then led to Donald Trump in the White House.[37] People came to see themselves as individual contractors and, eventually, as members of issue and lifestyle networks. This transformation led to the rise of interest groups and the decline of parties in the electorate, the rise of interest group politics, and marketed politics. In response, the parties invested a great deal in market research and learned that not everyone in every place was equally likely to vote for their candidates or supported their issue positions. Thus, the parties began to allocate resources in the places and on behalf of the candidates that were most likely to bring them the best return. At the same time, campaigns and candidates began trying to match types of appeals to voter profiles. This was in keeping with the way in which the country was realigning itself geographically, demographically, and culturally. Marketers were able to break the country up into a variety of different audience segments and those audience segments were able to segregate themselves into communities of the like-minded.[38] This trend was further accentuated by the rise of social media and the development of the kinds of large databases and tracking technologies that meant that multiple conversations could take place within but not across groups and political marketers were able to shape these conversations in ways that their 1960s predecessors could barely have envisioned.[39] The upside for political marketers and the like-minded was that it was now much easier to find and stay within one's ideal group than it had once been. The downside is that this sorting came at the cost of cross-group communications that have the potential to build a society instead of reinforcing segments.[40] Thus, politics became just another form of branded and marketed activity.

Donald Trump's use of public relations techniques to win the Presidency resembles the concepts that Edward Bernays presented in his works Propaganda (2004) and the Engineering of Consent (1955). Trump posited that he represented what people really wanted and, once in office, would listen to them and deliver for them. Bernays argued that public relations techniques could be used to build awareness of public affairs and public figures but could also be used by public figures to understand what the voters wanted and through this process social consensus might be produced. Trump's team used market research and his own marketing expertise to understand his customers. His team broke the audience up into smaller pieces to communicate precise messages that resonate with specific audiences. Bernays wrote at a time when the American population was not as educated, diverse, or geographically spread out as it now is. The country has become sorted geographically and along lifestyle lines. This has produced a situation in which entire regions of the country vote for one party or another and are culturally insular.[41] This clustering of the like-minded has extended beyond physical space into media and online in which people are broken down into specific groups and then served with targeted messaging.[42] Bernays thought that there were common interests that an elite could identify and discuss with the mass of the population, but he wrote in a time when fewer people were educated. He wrote well before the social revolutions of the 1960s and the communications revolutions of the late twentieth and early twenty-first centuries occurred. As Donald Trump's win shows, this might not be something a candidate has to do but Trump's experience in office shows that success in governing might depend on it.

Donald Trump became the GOP standard bearer partly in response to the GOP's ongoing product problem. The Conservative brand traditionally emphasized (1) low taxes, (2) deregulation, (3) market economics, (4) strong defense and American engagement in the world, and (5) traditional moral values. The GOP brand was damaged because of a series of product failures during the Bush years then Republicans spent the Obama years mired in a factional battle over the party's product offering and ideological leanings. While there were many who called for moderation on tax, regulatory, immigration, and cultural issues, there were others like the Freedom Caucus that argued that the party should stick to its Reagan roots and double down on its policy positions. McCain and Romney ran civil campaigns that argued for GOP moderation. Both lost the general election, and their defeats made a big impression on Mr. Trump who faulted them for not being tough enough.[43] Donald Trump is a branding expert who is well versed in reading market trends. Trump's TV show, "the Apprentice" scored well with a diverse audience yet Trump's political brand was heavily targeted at older, white voters.[44] This is partly because Trump's data team figured out that these voters were underperforming in terms of turnout and could be mobilized in bigger numbers thus shifting the ideological positioning of the Republican Party and paving the way for a Trump victory.[45] This shift too shows how branding is combined with segmentation to produce a tightly targeted political product.

Donald Trump's electoral victory shows the importance of marketing in American politics but his tumultuous administration and electoral defeat in 2020 show its risks and limits. Trump's use of branding and marketing is not unique among recent Presidents but the obsessive personal focus on branding and marketing stands apart. In the White House, Donald Trump was a performer and marketer more than a manager.[46] Trump's career, before entering politics, focused on selling consumer products. He had sold everything from wine to casinos, appeared in commercials for other companies and appeared in professional wrestling broadcasts. He was an accomplished promoter and multimedia performer. While. Trump had his own celebrity brand. He was not the first President who made use of the brand strategy, but he updated the strategy and tactics associated with it for the social media age. Reagan, Clinton, and Obama all built emotively optimistic brands. Reagan wanted to "Make American Great Again," George H. W. Bush sought a "kinder, gentler" Reaganism, Clinton was "The Man from Hope" George W. Bush sought to be a "United Not a Divider" and Barack Obama sought "Change You Can Believe In." The key differences between Trump and these recent predecessors are Trump's use of sticky branding and omnipresence strategies. For the other Presidents who have used it, branding was a tool but for Trump it was the administration's central focus. His predecessors used marketing techniques more sparingly once in office but made extensive efforts to broaden their appeal to make their presidencies more representative of the country. Consistent with the way in which sticky branding works, Trump was focused on building community with his best customers and creating a sense of omnipresence. Consistent with the sticky brand's emphasis on service, argued, to his customers, that he had run for President to help the country, not for ego or personal gain. He donated his Presidential salary to charity and presented himself as a business tycoon. Donald Trump has professional experience using these techniques and, unusual for a President, did not depend on a retinue of advisors to speak for him instead he does it himself. He tweeted, he called reporters, and would do sit-down interviews even with those who did not write flattering things about him. Some of his predecessors did some of these things but none of them did them to the extent Trump did nor did they try to function as their own media department as Trump did. The contrast between the way in which the Biden Administration and the Trump Administration approached public relations proves the point. Biden sits above several layers of specialized communications staffers and rarely appears in the media without a script. This is the opposite of the approach that Trump took.

Trump built an emotive brand around the idea that the country had lost its way and that he could restore it to its lost glory. Everything brands and communicates, thus looking at Donald Trump's behavior through the prism of branding theory is a logical thing to do.[47] Trump's personal presentation fits his brand. He mostly wears a dark business suit, a red tie, and a white shirt. This is typical attire for an American chief executive officer. He frequently pointed out that because he had a lot of money, he would not become corrupt in office. He used his residences, his businesses, and even his air fleet to give validity to his claims. Ever the marketer, Donald Trump focuses on his brand, his product, and his customers exclusively. In office, Trump was totally focused in keeping brand promises. He nominated people to key government positions of whom his supporters would approve and promoted policies that they would favor. Doing this has been a continuation of the targeted brand story Trump told on the campaign trail and perpetuated us versus them mentality that has developed in the country in recent decades.

Trump: The American Variant in the Populist Moment

Trump's brand strategy succeeded in 2016 because it fit a populist mood in the country. Trump gave voice to those who thought the elites has undermined the country's culture and economy. Like any marketers, political marketers need to understand the marketplace in which they are trying to sell. Donald Trump and his team read the populist mood in the United States correctly in the run up to 2016 then found big enough audiences in enough states to win the Presidency. There have been other populists who have risen to prominence in the United States, but Trump won the Presidency using populist themes and his branding is a big reason he did so.[48] Populism has developed in response to socio-economic dislocation meaning Trump's brand can be taken as one response to the Financial Crisis, Mass Immigration, and rapid cultural change.[49] Populism has not just risen in the United States in recent years.[50] Trump's populism was the response to the 2007 financial crisis, a permanent American military establishment, a global economic order the United States built that might have outlived its usefulness, and mass immigration that combined with rapid cultural change led some people to feel that their country was disappearing before their eyes.[51] Trump's success was at least as much a reflection of the sentiment that the elites in both parties were out in front of what the public in both parties was willing to support meaning that he sold himself as an insurgent bringing back a better past that was better than the elite manufactured presently.[52] The policies that activated these Americans in support of Trump had been promoted indirectly through battles over judicial or cabinet nominations that had themselves been used as marketing opportunities by both parties.[53] Typical of the battle between the cosmopolitans and the nationalists that is raging globally, Trump and his opponents have the same overly negative view of each other and instead of talking with each other just point out what they hate about the other group and refuse to compromise on anything.[54] This fits perfectly with Mason's argument that suggests that segmentation and sorting are the cause of our current ills, and both fit with the idea that branding is really driving all of it.[55]

Donald Trump's election reflects a populist challenge to the modern liberal order by populists.[56] Trump appealed to people who felt themselves excluded from the cosmopolitan liberal order. Some of their alienation is the result of elite policy choices like free trade, liberal immigration and refugee policies, and an emphasis on secularism and diversity.[57] The context in which Donald Trump operated differed from his European counterparts because the United States has a long history of populism and Europe does not.[58] Americans have seen populist candidates from the right and the left run and gain traction.[59] Running against elites and the government they seek to head is something of a long-standing tradition for American politicians. Indeed, Eatwell and Goodwin present the real battle that Trump and his European counterparts fought as being like the one that Bendix (1980) described in his book Kings or People. Bendix looked at the process through which nations became either monarchies or representative systems. One can see the European Union, other international institutions, and the American elite in both parties as a modern equivalent to the Aristotelian guardian class out to stifle the popular will while serving its self-defined good. The elite believe that more integration will produce more stability and that the nation-state has or will soon have outlived its relevance in a highly connected world. This misses the key role that culture and national identity play in shaping the day-to-day understanding many people have of the world.[60] Donald Trump's branding and rhetoric tapped into this sense. Like the Italian Five Star Movement had, Trump argued that people knew better than the elite and that direct communication could replace some of the existing institutions of state. Five Star, however, went further than Trump by arguing that technological changes had made the time right for direct democracy.[61] Trump's critique stuck to the notion that the elites were stupid, corrupt, or both and that average people had been forgotten but made to pay for a system that did not benefit them, it benefitted the elite. Trump mostly focused his ire on the political elite, but it was easy to see how his audience could have taken him as speaking about the creative class housed in big coastal cities who were more cosmopolitan in orientation than were they. Trump's branding reflects his populist nationalism in culture, economics, and international affairs. His actions in office were true to the brand promises he made on the campaign trail.

Trump won the election by taking ideas from the left and right then turning them into an emotional sticky brand. This brand engaged a few segments of the electorate that had not voted in a long time in a big way and kept enough Republicans on board in the right places to win. Trump articulate the themes of strength, security, and economic growth that conservatives work with across the world but added in things that would be more familiar to leftist populists: the economy is rigged, free trade has been bad for you and good for the elites, and that the voices of ordinary Americans have been locked out of government for too long. Trump represented himself as being just an average guy who happened to have a lot of money and specifically not a member of the cosmopolitan elite.[62] His brand story rejected the cosmopolitans and the world that they had made. While Trump himself is a very wealthy Ivy Leaguer, his brand persona is a working-class everyman like the protagonist on the 1970s TV show "All in the Family" Archie Bunker.[63] Trump weaved a brand story in which he would restore growth and order to the country but also make people proud to be Americans again while making the elite in both parties uncomfortable something All in the Family creator Norman Lear noted by saying "I think of Donald Trump as the middle finger of the American right hand."[64]

NOTES

1. Rahm Emmanuel It's Time to Hold American Elites Accountable for Their Abuses If Democrats want to address simmering middle-class anger, they need to deliver justice. May 21, 2019. https://www.theatlantic.com/ideas/archive/2019/05/middle-class-americans-are-sick-elite-privilege/589849/.
2. Ibid.
3. Mark Leibovich. "This Town Melts Down." *The New York Times*. July 11, 2017. https://www.nytimes.com/2017/07/11/magazine/washington-dc-politics-trump-this-town-melts-down.html, accessed July 31, 2019. And This Town, 2014.
4. See Mark Leibovich This Town (2013) for an in-depth examination of how Washington's culture had diverged from that of the country at large prior to the Trump years.

5. See Alan Abramowitz and Steven Webster. "The Rise of Negative Partisanship and the Nationalization of U.S. Elections in the 21st Century." *Electoral Studies*. Volume r1, March 2016, pp. 12–22.
6. As Pollack and Schweikart (2017, p. 5) note there are legitimate questions about the extent to which Barack Obama's popularity was as high as the polls claimed it to be by 2016.
7. Steve Bertonia. "How Jared Kushner Won Trump the White House." https://www.forbes.com/sites/stevenbertoni/2016/11/22/exclusive-interview-how-jared-kushner-won-trump-the-white-house/#17d702 ad3af6, accessed November 22, 2016.
8. Richard Krietner. "What Time Is It? Here's What the 2016 Election Tells Us About Obama, Trump, and What Comes Next." *The Nation*. November 22, 2016. https://www.thenation.com/article/what-time-is-it-heres-what-the-2016-election-tells-us-about-obama-trump-and-what-comes-next/, accessed November 22, 2016.
9. See for example: Tanzina Vega. "Campaigns Use Microtargeting to Attract Supporters." *New York Times*. February 20, 2012. https://one drive.live.com/edit.aspx?cid=77f030235b4a5a8e&page=view&resid=77F 030235B4A5A8E!2663&parId=77F030235B4A5A8E!101&app=Word& wacqt=mru, accessed February 27, 2020.
10. Axelrod: I Missed It, But Trump '16 Is Obama' 08 Former Obama aide says open presidential elections reflect on the incumbent, and voters like contrast. Gabrielle Levy. "Axelrod-i-missed-it-but-trump-16-is-obama-08." https://www.usnews.com/news/articles/2016-01-25/.
11. Josh Hafner. "Donald Trump Loves the 'Poorly Educated'—and They Love Him." USA TODAY. February 24, 2016. https://www.usatoday. com/story/news/politics/onpolitics/2016/02/24/donald-trump-nev ada-poorly-educated/80860078/, accessed January 6, 2020.
12. See Pew Research Center US Politics and Policy. "An Examination of the 2016 Election Based on Validated Voters." August 8, 2018. https://www.people-press.org/2018/08/09/an-examination-of-the-2016-electorate-based-on-validated-voters/, accessed February 28, 2020.
13. Emily Ekins. "The Five Types of Trump Voters: Who They Are and What They Believe." The Democracy Fund Voter Study Group. June 2017. https://www.voterstudygroup.org/publication/the-five-types-trump-voters, accessed January 6, 2019.
14. Ibid.
15. Ibid.
16. See for example Lisa Lerer and Reid J. Epstein. "Democratic Leaders Willing to Risk Party Damage to Stop Bernie Sanders." *New York Times*.

February 27, 2020. https://www.nytimes.com/2020/02/27/us/pol
itics/democratic-superdelegates.html?action=click&module=Well&pgt
ype=Homepage&section=Politics, accessed February 27, 2020.
17. David Greenberg. "The End of Neutrality: Society's Shared Middle
   Ground Is Quickly Turning into a Battlefield. What Will That Do to
   Democracy?" Politico Magazine. September/October 2018. https://
   www.politico.com/magazine/story/2018/09/06/common-ground-
   good-america-society-219616, accessed September 20, 2018.
18. "Donald Trump and Hillary Clinton's Final Campaign Spending
   Revealed FEC Report Shows Donald Trump Laid Out $94 m in
   Last Push for White House While Hillary Clinton Spent $132 m and
   Cemented Herself as Biggest Fundraiser." The Guardian. December
   9, 2016. https://www.theguardian.com/us-news/2016/dec/09/trump-
   and-clintons-final-campaign-spending-revealed, accessed January 7, 2020.
19. Judis (2018, p. 53).
20. Tom Goodmanson. From Omnichannel to Omnipresent: The New
   Customer Experience. https://www.websitemagazine.com/blog/from-
   omnichannel-to-omnipresent-the-new-customer-experience, accessed July
   4, 2019.
21. Josh Barney. Omnipresence in Marketing: The Power of Being Everywhere (and How to Get There). https://www.einsteinmarketer.com/omn
   ipresence-in-marketing/, October 29, 2018, accessed July 4, 2019.
22. Ibid.
23. Michael Moore. "Five Reasons Why Trump Will Win." https://michae
   lmoore.com/trumpwillwin/, undated, accessed July 19, 2019.
24. Bill Snyder. Phil Knight on the Controversial Kaepernick Ad and
   Nike's Never-Give-Up Attitude. "It Doesn't Matter How Many People
   Hate Your Brand as Long as Enough People Love It." February
   14, 2019. https://www.gsb.stanford.edu/insights/phil-knight-controver
   sial-kaepernick-ad-nikes-never-give-attitude, Stanford Graduate School of
   Business, accessed July 3, 2019.
25. John D. Stoll When It Comes to Colin Kaepernick, the Flag and Nike,
   It's Just Business. https://www.wsj.com/articles/when-it-comes-to-
   colin-kaepernick-the-flag-and-nike-its-just-business-11562161561?mod=
   hp_listb_pos1, July 3, 2019, accessed July 3, 2019.
26. John D. Stoll When It Comes to Colin Kaepernick, the Flag and Nike,
   It's Just Business. https://www.wsj.com/articles/when-it-comes-to-
   colin-kaepernick-the-flag-and-nike-its-just-business-11562161561?mod=
   hp_listb_pos1, July 3, 2019, accessed July 3, 2019.
27. @realdonaldtrump tweet dated July 3, 2019, accessed on July 4, 2019.
   https://twitter.com/search?q=%40realdonaldtrump&src=tyah.
28. @realdonaldtrump tweet dated July 3, 2019, accessed July 4, 2019.
29. @realdonaldtrump tweet July 3, 2019.

30. @realdonaldtrump tweet July 3, 2019.
31. @realdonaldtrump tweet July 3, 2019.
32. For an in depth examination of how the Obama and Romney campaigns used data based targeting see Sasha Issenberg. "How Obama's Team Used Big Data to Rally Voters." *MIT Technology Review.* December 19, 2020. https://www.technologyreview.com/2012/12/19/114510/how-obamas-team-used-big-data-to-rally-voters/.
33. For a book length treatment see Greenberg (2016).
34. See for example Kathleen Hall Jamieson Packaging the President.
35. See Bishop (2009) for a book length treatment on the impact of social sorting in contemporary America.
36. See Skocpol (2013) for a book length treatment on the transformation of social arrangements in the country.
37. See for example, Murray (2012, pp. 46–64).
38. Turow, Breaking Up America (2007).
39. Turow Niche Envy (2008).
40. Turow, Breaking Up America (2007).
41. For a book length treatment see Bishop (2009).
42. Turow Breaking Up America (2007) and Niche Envy (2008) combine to show how niche narrowcasting and segmentation have changed the way the advertising and media worlds operate.
43. Coppins, 215 contains several incidents of Trump saying similar things.
44. Green (2017, p. 96).
45. Green (2017, pp. 98–102).
46. O'Brien (2015 especially p. 81).
47. Sergio Zyman (2000), Zyman and Brott (2002) presents two book length studies on the importance of consistency in branding.
48. John Judis (2016, 2018).
49. Ibid.
50. Eatwell and Goodwin (2018).
51. Judis (2018, p. 45).
52. Ibid.
53. Ibid.
54. Ibid.
55. Mason (2018).
56. Eatwell and Goodwin (2018 especially p. 79).
57. Ibid.
58. Eatwell and Goodwin (2018, p. 17).
59. Judis (2018, p. 57).
60. Eatwell and Goodwin (2018, pp. ix, xii).

61. Darren Loucaidis. "Building the Brexit Party: How Nigel Farage Copied Italy's Digital Populists." *The Guardian*. May 21, 2019. https://www.theguardian.com/politics/2019/may/21/brexit-party-nigel-farage-italy-digital-populists-five-starmovement?fbclid=IwAR07r7DMtJB_BVYwAXCeKid9qRZ8ch3oBOWahtw8bP7J4PvSU0gAD8F0_CY, accessed May 30, 2019.
62. Judis (2018) provides a book length analysis that partly argues current events can be seen through the prism of a conflict between cosmopolitanism and nationalism.
63. Nolan McCaskill. "Norman Lear: Trump Is a Real-Life Archie Bunker." Politico. June 3, 2016. https://www.politico.com/story/2016/06/norman-lear-trump-archie-bunker-223875, accessed July 19, 2019.
64. Ibid.

References

Adams, Scott. *Win Bigly: Persuasion in a World Where Facts Don't Matter.* Penguin, 2017.
Bachner, Jennifer and Benjamin Ginsburg. *What Washington Gets Wrong.* Prometheus, 2016.
Bendix, Rheinhard. *Kings or People: Power and the Mandate to Rule.* University of California Press, 1980
Bernays, Edward (Ed.). *The Engineering of Consent.* University of Oklahoma Press, 1955.
———. (Introduction by Mark Crispin Miller). *Propaganda.* Ig Publishing, 2004.
Bishop, Bill. *The Big Sort.* Mariner Books, 2009.
Eatwell, Roger and Matthew Goodwin. *National Populism: The Revolt Against Liberal Democracy.* Pelican, 2018.
Green, Joshua. *Devil's Bargain: Steve Bannon, Donald Trump and the Storming of the US Presidency.* Penguin, 2017.
Greenberg, David. *Republic of Spin.* New York: Norton, 2016.
Judis, John B. *The Populist Explosion.* Columbia Global Reports, 2016.
———. *The Nationalist Revival: Trade, Immigration and the Revolt Against Globalization.* Columbia Global Reports, 2018.
Mason, Liliana. *Uncivil Agreement: How Politics Became Our Identity.* Chicago. University of Chicago Press, 2018.
Miller, Jeremy. *Sticky Branding: 12.5 Principles To Stand Out, Attract Customers and Grow an Incredible Brand.* Page Two Books, 2015.
Murray, Charles. *Coming Apart; The State of White America.* Crown Forum, 2012.

Norris, Pippa and Ronald Inglehart. *Cultural Backlash: Trump, Brexit and Authoritarian Populism*. Cambridge University Press, 2019.

O'Brien, Timothy L. *Trump Nation*. Open Road Media, 2015.

Pollack, Joel B. and Larry Schweikart. *How Trump Won: The Inside Story of a Revolution*. Regenery, 2017.

Skocpol, Theda. *Diminished Democracy: From Membership to Management in American Civic Life* . University of Oklahoma Press, 2013.

Skowronek, Stephen. *The Politics Presidents Make*. Belknap Press, 1997.

Skowronek, Stephen, John Dearborn, and Desmond King *Phantoms of a Beleagured Republic*. Oxford University Press, 2021.

Turow, Joseph. *Breaking Up America*. Chicago: University of Chicago Press, 2007.

———. *Niche Envy*. MIT Press, 2008.

Zyman, Sergio. *The End of Marketing as We Know It*. Harper Business, 2000.

Zyman, Sergio and Armin A. Brott. *The End of Advertising as We Know It*. Wiley, 2002.

CHAPTER 3

Segmentation and Trump

Abstract This chapter argues that Donald Trump's campaign and Presidency show how data fuels political marketing. In the wake of Trump's success, media, commercial and interest group concerns have adjusted their brands to be emotionally opposed or aligned with the Trump brand. Trump's efforts show that geography, demography, and psychographics are key elements of a contemporary political marketing campaign that can be combined to find the right audiences and then understand which emotional appeals would resonate with them rather than employing society making messages. Across platforms, Trump told his audiences an emotive brand story that resonated with them while simultaneously alienating other audiences. All of which differ significantly from American politics in the pre-branding, marketing age.

Keywords Segmentation · Targeting · Data-driven campaigning · Team Trump · Dwight D. Eisenhower · Partisan media · Franklin D. Roosevelt · Disinformation · Trump Rallies · Brand story · Border Wall · Elizabeth Warren · Bernie Sanders · Presidential Election of 2020 · Presidential Election of 2016

In the early twenty-first century, the number of media platforms, distribution channels, and content that Americans could access increased significantly. The explosion of content, channels, and platforms was a key part of the reason Donald Trump's development of an emotive sticky brand was strategically wise. The world in which Americans lived had become noisier and the proliferation of platforms meant the audience was more fragmented than ever, but an emotive sticky brand offered a way for Trump to make his offering stand out.

These new platforms produced much more data about their users than once was available. Political and commercial marketers used it to build databases to understand their customers. An example of the way in which this worked in the late twentieth and early twenty-first centuries is provided by the Prizm system. Prizm was developed by Claritas.[1] Prizm and other databases like it let the marketer see what consumers do as opposed to what they claim to have done. This behavioral data can be overlain with geographic and demographic data to build very precise customer profiles at which messages can be precisely targeted. Both parties and many campaigns maintain such databases to help them develop and distribute their branded political products. These databases can help marketers understand which of their audience targets are performing well and those on which they need to focus to increase turnout and donations. The databases can track contact with elected officials, event attendance, and merchandise sales. Both parties have a good sense of which issues specific customers will respond to and tailor their pitches accordingly. Donald Trump took a data-driven approach to find an underserved audience of working-class people, engage it, and turn it out in 2016 and 2020.

Tracking technologies like website cookies give political marketers an understanding of consumer behavior, where they are going, and what they are consuming as opposed to simply taking the customer's word for these things.[2] For example, the 2020 Trump campaign stated that it used web beacons that let it see the location of mobile devices, how close the user's device was to the measuring device and how long the two were in contact.[3] The ability to generate data using beacons, cookies, and tools that can find similar users that resemble those being targeted lets political marketers fire undesirable audiences while digging deeper into desirable ones. Like commercial marketers, political marketers reward high-performing customers with special benefits or praise while shaming or sometimes firing their underperforming ones (Issenberg

2013). Contemporary political campaigns are more akin to a string of targeted niche campaigns than they are a single mass campaign. Candidates and campaigns no longer try to appeal to all voters. Instead, politicians divide the electorate into specific segments toward which they devote various levels of attention. On the other hand, the proliferation of content and platforms has made it possible for Americans to opt into communities of like-minded individuals meaning that they seldom encounter people with whom they disagree as Bishop (2009) noted. Politics has become like a sporting contest in which one side must win at the expense of the other as Mason (2018) and Turow (2007, 2008) have suggested and in which discussions take place within but not across audience segments.[4] Political polarization has developed in part because campaigns can quantify what constitutes the strategy that gives them the chance of winning. This usually means appealing to specific audiences, ignoring others, and doing so away from the prying eyes of the media and their opponents.[5]

Our current politics is as much a battle of technological innovation as it is about having the best candidate, organization, or policies. The battle between established and disruptive technologies has been raging for the last century in this country. The twentieth century saw major developments in the ways in which political candidates were presented to the public and significant changes in the ways in which politics took place in the country. Further, the people who presented politicians to the public often became household names themselves as was the case for Edward Bernays a century ago and a slew of political consultants today. In addition to tapping into new forms of expertise and new types of experts, politicians have often been early adopters of innovative technologies. FDR took advantage of the innovative technology of radio to speak directly with the voters thus building deep relationships with them in the process, the New Deal itself was a brand and it contained many branded agencies and programs to sum up what amounted to a large governmental intervention into many areas of American life.[6] John F. Kennedy pioneered the modern press conference and took the use of commercial advertising to a much higher level than what its pioneer, Dwight Eisenhower had reached.[7] Ronald Reagan brought a full marketing model into American politics (Cosgrove 2007). George W. Bush began to make extensive use of the web in his 2004 campaign, and Barack Obama and Mitt Romney made widespread use of the tracking cookies and niche targeting strategies with which we remain familiar.[8]

Politicians, policies, and parties are branded as are most consumer products. Contemporary politicians and parties usually research and segment their target audiences, build a political product, and develop a full marking communications plan prior to their launch. Political campaigns are often understood as being equivalent to a start-up company.[9] Thus, they go through the same trial and error processes as are commonly found in the startup world.

Trump ran his campaign like a startup meaning that staff turnover was more of a feature than a bug. What could be seen by some as instability could be seen by others as representing creative destruction. In keeping with the startup model, the Trump team was unafraid to try things and then scale the ones that worked to a general audience.[10] Trump did a lot of his own marketing, but his first campaign was staffed by a veteran team of conservative activists and operatives. Trump's traditional GOP team included Roger Stone and Paul Manafort who had been involved with GOP campaigns back to the Nixon years, Rudy Giuliani, a former Presidential candidate and Mayor of New York City, and Newt Gingrich. These people were well versed in the use of political marketing techniques. For example, Newt Gingrich has a long record of accomplishment in Republican political marketing. Gingrich has always stressed differentiation and branding in his political pursuits. His biggest success was the Contract with America through which Republicans gained control of the House of Representatives for the first time in forty years in 1994.

Trump was willing to take on people who other Republican campaigns had either kept at arm's length or had specific skill sets like working digital media at various times to augment its veteran core group's skills. He added David Bossie, Cliff Fletcher, and Steven Bannon to his team at various times. Each of these three men was part of a niche conservative media universe meaning that their hiring represented Trump trying to add the ability to drill down deeply into specific conservative audiences. As activists in those audiences, they had their own objectives in working for Trump. Bannon and Fletcher had been involved in conservative-themed media and thus understood how niche media could reach niche audiences and advance the Trump effort.[11] Bannon articulated ideas of the heroic narrative and epic clash that are standards in the branding.[12] In Trump, they might have had a vessel that was flawed in many ways but his skills as a marketer and performer made him the ideal face for an insurgent effort to reposition the GOP in a more populist direction.[13] Bannon saw Trump as being akin to Ronald Reagan in his willingness to speak for forgotten Americans, his willingness to face off against evil (Communism for Reagan, Islamic terrorism for Trump), and the way in which each could be presented as being a national savior.[14] Trump's start-up like campaign tightly targeted its messaging in order to take advantage of innovative technology, lessons from web-based startups like Facebook, and an understanding of what the audience wanted but also its reactions to Trump's words.[15]

His team could make strategic targeting decisions because they had a data-driven understanding of their customers.[16] This data-driven operation shaped spending, audience targeting, and travel decisions.[17] Having a team of experts, more data, and more advanced analytical techniques meant that the campaign could efficiently use its resources. It did a better job of doing so in 2016 than it did in 2020 but this could be a function of the differences in the marketplace and in Trump's strategic position in each cycle. These experts and techniques helped the campaign build an emotional brand that could be distributed to a niche not mass audiences and that they could see as sharing a brand heritage with Ronald Reagan something that was a strong selling point given the age of Trump's target audiences. One of the issues that Trump's 2020 campaign had was that most of this cast of characters was gone. Instead, the campaign's 2016 digital director, Brad Parscale, started out as its manager but he was removed from that position in July 2020 after a disastrous rally in Tulsa, Oklahoma, and a cyber-attack on some of the campaign's platforms. Parscale was replaced with former New Jersey Governor Chris Christie staffer Bill Stepien. Stepien was very experienced in Republican politics and data-driven campaigns.[18]

Donald Trump's success building and deploying a political brand reflected broader trends in marketing and American society. He did not cause the social sorting that has led to our national divisiveness but capitalized on it to win office in 2016. In office, he followed the segmented brand strategy because he focused on keeping his best customers happy.[19] Trump was a commercial marketer who adjusted his brand for politics as he had adjusted it to fit other endeavors. In 2016, Trump made promises without mentioning costs or downsides just as Bernie Sanders and sometimes Joe Biden did in 2020. This is consistent with branded American politics. Each party cherry-picks aspects of public policy that build its brand and offer benefits to its target audiences. For example, Democrats are fond of talking about the 90% income tax rate the United States had during the Eisenhower years but seldom mentioned the 26% minimum tax rate and the much higher tax participation rates, as well as the voluminous US tax code and its many deductions that existed during that time.[20] Also left out of this construction is Ike's national security rationale for high tax rates and broad tax participation.[21] Instead, the Democrats talk about tax fairness and income inequality. The impact such techniques has had on our politics is clear when we look at the way Ike thought about taxation versus the ways in which Ronald Reagan talked about welfare queens or Barack Obama presented people making $250,000 a year in salary as "millionaires and billionaires" something he did to demonstrate that he like his Democratic predecessor, Bill Clinton, could raise taxes yet not wipe out economic prosperity.[22] The difference between Eisenhower and the modern politicians is a reflective of the ways in which the nation's values have become much more individualistic (Bellah 1985) and consumeristic (Barber 2008) since Ike was in office. As our politics have become another form of consumeristic activity thus the importance of marketing and branding.

There are many more communicative channels available to political marketers today than there were in Ike's time. There is much more frequent coverage of public affairs than existed in Ike's time. Trump's omnipresent brand strategy made sense because politics itself has become omnipresent in recent decades. The imperative to brand and target audiences increased throughout the series of innovations represented by cable television, the internet, the mobile phone and web, social media, and streaming media services. Trump pursued brand omnipresence. This strategy fits the social media age in which communication is instant and we are all inundated with information. If Reagan's introduction of the political marketing model represented an evolution of politics to fit the cable TV era, Trump's brand omnipresence strategy pushed it forward into the social media age.

The Trump media circle shows how both parties have media systems that their best customers consume. The partisans of the other persuasion focus on one prominent outlet like Fox News or MSNBC as the driver of their opponents' wrongheaded beliefs. They seldom consider the notion that these outlets are important, but not the only, aspect of a message distribution system aimed at several different sub-audiences. Trump's team used alternative media platforms to reach its targeted audiences. That the viability of Trump's candidacy in 2016 and the surprise at how close he came to winning in 2020 did not attract more notice is itself a symptom of a deeply segmented society. The world has changed since Ike was President because the parties have much more data about who their voters are, have an ability to divide up the electorate very precisely, and have much more information about what the ways in which the voters that they are targeting behave than Ike could have thought to have been possible. Part of the reason such data exists is that the technology to generate and maintain it exists now unlike in the 1950s, because the population is more diverse in a number of ways than it was in the 1950s, because there were many fewer media outlets and platforms in the 1950s and because media demography in the 1950s was more homogenous than it is today. It was a slower, simpler world in which it was not possible to aim specific messages at specific audiences or to develop a detailed data-based understanding of specific niche audiences. When Ike was the President, phones plugged into a jack, a camera required film, and the media had a much cozier relationship with politicians it was covering than it does at present. The technology and culture of that time militated against some of Trump's more extreme or ill-informed statements ending up in the public eye without significant editing and reducing the chances of someone like Trump being elected in the first place.

On the one hand, Branding and marketing offer politicians who are disciplined in their use a level of protection against ending up in damaging or embarrassing situations. On the other hand, technological changes and the explosion in the number of media outlets mean that it is impossible to insulate a politician from negative coverage. Trump's pursuit of an omnipresence strategy made him more vulnerable to negative coverage simply because he was very available, and this problem was compounded by Trump's long history in the public eye. It was partly ameliorated because Trump was an accomplished marketer and communicator. For example, in 2016 one of Donald Trump's bigger problems was a tape recorded long before he ever ran for President in which he made disparaging remarks about women to Billy Bush host of the TV program "Access Hollywood." This tape appeared a few days before a Presidential debate. Trump apologized but then flipped the script by holding a press conference with many of the women who had accused Bill Clinton of inappropriate behavior toward them in attendance. The political environment in which Donald Trump became President featured a continuous news cycle, an ability for active citizens to produce content about candidates that might have been off their message (the Mitt Romney comments in 2012 about 47% of the public automatically supporting Barack Obama's reelection because they got government benefits but paid no taxes was recorded by a bartender at a fundraiser who uploaded the comments to YouTube, Presidential candidate George Allen was undone by a young man working as a video tracker for his opponent whom he called a racial slur while the camera was running and Hillary Clinton made remarks at a private fundraiser about some Trump supporters fitting into a "basket of deplorables"). [23] Contrast their failure to change the story with what Trump was able to accomplish in 2016 and his dexterity with branding is clear. Trump tried to something similar in the face of a persistent policy problem in the form of the pandemic by trying to highlight a laptop that belonged to Hunter Biden as part of his campaign close in 2020. The idea seemed to be to show that Joe Biden was just another Washington insider, but the effort failed to gain traction beyond the New York Post and was suppressed by social media companies as "Russian Disinformation." Trump's press statements and his campaign's efforts to produce witnesses gained little traction as a result. It was also hard to see exactly what this had to do with Joe Biden himself beyond some vague accusations of corruption or how it spoke to the concerns of average Americans. In 2016, it was obvious that the Trump messaging was his opponent, would say one thing, do another, and was untrustworthy. In 2020, the same kind of messaging effort fell flat. Trump told a more relevant story in 2016, more people saw or heard about it, and it was more impactful as a result.

Donald Trump would road test material in a few venues and then either drop it or add it to his messaging depending on the audience's reaction to it (Green, 2017). Over time, brand stories are developed that present target audiences with stories to justify their worldview or the benefits that these policies offer to them. Brand stories can also be used to show how some people who either would not benefit from policy chances or do benefit from existing public policies do not deserve to do so. Some, like Jardina (2019) argue that Donald Trump developed a brand story to present whites with a rationale for his campaign and policies that would assure their material well-being and continued cultural preeminence. This is entirely consistent with the way in which a brand narrative is built and how brand loyalty is established. The ability to build a durable relationship with an audience that lets them quickly understand why they should buy the product or support the politician is the rationale for branding and why the brand can be an effective tool in political marketing. Some of the instability around the Trump campaigns and administrations was simply a result of using a startup model and, while it might have produced innovation on the campaign trail, it produced instability in government.

Trump's brand strategy bore some similarity to the ways in which Ronald Reagan used welfare Queens and Barack Obama presented $250,000 annual salary earners (usually dual-income couples living in expensive real estate markets as "millionaires and billionaires" flying around on corporate jets).[24] Reagan, Obama, and Trump all used branding to simplify a complicated reality, to present the other as undeserving or as a threat, and to justify policies that specifically distributed costs and benefits. Political brand stories can explain why those receiving a negative or a positive outcome are not being victimized or unduly reward, they're getting what they deserve or finally being treated fairly after decades of accruing benefits unfairly. While Trump may have switched targets from the racialized images Reagan used of welfare queens to Mexican immigrants, the point of the exercise was the same: show a target audience that this product was for them then build a sense of brand identity with and loyalty for the brand. It could be argued that both pitches worked with a sense of racial identity as well. In the case of the $250,000 annual salary millionaires, Obama specifically picked the number to build fellowship with the Clinton Administration that had similarly raised taxes but managed to keep a prosperous economy.[25]

Another version of this features Democrats claiming that "the rich do not pay anything" or "don't pay their fair share of taxes." What constitutes rich is never defined nor is the term fair share. The use of these terms injects issues of class and social responsibility into a progressive brand while also allowing progressives to advocate for more spending that would benefit many of their target audiences. This pitch allows progressives to argue that they will tax rich people who've either been underpaying for years or those whom the market has unfairly rewarded. Consistent with the brand strategy, individual corporate or individual tax avoidance cases are sometimes presented as representing the behaviors pursued by every affluent American even though the data shows this is not the case. The United States has a highly progressive federal tax code and is heavily dependent on a small group of ratepayers to fund its government.[26] This too is a consequence of branding and marketing because politicians are, like retail marketers, trying to offer their customers the best deal at the best price.

Another version of the brand narrative strategy was the one that Donald Trump used to argue that the Government of Mexico would pay for a wall along its border with the United States. Anyone familiar with either international relations or the process involved in building a wall knew that a wall was not likely to be paid for by the Mexican Government or be built very quickly. The idea that it would be built quickly and paid for by others might sound plausible to people who do not understand or have full information about the reality of a given situation. A brand is the informational shortcut that lets people feel that they know enough to make an informed decision about a product, policy, or politician. The tax and wall assertions offer easy quick solutions to complicated problems and, in both cases, do so in ways that pass no cost onto most consumers. It certainly sounded good though and, as brands do, offered emotional satisfaction to audiences that bought into their promises. Trump's story offered an easy, quick solution to the nation's complicated immigration problem, the issues that exist with cross-border criminality, and for those attracted to Trump for reasons of racial identity held out one quick solution to deal with the nation's changing demography and culture.

The experiences of two Democrats in the 2020 primaries show why politicians are incentivized to deal in brand stories but not policy specifics. Elizabeth Warren's team presented her as an advocate for "big structural change," something that can be seen as aspirational branding and she rolled out a series of plans to keep the brand promise with one big exception: healthcare.[27] When she finally released the specific heavy plan, her opponents tore into it, it was complicated thus intermittently attentive audiences only heard a few things about it including that it involved new revenue and momentous changes.[28] Warren's momentum slowed after that.[29] In contrast, her progressive competitor, Bernie Sanders, kept repeating the same brand aspects, values, and story but mentioned few specifics about healthcare. He took a similar approach in this case to the one Trump has adopted across subjects. The advantages of the brand strategy over delving into the specifics of politicians remain clear. Contemporary politicians, political parties, and interest groups consciously construct brands for themselves and their policies.

The brand story offers its users a way to provide consumers with emotional engagement, moral clarity, and the possibility of a happy conclusion. The world of politics and policy is often much messier than the brand story claims it to be. The rise of political marketing has produced an incentive for marketers and politicians to always find problems to solve. Problems are a key tool through which specific segments of the population can be mobilized at election time. While Ike might have worked with society making themes and issues like income tax for all and building the interstate highway system, political marketing and branding have raised the individualistic question that Ronald Reagan asked in 1980, "ask yourself, are you better off now than you were four years ago?" to paramount importance. Given the many ways that self-interest can be defined, how the public has assumed that the President can solve all problems and that the government is responsible for producing economic prosperity, it should not be surprising that the elite consensus that developed in the age of Ike ran into trouble in the age of social media and was faced with an onslaught of challengers from the right and the left.[30]

While Bishop (2009) and Mason (2018) suggest this is a function of sorting, sorting would not have happened without targeted marketing and would not continue to happen without targeted branding. Branded, tightly targeted political products build loyalty within not empathy across audiences meaning our politics have become akin to a sporting contest between the red and blue teams. Brand loyalty for the party brand within the core audiences has strengthened. At the same time, both parties have become more susceptible to personally branded politicians taking advantage of the more open party nominating processes that exist now to promote themselves and their personal brands and agendas. Donald Trump's success in 2016 and Bernie Sanders's giving the Democrats a run for their money in 2020 underscore this point. Gone are the days in which both teams could win because creating that environment would require both parties to exercise more control over their nomination processes and expand their product offerings to include items that sold better outside their core audiences and regions (instead of nationalizing everything) than they did within them weaken their brands. In modern politics, if one team is winning then the other must be losing and the winning team must have cheated in some way to do so.

Donald Trump's Presidency was the result of branded politics. Trump only focused on building his brand's favorability within its target audiences. The Trump campaign and administration knew which audiences it targeted. Trump campaign manager Brad Parscale argued that the possible voter universe for Donald Trump was about one hundred million people for the 2020 election.[31] As the result of that contest showed, Trump did get more votes than he had in 2016 but not enough to win. Trump's team relied on data gleaned from its rallies to build a live customer base (it took a working mobile phone number to enter) instead of polling data because current polling was not as reflective of public opinion as it had been because America is much more complicated than when landline polling was developed and was further biased because nobody would pick up a phone call now from people, they did not know whereas in the past they might have.[32] By requiring people to provide a working number to enter a rally, the Trump team generated more data about their customers than they might otherwise have been able to get including voting histories.[33] It could then segment the audience and communicate with its targets in ways that those outside its target audiences will never see and this, Parscale argued, explains why so many media figures and citizens who only saw public polling were blindsided by the result in 2016.[34] He noted that because the world was more complex than it once had been, the Trump campaign used methods beyond polling including data mining and artificial intelligence to understand its customer base.[35] The campaign had different messages for different audiences. The Trump campaign used several distinct kinds of segmentation including demographic and geographic to which it added the study of what people do (psychographic segmentation) to its tool kit.[36] They took advantage of the ways in which people use social media platforms like Facebook and Twitter and the data provided by signing up for entry to Trump rallies to figure out who their customers were likely to be.[37]

The Trump campaigns showed how a candidate can work with the party as organization to build a data juggernaut. Trump's campaign was able to acquire data about its customers using their rallies, by hiring the now infamous Cambridge Analytica firm, and, most importantly, by tapping into the resources and expertise that the Republican National Committee had developed since 2012.[38] In 2012, the Romney campaign thought that it was going to do win on election night. The events of the evening proved that the party had a data and analytics problem. It solved this by studying the Obama campaigns and by investing over a hundred million dollars in a new data and analytics program that the Trump campaign tapped into during 2016 and this allowed it to offset some of its own faults in this area.[39] All of this is dramatically different from the ways in which campaigns were mass-market affairs and in which they dealt with popular themes and issues aimed at mass audiences during Ike's era.

Trump's team took all the virtual and media tools and then combined them with big events that let people experience the Trump brand themselves. Instead of door knocks like one of the Democratic disruptors

Representative Alexandria Ocasio-Cortez used to build contact with her customers, Trump used rallies to connect with his. In the 2020 Democratic primary cycle, Bernie Sanders used a similar rally strategy only his campaign added musical acts like "The Strokes" and "Public Enemy" to signal target audiences about Sanders's interest in their business. These three approaches all have a commonality: they provide the target customer with a direct brand touch point that they can experience in person. A brand touchpoint is designed to give the customer a positive experience and can be defined as "interaction between a brand and its customers."[40] Through these kinds of activities people get to interact with the brand and provide data about themselves to better target the pitches that they receive or feedback about their likes and dislikes so that the campaign can improve its product offerings.

The segmented emotional brand is a perfect tool for what American politics has become. As Norris and Inglehart (2019) note one way to understand American politics at present is as a fight over values. These values fights get translated into fights about materialist and postmaterialist values. Trump's values-based campaign focused on order, tradition, and freedom, and these values were applied to many policy areas including the extent to which the country should either shut down or remain fully open as normal during a pandemic. Trump's values were expressed through the brand. Like most contemporary national politics, much of what he talked about was based on decisions made by judges and bureaucrats but not Congress and focused on rights and values. Since the 1960s, Democrats have supported a series of rights-based movements modeled after the Civil Rights movement.[41] This was partly because of their belief in the righteousness of the causes but also because the party had lost a long-standing area of its strength: unionized workers. Further, Democrats have struggled with working-class voters overall whose share of the Democratic audience has steadily dropped in recent decades.[42] Simultaneously, Republicans went from an even split of voters without a college degree in 1999 to a fifteen-point advantage by 2019.[43] Trump built on but did not create this advantage.[44] Consistent with the segmentation model used by Trump's team, Jones notes that "Trump's politics and his policies on issues like immigration, the Affordable Care Act and abortion have helped increase the party's appeal to whites without college degrees, but they may be a double-edged sword if it is also driving white college graduates away from the party".[45]

Trump added class and race conscious messages aimed at whites to a politics in which emotional branding and audience segmentation were ascendant. Trump's brand story articulated the other side of the rights-based movements as enhanced the representativeness of the idealized American political story. Market research and Trump's personal skill as a marketer helped the campaign find an audience that was concerned about these rapid changes. Trump's brand story appealed to their concerns and, as a result, built deep loyalty for his product. One example of this is the way in which Trump used judicial nominations to reach conservative Christians. Much of the battle over rights and values that has taken place in the United States since the 1960s has been decided around a series of court and administrative agency rule-making decisions. The staffing of courts and the senior positions in the bureaucracy are key tools to shape the outcome of the broader policy battle in which the country has been enmeshed since the 1960s.

As a candidate in 2016, Donald Trump circulated a list of potential nominees to Christian Conservative groups and floated names of potential cabinet and administrative agency leaders on the campaign trail. Developing and circulating such a list was a form of signaling about what the Trump Administration's policy priorities would be in office. He continually pointed to the appointments that he had made from this list as an example of having kept a promise. He also talked about the tax cuts he had worked to pass through Congress, the trade deals he had made and the economic confrontations his Administration had gotten into especially with China. Free market and Christian conservatives might not like Donald Trump's personal traits, his working-class brand persona, or his trade policy and moralists might not approve of him at all but such signaling showed that Trump would be friendly to their interests and surrounded by people like themselves. This is a big part of the answer to the question of why so many Republicans were willing to put up with his undesirable traits: they liked the policies and the nominees even if they did not like him.

Trump was hardly alone in using nominations for cabinet and judicial nominations as part of a marketing strategy but by outlining who it would put in these positions in advance of the 2016 election, he was more aggressive in their use as a marketing tool. These positions have become vital tools through which candidates signal specific audiences about policies once they got into office. In office, Trump used his many nominations to show that he had kept his campaign promises. Judicial and executive branch agency head nominations have become major marketing and brand-building opportunities for politicians, parties, interest groups, and media outlets. Gradually, political discourse has developed among members of both parties that their rights and way of life will be threatened when the other party gets control of the courts and bureaucracy. This rhetoric is used to justify all out fights over Presidential nominations. Issues like LGBTQ2SIA+ rights, immigration, racial and ethnic rights, affirmative action, reproductive rights, the role and behavior of the police in society, the rights of religious groups of all sorts, and environmentalists are ideal areas for these kinds of marketing campaigns. Legal and regulatory battles have served as fodder for an interest group, candidate, and party marketing campaigns at least since the Reagan years. Trump intensified all of this through his highly emotional branding and brand story in which he sounded completely authentic and determined to make words into actions. This meant that he riled up his supporters and opponents to the point that both were willing to fight with all they had to achieve or avoid the nominees and policies Trump proposed. The legal and regulatory back and forth over these matters has increasingly allowed interest groups, both parties, and individual politicians to market themselves to their core audiences something that intensified in the age of Trump. A campaign can run multiple targeted campaigns just as companies have many line extensions of their brands to sell new products. The segmented brand must only tell a coherent story within each audience that it has targeted. The story does not have to make sense in specifics in all its elements but must be centered on an overall emotive concept to provide customers with a consistent brand experience. Therefore, when Trump's political and media opponents focused on facts to the extent that they missed the point of his behavior and the significant levels of engagement it produced.

Donald Trump's election provided liberal interest groups, media, and the Democratic Party with their own significant brand-building opportunities. The American Civil Liberties Union is a case in point because it once had a mission of upholding free speech but that morphed into a broader mission to oppose Donald Trump's policies. This was a marketing homerun given that its membership numbers tripled, and its online fundraising went from between $3 and 5 million to about $120 million annually.[46] Such an impressive return on investment showed the power that a targeted emotional brand can have to help to change a business's fortunes. It was not just interest groups that made hay from this kind of marketing during the Trump era and, while their businesses thrived, the country suffered.

These successes present several problems for the functioning of the political system. First, both parties catastrophize what the results of their rivals getting their way would be for their target audiences. Second, both parties have elevated most issues to moral crusades thus producing gridlock in government. Third, media outlets, eager to attract eyeballs and higher ad fees, exaggerate the significance and extent of these conflicts. The net result is to give the public a sense that the country is far more polarized than is the case. Media companies rushed to position themselves as opponents or supporters of Donald Trump. This was a winning strategy as MSNBC, Fox, and the New York Times all saw upticks in their numbers. All of them found large audiences through segmentation and built emotional brands arounds their support or opposition for Donald Trump. One obvious example of a media outlet that did not do that was CNN. While much of CNN's content featured anti-Trump news analysts, the channel's branding was not specifically built around opposition to Trump. Branding is a key tool to signal audience about things that they should or should not be interested in. CNN's more successful competitors reaped the benefits of the segmented emotional branding that they developed while CNN posted more modest results. Segmented emotional branding is a powerful tool that can be used to increase business across sectors and its use can produce great benefits beyond the world of politics.

Trump and his team continue to pursue their targeted strategy even though Trump is out of office. Their targeted approach can be effective provided it attracts enough voters to win and enough donors to keep the political organization operating. Trump's expertise is in selling. This meant that he never spent much time in government figuring out to work with Congress. Even in the case of the controversial Kavanaugh nomination, Trump's team prodded the nominee to mirror Trump brand. He did not try to mobilize these supporters to lobby Congress while President with very few exceptions like the Brett Kavanaugh nomination battle. The one time he made a determined effort to mobilize his supporters to come to Washington and present themselves before Congress, the result was an afternoon of death and disorder. Holding a campaign-style rally that presented the entire Trump emotive sticky brand to a large crowd just before it walked up the National Mall to Congress on January 6, 2020, was neither wise nor an ethical use of branding and marketing. Donald

Trump might be an expert at the use of these techniques, but he has a long history of ethically dubious behavior in use of them.

Trump tapped into extant political cultures but did so using the tools that made the sorting happen: branding and segmentation. Americans sorted in response to pitches made to them about many things as Bishop (2008) noted. The trends of sorting and the ability to live in an information bubble of the like-minded were trends Trump and his team noticed and exploited to win an election. They did not create or cause these phenomena. Donald Trump noticed these trends. These trends were reinforced by made even stronger by social media and the internet. People can use these tools to wall themselves off into communities of the like-minded something Turow anticipated in his 1997 and 2006 works. It is possible for people who voted for Trump in 2016 to never encounter anyone who did not vote for him and vice versa. Trump's election showed the power of geography in the American system. Geographic segmentation is commonly used in marketing. Trump's campaign staged events and developed messaging for their campaign aimed at the places that would help them get the biggest amounts of the right votes in the places that they needed to get them. Given the uneven nature of the Obama economic recovery geographically, demographically, and occupationally, the idea that some parts of the electorate in some well-positioned declining industrial states might support a candidate calling for real change should not come as a surprise.[47] That Trump barely lost some of the same states in 2020 that he won in 2016 is a testament to the power of his brand. The environment in the country in 2020, the enmity he had engendered among his opponents and the Democrats nomination of Joe Biden, who could present himself as a moderate working-class centrist, meant that Trump faced a much tougher challenge in 2020 than he had faced in 2016.

Trump's 2016 Electoral College win resulted from the strength of the campaign's emotional brand and how it was designed to take advantage of a segmented America. Trump's brand was aimed at specific voters in specific places. The Clinton campaign resonated in coasts and in cities. The Trump campaign resonated inland and in rural areas. Further, the racial and ethnic diversity of the country is not evenly distributed across all fifty states. Some states have populations that are a lot older, a lot whiter than others and there is tremendous economic diversity across the country. States with older, whiter, more conservative populations that had economies based around manufacturing or resource extraction offered better opportunities for Trump than did states with young, diverse populations and post-industrial economies. In the American system, geography plays at least as key role as demography thus the idea that the country's rapidly changing demography would favor Democrats is overstated because this growth was concentrated in a few states meaning its overall impact would be muted in national politics.[48] Given how people can wall themselves off into their own media, web, and social media worlds, it is not surprising that Trump had a tough time working with Congress, building social consensus, and did not enjoy popular support in opinion polls despite a surging economy. Nor is it surprising that he was impeached given the elevated levels of partisan polarization in Congress. On the other hand, his approval ratings increased as the impeachment process bled into the 2020 Democratic primaries showing that his segmentation, branding, and targeting strategy offered the prospect of at least holding onto most of the audience he attracted in 2016. Further, he might be able to attract others depending on who his general election opponent was. Especially for swing state suburban voters, a far-left nominee might have made Donald Trump appear to be attractive in comparison. Joe Biden was presented as a moderate and this is part of the explanation for why Joe Biden presented Trump with such a stiff challenge. A leftist Democratic nominee could have aided the Trump reelection effort by either attracting new voters to his cause or keeping turnout down on Election Day.[49]

All of this is a long way away from the era of Ike. Ike had a public persona and a nickname based on his service in World War II. His campaigns pioneered the use of television advertising with long-form question and answer ads that look stilted in comparison to modern political marketing pitches. Ike appeared in ads in which he spoke in long-form or featured repetitive jingles. While these techniques can build product awareness through advertising, they are quite different from modern political marketing campaigns with their emphasis on market research, brand, segmentation, and narrowcasting. Ike's themes and issues were society making not segment making. He spoke in long form and stressed themes and issues that would make society stronger not segment targeted brand stories telling us some undeserving individual or crooked corporation is defrauding benefits, not paying their "fair share" of taxes, being made morally weak by dependence on government because they have an opportunity to buy subsidized health insurance (that came with death panels to determine coverage levels) to note but a few prominent examples. Ike was the standard bearer of a GOP that was less geographically constrained and, unlike Trump and his rivals, did not just target a few audiences. Ike appealed to a variety of different interests just as his Democratic rivals attempted to do. Part of the reason America has a large urban/rural and coastal/hinterland divide is because social sorting and market segmentation have encouraged politicians to market too narrowly not broadly and emotively not substantively. Better databases and social media, niche media that encourage niche narrowcasting and branded legacy media incentivize politicians to find and mobilize ever more of their best performing audience segments and deemphasize the rest. This is as true of political as it is of consumer marketing. Donald Trump did not cause this environment but has used it effectively. He only says and does things that please his best performing customers. His 2016 win exemplifies the trend. The outcome was decided in a few swing states that were narrowly won or lost after both candidates had developed bastions of strength based on their dominance in other states and Trump won 71 Electoral College votes in 2016 in states decided by 1.5 points or less.[50] Building a brand that turned out the target audiences in bigger numbers than previous Republican candidates clearly paid off in this instance for the Trump campaign. The incentive of the age is to focus on issues that emotionally engage to attract specific parts of the electorate as the 2016 cycle shows.

Notes

1. Claritas Prizm website. https://www.claritas.com/prizmr-premier, accessed March 1, 2020.
2. For an in-depth explanation see Jessica Leber. "Campaigns to Track Voters with Political Cookies." *MIT Technology Review.* June 27, 2012. https://www.technologyreview.com/s/428347/campaigns-to-track-voters-with-political-cookies/.
3. Matt Binder. "Trump Campaign Says It Can Follow Your Phone." Mashable. September 26, 2019. https://mashable.com/article/trump-campaign-beacons-privacy-policy/, accessed March 4, 2020.
4. Joseph Turow Breaking Up America (2007) and Niche Envy (2008).
5. (https://www.forbes.com/sites/stevenbertoni/2016/11/22/exclusive-interview-how-jared-kushner-won-trump-the-white-house/#2f1f49 53af68, accessed November 22, 2016).

6. For a detailed explanation of how technology has changed the kinds of politicians who run for office and how they run for office see Postman (1985).
7. For a detailed examination of the way in which Presidential advertising worked for most of the second half of the twentieth Century see Hall-Jamieson (1996).
8. For a detailed examination see Sasha Issenberg. "How Obama's Team Used Big Data to Rally Voters." *MIT Review*. December 19, 2012. https://www.technologyreview.com/2012/12/19/114510/how-oba mas-team-used-big-data-to-rally-voters/ or David McCoy. "The Creepiness Factor: How Obama and Romney Are Getting to Know You." *The Atlantic*. April 10, 2012. https://www.theatlantic.com/politics/archive/ 2012/04/the-creepiness-factor-how-obama-and-romney-are-getting-to-know-you/255499/.
9. Matt McDonald. "The Fastest Startups in the World." Medium. June 4, 2015. https://medium.com/hps-insigh, accessed March 4, 2020.
10. Lewandowski and Bosse (2017, pp. 172–178).
11. Sims (2019, pp. 21–22).
12. Green (2017, pp. 84–93).
13. Scott Shane. "Combative Populist Steve Bannon Found His Man in Donald Trump." *New York Times*. November 27, 2016. https://www. nytimes.com/2016/11/27/us/politics/steve-bannon-white-house.html, accessed March 7, 2020.
14. Ibid.
15. Ibid.
16. For a general presentation on the topic see Alexander Nix "Cambridge Analytica—The Power of Big Data and Psychographics." Presentation to the Concordia Annual Summit, 2016. https://www.youtube.com/ watch?v=n8Dd5aVXLCc, accessed July 31, 2019. On the topic of the Trump campaign's use of analytics see Stephen Bertoni. "Jared Kushner in His Own Words on the Trump Data Operation the FBI Is Reportedly Probing." May 26, 2017. https://www.forbes.com/sites/stevenbertoni/ 2017/05/26/jared-kushner-in-his-own-words-on-the-trump-data-ope ration-the-fbi-is-reportedly-probing/#6df9207ba90f, accessed July 31, 2019.
17. For a detailed investigation of analytics and data driven campaigns see Issenberg, 2012.
18. Kaitlin Collins et al. "Trump Shakes Up Campaign Leadership as He Struggles in latest Polls." CNN.com. July 15, 2020. https://www.cnn. com/2020/07/15/politics/trump-campaign-manager-demoted/index. html.
19. For a detailed investigation of analytics and data driven campaigns see Issenberg (2013).

20. Hitchcock (2018).
21. Ibid.
22. Andrew Ross Sorkin. "Week in Review: Rich and Sort of Rich." *New York Times*. May 14, 2011 https://www.nytimes.com/2011/05/15/weekin review/15tax250copy.html.
23. Aaron Couch. "Bartender Who Recorded '47 Percent' Romney Remarks Reveals Identity." *Hollywood Reporter*. March 13, 2013. https://www.hol lywoodreporter.com/news/bartender-who-recorded-47-percent-428527. Bill Bartel. "What Ever Happened to SR Siddarth, the Tracker Who Sparked the Demise of US Senator George Allen?" *Virginian-Pilot*. November 20, 2016. https://www.pilotonline.com/government/vir ginia/article_c8cf9d51-3905-5d1c-90e0-80a9c939349b.html. Transcript. "Read Hillary Clinton's 'Basket of Deplorables' Remarks About Donald Trump Supporters." *Time*. September 10, 2016. https://time.com/448 6502/hillary-clinton-basket-of-deplorables-transcript/, accessed March 4, 2020.
24. Andrew Ross Sorkin. "Rich and Sort of Rich." *New York Times*. May 14, 2011. https://www.nytimes.com/2011/05/15/weekinreview/ 15tax250copy.html, accessed March 4, 2020.
25. Ibid.
26. For a recent breakdown of who pays taxes and how much they pay see Robert Bellafiore. "Summary of the Latest Federal Income Tax Data, 2018 Update." Tax Foundation. https://taxfoundation.org/summary-lat est-federal-income-tax-data-2018-update/, accessed March 1, 2020.
27. Alex Thompson. "Bailey Versus Blood and Teeth." Politico. March 6, 2020. https://www.politico.com/news/2020/03/06/warren-team-won ders-how-they-blew-it-122628?fbclid=IwAR2LnYhTNTq95k0jP-GWY vhWxJrhw-xac7gPIRQ16oBY_4MXtczxPSfyo44.
28. Ibid.
29. Ibid.
30. For an in-depth discussion of the Presidency and the ways in which the realities of the job misalign with the public expectations people hold about the institution see Jeremi Suri (2017).
31. Major Garrett. "The Takeout." CBS News. https://www.cbsnews.com/ video/brad-parscale-on-the-takeout-62119/, accessed June 21, 2019.
32. Ibid.
33. Ibid.
34. Ibid.
35. Ibid.
36. Ibid.
37. Ibid.
38. Lewandowski and Bosse (2017, pp. 172–178).

39. Ibid and for an example of GOP reverse engineering of the Obama effort
    see Patrick Ruffini. "Inside the Cave." PowerPoint Presentation https://
    enga.ge/wp-content/uploads/2018/01/Inside_the_Cave-1.pdf.
40. Amy Aitman. "How to Define Brand Touchpoints for a Winning
    Customer Experience." Canny. https://www.canny-creative.com/how-to-
    define-brand-touchpoints-for-a-winning-customer-experience/, accessed
    March 4, 2020.
41. See for example Thomas Edsall and Mary Byrne Edsall Chain Reaction,
    (Norton), 1992 for an in-depth discussion of these topics.
42. Ruy Teixeira and Alan Abramowitz. "The Decline of the White Working
    Class and the Rise of a Mass Upper Middle Class." Brookings Working
    Paper, April 2008. https://www.brookings.edu/wp-content/uploads/
    2016/06/04_demographics_teixeira.pdf, accessed October 11, 2019.
43. Jeffery M. Jones. "Non-College Whites Had an Affinity for the GOP
    Before Trump." Gallup. https://news.gallup.com/poll/248525/non-col
    lege-whites-affinity-gop-trump.aspx, accessed October 11, 2019.
44. Ibid.
45. Ibid.
46. Nick Visser. "ACLU Quadrupled Membership, Gained $120 Million
    in Donations After Trump's Election." *Huffington Post.* July 5, 2018.
    https://www.huffpost.com/entry/aclu-membership-skyrockets-trump_
    n_5b3db75de4b07b827cbd69b8.
47. Zito and Todd (2018) discuss this topic in depth.
48. John Judis. "The Emerging Republican Advantage." Carnegie Endow-
    ment for International Peace January 31, 2015. https://carnegieendo
    wment.org/2015/01/31/emerging-republican-advantage-pub-58932,
    accessed July 30, 2019.
49. Cosgrove and Shrader in Moufahim (2021).
50. See Nate Cohn. "Why Trump Had an Edge in the Electoral College."
    New York Times. December 19, 2016. https://www.nytimes.com/2016/
    12/19/upshot/why-trump-had-an-edge-in-the-electoral-college.html,
    accessed March 1, 2020.

References

Barber, Benjamin. *Consumed.* W.W. Norton, 2008.
Bellah, Robert N. *Habits of the Heart.* Harper Collins, 1985.
Bishop, Bill. *The Big Sort.* Mariner Books, 2009.
Cosgrove, Kenneth. *Branded Conservatives.* New York: Peter Lang, 2007.
Cosgrove, Kenneth and Nathan R. Shrader. Political Branding in the USA Elec-
    tion of 2020. In Mona Moufaim (ed.) *Political Branding in Turbulent Times.*
    Palgrave, 2021.

Green, Joshua. *Devil's Bargain: Steve Bannon, Donald Trump and the Storming of the US Presidency.* Penguin, 2017.

Hall-Jamieson, Kathleen. *Packaging the Presidency: A History and Criticism of Presidential Campaign Advertising* (3rd Edition). Oxford University Press, 1996.

Hitchcock, William. *The Age of Eisenhower: America and the World in the 1950's.* New York. Simon and Schuster, 2018.

Issenberg, Sasha. *The Victory Lab: The Secret Science of Winning Campaigns.* Broadway Books, 2013.

Jardina, Ashley. *White Identity Politics.* Cambridge University Press, 2019.

Lewandowski, Corey R. and David N. Bossie. *Let Trump Be Trump: The Inside Story of His Rise to the Presidency.* Center Street, 2017.

Mason, Liliana. *Uncivil Agreement: How Politics Became Our Identity.* Chicago. University of Chicago Press, 2018.

Norris, Pippa and Ronald Inglehart. *Cultural Backlash: Trump, Brexit and Authoritarian Populism.* Cambridge University Press, 2019.

Postman, Neil. *Amusing Ourselves to Death: Public Discourse in the Age of Show Business.* Viking Penguin, 1985.

Sims, Cliff. *Team of Vipers: My 500 Extraordinary Days Inside the Trump White House.* St. Martin's Press, 2019.

Turow, Joseph. *Breaking Up America.* Chicago: University of Chicago Press, 2007.

———. *Niche Envy.* MIT Press, 2008.

Zito, Salena and Brad Todd. *The Great Revolt.* Crown Forum. 2018.

CHAPTER 4

Trump: Direct-to-Consumer

Abstract Donald Trump shows how to use social media platforms to reach consumers directly and build brand omnipresence. Cosgrove notes that Trump's election resulted from gaining earned media and using social media to build strong customer relationships. Trump's team used analytics to win efficiently meaning their interest in winning the Electoral College was minimal. His campaign used data to target its message to specific audiences. The difference being that once elected President, Donald Trump has struggled to expand beyond his efficient data-driven approach and become a symbolic leader for the entire country.

Keywords Social media · Celebrities · Presidential leadership · Positioning · Twitter · Facebook · @realdonaldtrump · Donald Trump relationship with media · Direct-to-consumer marketing · Brand omnipresence · "Sleepy Joe," Joe Biden · First Trump Impeachment

Modern American politics is about marketing and branding. Political practitioners and organizations develop emotional brands around their candidates and policies. Political marketers usually try to combine a direct-to-consumer and earned media strategy to get the most impressions for their brands as possible at the least cost. Donald Trump long relied

K. M. Cosgrove, *Donald Trump and the Branding of the American Presidency*, https://doi.org/10.1007/978-3-030-30496-6_4

on earned media to make people aware of his brand and the products it has supported over the years.[1] Before adopting social media as a direct-to-consumer marketing platform, Trump bought ads, appeared regularly in mainstream news coverage and celebrity gossip columns to build brand awareness.[2] Two examples of largely non-political outlets through which Trump built his personal brand are Forbes magazine that regularly included him on its richest list and the 1980s Zeitgeist themed "Lifestyles of the Rich and Famous" because: "these channels presented Trump generally uncritically (when he had financial problems, Forbes wordlessly dropped him)".[3] Trump has always had a selling orientation, known how to earn media coverage, and understood how to build a brand. Politics was a new endeavor but the marketing techniques and media strategy he used to promote himself in this field were like those he had used to promote himself in other fields. Trump used social media as a form of direct-to-consumer marketing aimed at building brand omnipresence and, in doing so, he reduced the distance between the public and the President.[4] He appeared in our newsfeeds along with pictures of our friends and families, information about the activities we enjoy, or companies that have built longstanding relationships with us. No President got quite as close to us daily as Donald Trump did. George W. Bush and Barack Obama experimented with social media and web-based campaigning but did not try to build an omnipresent brand as Trump attempted to do. Bush and Obama were not continuously devoted to brand building and dissemination as is Donald Trump. On the other hand, because he focused on his brand and building omnipresence for it, he never really transitioned into the role of President as a unifying symbol. Instead, he was more like a national brand manager hawking a product that people either loved or hated. Trump used social media and the web to shape a national conversation and directly speak to his audiences. He used social media right up until January 6, 2021, after which he was banned from it because of his activities between Election Day 2020 and the events of that day which many Americans feel that he incited. Even after that, Trump has not given up on having an omnipresent brand despite the communications obstacles that the social media restrictions have placed upon him.

As President, he continued building relationships with all sorts of journalists including those whom he regularly and publicly attacked. Trump used these contacts to rail about the unfairness of his coverage regarding the work he has done and to argue that the media did not recognize his excellent performance. [5] Trump cut a unique figure in the Presidency because he was so accessible to media and the public as part of the brand omnipresence strategy. Many of the people who cover him think he would like to have more contact with journalists himself.[6] As one observer noted: "In all these conversations, Trump toggles back and forth between on-the-record, on-background, and off-the-record—betraying a fluency with reportorial rules of engagement that is more typically found in operatives than in principals."[7] This is a function of Trump's expertise as a marketer but also a product of his extensive experience in generating publicity for himself in the New York media. He even went so far as to develop a fictitious media spokesperson persona: John Barron.[8]

Trump took the office of the Presidency from exalted status to daily presence in social media feeds alongside friends, interests, media outlets, journalists, and interest groups. His strategy was the next step in a process of bringing the President and the Presidency into the marketing world that began at least a century ago. Candidate and President Trump worked to build deep relationships with his targeted audience every day. His efforts to build an omnipresent brand put people in direct contact with their President in ways no prior generation of Americans had ever been. Like Jimmy Carter, who tried to use political marketing to be a Presidential everyman (Hall-Jamieson, 1996), Trump democratized access to the President's words. Anyone could read what he posted on social media or watch his media availabilities for themselves. Trump's persona was engaging and easy to understand. It provoked wildly different responses from proponents versus opponents. His social media activities seldom consisted of speeches. Instead, they used common language, were brief, and were easy to read. His social media activity functioned as a brand distribution platform. He used this platform to build enduring relationships with the audience, tell the brand story stories efficiently and drive news cycles to build omnipresence. Even Trump's Twitter handle, "@realdonaldtrump," was part of the brand distribution effort because it contained a touch of authenticity in it. It positioned him as being "real" Donald Trump in contrast to the "fake news," the cartoon conservatives or out-of-touch Washington establishment he railed against. The emphasis on the authentic Trump gave the observer a choice between real and fake. Most people given a choice will take the real thing over the fake one as the success of Coca-Cola (which markets itself as the real thing) over imitators shows.[9] The Twitter handle was a positioning statement but also an effort by Trump to call into question the mainstream media's credibility in a way that built fellowship with the decades-long conservative critique of liberal media bias.

Trump's media and direct-to-consumer marketing campaigns took some of the mystery and majesty out of the Presidency. Instead of seeing this President as a policy superhero able to tame the separated system without breaking a sweat, leading intellect, and person to emulate. Trump's Twitter feed showed that he was a lot more like our cranky relatives who complain about politics than a mythic figure. This reduced the prestige of the office and empowered his opponents to challenge him in ways they might not have faced off against a more conventional President who used the trappings of office to create a more magisterial image. Trump would not stop tweeting once in office and his rationale for continuing was that of the marketer: taking away Twitter would be taking away his voice.[10] This is what happened once Twitter and Facebook banned Donald Trump. He issued press releases, tried and operate his own website but none of it had the impact that presented his brand through the market leaders in the social media category had to build brand omnipresence.

Trump got that, in the social media world, brands must be omnipresent to really build customer relationships. Many brands have become values-based and oriented toward social causes. While Trump was cause-oriented too, the causes he supported were not usually ones that were popular with the nation's elite or voters outside of Trump's target audiences. The problem from a Presidential leadership perspective was that he did not reach out to the bulk of the people who did not support his campaign. Instead, he focused on selling to his best segments as marketers often do. Twitter was a useful platform for Mr. Trump because it allowed him to get his message out directly to some of his target audiences. It was also of use to him because it generated a lot of earned media coverage. Much of what Trump tweeted was reported in some form by the media meaning that it was a way to reach his audiences who watched TV, listened to the radio, or read newspapers but were not social media users. What he said on social media platforms was retweeted and reported on in real-time meaning that he earned a steady stream of brand impressions. He explained his strategy to a White House audience by using the example of a policy announcement relevant to US policy toward the Golan Heights:

And I said, "We recognize the Golan Heights as being part of Israel."
It was a big thing. I go, "Watch this." Boom. I press it and, within two
seconds, "We have breaking news." John Roberts of Fox was over, and he
said, "We have breaking news. Please, break it up." Doesn't matter what
they're talking about, John, does it? He breaks it up. Now, that's Twitter.
That's social media. I call Twitter a "typewriter." That's what I really call
Twitter, because it goes onto Facebook automatically and it goes onto
Instagram. And it goes onto television — more so Fox than it does CNN.
If it's something bad, they'll put it on.[11]

Trump would take whatever publicity he could get and believed that any
attention was better than none:

> "It would be like a rocket ship when I put out a beauty. (Laughter and
> applause.) Like when I said — remember I said somebody was "spying on
> me"? That thing was like a rocket. I got a call two minutes later. "Did you
> say that?" I said, "Yeah, I said that." "Well, it's exploding." (Laughter.)
> "It's exploding." I turned out to be right. I turned out to be right. And
> we turn out to be right about lot of things.[12]

And even more telling about his personal involvement in developing a
brand-building strategy through social media and how it is used to drive
all other aspects of Trump's branding and media efforts:

> "I put out a social media statement. And I was telling Kellyanne the other
> day, I said, you know, I used to put out like a press release, right? And
> people would pick it up, sort of, you know, in the next day, two days.
> They'd find it sitting on a desk. If I put out — we hardly do press releases
> anymore because if I put out, on social media, a statement — like I'm
> going to in a little while on something totally unrelated, but a very impor-
> tant statement. Now they're going crazy. "What it is? Tell me what it is."
> Watch. (Laughter.) But it's very important.
> But if I put that out in a press release, I'm telling you, Kevin, people
> don't pick it up. It's me — same. If I put it out on social media, it's like
> an explosion. Fox, CNN, crazy MSNBC — they're stone-cold crazy".[13]

Trump used Twitter as a brand distribution channel even though Twitter's user profile does not fit his brand's best-performing segments.
Twitter's audience is younger, better educated, and more Democratic-
leaning than the general public.[14] Twitter users lean toward Democrats
on race, immigration, and gender issues. Trump's positions were far

from theirs meaning that they were not his target audience.[15] Even more daunting is the finding that the most active Twitter users are female.[16] Women, especially not younger women, women of color, or better-educated women, were not strong Trump supporters. Given that most of the Twitter audience did not overlap with the Trump audience, it is obvious that he was on Twitter to reach journalists and earn media coverage to distribute his brand. This media coverage equaled no-cost brand impressions and contributed to the sense that Trump was omnipresent. Trump was on Twitter to connect with journalists who often both criticized his tweets and reported them verbatim thus acting like the typewriter and replacing the press release as President Trump noted above. Trump changed the way he used Twitter in office to attack the media as a single entity rather than calling out specific journalists.[17] While he tweeted less in the White House than he did as a 2016 candidate, the number of attacks he has launched against the media was up from 9% as a candidate to 11% in the White House.[18]

Trump used social media to tell a brand story, reinforce that story and get it out to the public quickly and cheaply. Trump was the hero in his brand story taking trying to restore greatness to the country and respect for his supporters. The villains in his brand story included the bureaucracy, federal courts that ruled against him, the liberal media, Democrats, the cultural elite, members of his own Administration that disagreed with him, and sometimes even conservative media outlets. In the brand story, these villains were trying to stop Trump from making the country great again for selfish reasons. He almost never discussed the nuances of policy or why anyone would disagree with him about policy. Pointing out this alleged unfairness let him explain way some of the things that he was not able to deliver on as President. His efforts might not have convinced anyone outside his target audiences but within them they built deep loyalty.

The way that Trump used social media to communicate directly with his audiences shows how these platforms have weakened the elite's ability to act as gatekeepers. One way to understand the fractiousness of the Trump years is through the lens of a battle for control of the national political party and media structures. A few journalists, party leaders, or organizations can no longer screen out either populist candidates or those whose ideas reside outside of a narrow portion of the political center. Elite journalists, party leaders and activists, and issue network leaders have functioned as gatekeepers regarding who was and was not qualified to be

President, what was and was not appropriate Presidential behavior and what issues were and were not important for national consideration for decades. Donald Trump's direct-to-consumer marketing via social and earned media challenged their gatekeeping status. Social media and the internet weakened their position because they lowered the cost of entry for those seeking to become media stars, increased the rate of speed at which information was disseminated and let candidates get an unfiltered message out to their audiences.[19] Social media helped Trump to get his message through a media filter that kept discounting his chances and to differentiate himself from a large GOP primary field.[20] Social media and the internet allowed a different kind of candidate, who was branded differently and had a different product from the traditional Republican product to win in 2016 and generate even more votes in a losing cause in 2020. Candidates and interest groups that emulate Donald Trump's strategy of seeing social media posts to earn media have the potential to build prominent national brands just like he did.

The Trump campaign made extensive use of Facebook as an advertising and earned media vehicle. Trump's Facebook advertising strategy generated complaints among his opponents and some in the media. The campaign's retort was that Barack Obama had done similar things but the same people who complained about Trump's activities said nothing when Obama engaged in them.[21] Facebook advertising let Trump's campaign speak directly to voters in targeted ways meaning that the gatekeepers never saw some of what the campaign activities and messaging were exactly. As Brad Parscale noted "it was controlling the eyeballs of the places we needed to win."[22] It could target extremely specific segments of states with awfully specific messaging so much so that Trump ran 5.9 million ads and wrote 50,000 unique ads between the conventions and Election Day.[23] Trump's rhetoric was one of the keys that made the strategy work because the controversial things he said attracted a lot of eyeballs and, while a lot of those eyeballs were appalled by what they saw, others loved it meaning that these advertising buys were relatively inexpensive and an efficient way to target the right people.[24] This efficiency in buying and targeting meant that Trump needed to raise less money than his opponents because he needed to spend less money to reach his voters.[25] The Trump team took things that it knew about Facebook users, like if they had given Trump money or been on a certain email list, then combined those with the platform's ability to see what they had done on the internet by reading their cookies. Facebook gave Trump, like it gives any advertiser, a custom audience for its message.[26] Facebook then searches that audience for friends who have similar likes and behavioral patterns as do the original targets something known as a Facebook lookalike audience.[27] Parscale noted that this was: "one of the most powerful features of Facebook" because it let them find new people who might be receptive to their messaging.[28] All of which gave the Trump team a precise way to distribute its branded products to its targets while not letting its opponents or the media see them.

In 2016, the Trump team worked with data models from Cambridge Analytica to identify supporters and bought lists from other GOP-leaning groups to build its own unique message distribution list on the top of what the GOP provided to it.[29] These tools offer the marketer an option to try to drive down turnout among groups not likely to support it and the Trump campaign took full advantage of this option by aiming negative messaging about Hillary Clinton at three of her key groups: white liberals, young women, and African Americans.[30] Each group was fed negative information about the candidate to persuade them to stay home on Election Day and thus create an electorate that was more favorably inclined toward Donald Trump.[31] This is something Parscale denied happened when asked by PBS Frontline.[32] Such use would partly explain why turnout among young and African American voters declined in 2016. Their use shows how politics has become just another form of commercial marketing as Parscale told Green and Issenberg "I always wonder why people in politics act like this stuff is so mystical, it's the same shit we use in commercial, just has fancier names."[33] As Martinez wryly notes the same techniques that are used to sell consumer goods like towels were used in 2016 to market Presidential candidates and by that time these were well-known techniques in the marketing world.[34]

Trump's social media operation was one way that team Trump generated interest in its website, its rallies, merchandising operation, and fundraising efforts. Social media advertising and website traffic can interest people in signing up for an email list, receiving text messages, donating, or buying merchandise. The efforts can create brand loyalty and sell branded merchandise. Selling branded merchandise generated money for Trump's campaigns. The merchandising mattered beyond raising money because, just as is the case for other lifestyle brands, having people wear branded merchandise gains impressions and can generate buzz around the brand. Between the merchandising, the earned media, and the social media, Trump went a long way toward building an omnipresent brand. His team augmented these efforts with paid advertising.

The 2016 Trump campaign did not have to spend as much on paid media as its opponents did because it used media coverage and social media statements to generate a lot of brand impressions for free. As President, Trump stopped the tradition of a regular White House press conference and briefing by the Press Secretary. He often handled such matters himself. He held his own press conferences that were of great length, gave interviews to favored journalists, called into favored outlets, and continued to be a dominant presence on social media. Trump's team has also launched lawsuits against media outlets claiming defamation. While these suits might be unlikely to succeed given the high legal standards that a plaintiff who is also a public figure must meet, they are another way to reiterate Trump's brand narrative about the veracity of the media and the treatment Trump received from it.[35] The 2020 Trump campaign did spend a lot of money, especially, early on paid advertising to disqualify its Democratic opponent and these early efforts had consequences later when the Trump campaign had to cut back on advertising for several weeks leaving the airwaves to the Biden campaign and after Trump had been faced with a hostile media scrutinizing his every word.

The Trump campaigns and the administration were branded and focused on selling in all their public manifestations. Trump's merchandising operation was a constant throughout his campaign and his term of office. Encouraging supporters to buy and wear Trump-branded merchandise made them into a street-level sales force that generated buzz about and showed momentum for the Trump brand. Such branded merchandise works just like a branded sports team or university merchandise does in that it indicates that one is a member of a specific community. For example, as any Division One college football fan can testify, wearing school colors during the season in any major American city will often generate a reaction from at least one other person. The Trump merchandise effort raised money, but it also showed that people were part of the Trump team, and this could show shy Trump supporters that there were other people like them who openly supported Trump. Encouraging people to wear Trump-branded merchandise, most notably the red "Make America Great Again" ballcap was a way to generate impressions for the brand, show that the campaign enjoyed popular support, and overcome hesitancy as much as it was about raising money.

Supporting Trump could be very controversial. Two examples involving hockey players prove the point. There was a firestorm of protest over members of the 1980 US Olympic Men's Hockey Team wearing the ballcaps as they appeared at a Trump rally.[36] The Trump campaign got a picture of its man surrounded by smiling Olympic heroes at a packed Trump rally. These Olympians, at least visibly, looked like one of Trump's bigger target audiences: middle-aged and older white men. Thus, intentionally or not, they helped to credential the Trump brand and present it favorably to its audience targets. The venue and the headgear fit perfectly with Trump's branding. The Olympians well might have believed they were simply acting to promote national unity but, in branded politics, everything, including headgear, can act to support a political brand. Thus, it should not have been a surprise that Trump's opponents raised questions about these activities.[37] Branded merchandise costs the Trump team little to produce. It has the potential to generate some revenue for the campaign and an enormous number of brand impressions at no cost to it. The second example involved hockey icon Bobby Orr who bought an ad endorsing Trump in the "Manchester Union Leader" days before the 2020 election. Like the Olympians before him, Mr. Orr was attacked by those who were not Trump supporters.

Trump achieved omnipresence through his tweets, his media availabilities, and his call-ins to conservative radio and TV shows. These activities-built brand awareness every day drove media narratives and generated a continuous buzz around the Trump brand. The brand omnipresence strategy helped Trump do transformational politics on the cheap. Trump's brand became the center of everything, all the time. The upside to Trump's omnipresence was that it reminded his supporters of why they liked him and let him show that he was both keeping promises and delivering for them. The downsides to pursuing omnipresence in the way that Trump did are that it has kept his opponents constantly mobilized and much of the rest of the country grew tired of him and all the conflict associated with him. Trump's brand is omnipresent but the problem with omnipresence is that it risks oversaturating the brand and exhausting the public.

This exhaustion partly explains why the House Democrats' decision to push ahead with the first impeachment did not catch on outside the party. Many Americans saw the entire episode as more partisan squabbling and paid it no mind or followed it then came to a similar conclusion.

For example, the Democratic primary field did not tie themselves to it because many of them were hoping to present themselves as either a return to normalcy or as a dramatic break with the status quo but the question is do the voters really want a dramatic break with the status quo or would they just like something less emotionally involved than the Trump omnipresent brand. Most survey data show that the latter is the case. Thus, it should not be surprising that Trump was trying to dig up dirt on the strongest centrist Democratic contestant during the primaries: Joe Biden. Biden proved to be a formidable foe for Trump because Biden could talk the same working-class talk Trump did but also appealed to more segments of the electorate. Trump had problems with Biden because the latter could use the Obama brand heritage thus helping him to appeal to liberal whites and a broad swath of voters of color meaning Biden could steal some of Trump's core audience and generate higher turnout among Democratic voters.[38] Hillary Clinton was not positioned to do either thing quite as well. Hillary Clinton's public persona was much different than Biden's and the way in which the 2020 campaign was conducted was starkly different than the way that the 2016 one was. People saw more of Hillary Clinton and her brand persona was not viewed as favorably as Biden's by a lot of Americans.[39] Trump's attacks wounded her in ways that they never did to Biden. In addition to presenting positioning problems for the Trump brand, Biden produced an electorate that was less favorable to Trump than the 2016 electorate.

Presenting Joe Biden as "Sleepy Joe" was an interesting choice given how much of the public has been exhausted by Trump's brand omnipresence strategy and how often Biden spoke of a return to normalcy.[40] More progressive Democrats like Bernie Sanders and Elizabeth Warren would have been easier for Trump to run against because they, like Trump, promised disruption. Unlike Trump or Joe Biden, who advocated for something closer to Obama-era policies, progressive Democrats promised to impose serious costs and disruptions on a broad swath of the public. Trump has asked people what they thought their 401k and stock portfolios would look like when "Crazy" Bernie or "Pocahontas" Warren got through with them. Sanders also offered a target-rich environment for red-baiting. Warren made many contradictory statements that could have undermined her credibility in a general election campaign as Trump himself told a rally in Manchester, NH: "I did the Pocahontas thing. I hit really hard, and it looked like she was down and out. But it was too long ago. I should have waited. But don't worry, we'll revive it."[41] Biden's offering was much more modest in policy terms and he sold himself as a moderate who was interested in toning things down. His endorsers played up stories of his personal decency and compassion. The combination made it more difficult for Trump to make a similar argument against his candidacy or to establish as clear a contrast between himself and Biden.

Trump's electoral win and loss show how important it is that political marketers understand their customers and be ready to adjust the brand story in response to changing customer concerns. In 2016, Trump found his customers, told them a powerful emotive story that resonated with their life experiences, brought the brand to life for them through his rallies, made the brand part of their lives by selling them merchandise and closed the sale. He continued selling once in office by continuing all the things that he helped him win in 2016. Trump made 46 more visits and outspent Hillary Clinton's campaign by 50% in the swing states that gave him the Presidency.[42] The Trump campaign focused on the rules of the game and the way in which one won the game not on being popular everywhere as Jared Kushner noted.[43] Thus, the Trump campaign developed a model that accounted for the importance of geography in the American political system meaning it focused on winning the Electoral College, not the popular vote.[44] The Trump campaign developed a strategy that fit John Judis's insight about the benefits of geography in the American system for Republicans and focused on winning the Electoral College while ignoring the popular vote contest.[45] Trump almost won in 2020 by using the same strategy.

Twitter was a useful platform for candidate Trump in 2016, but its value was mixed for President Trump and reelection candidate Trump. Twitter, along with other social media platforms, engaged in much more aggressive mediation in 2020 than they had in 2016 meaning Trump's strategy did not get quite the same results in the latter contest as it had in the former. Trump's words as President carried more meaning to more kinds of people in more places than did those of a Presidential candidate. As President, Trump had other platforms that he could and intermittently did use to get his message out. He did his own press briefings given how well he does in those, he could invite local reporters to the White House as Ronald Reagan did, he could invite favored reporters to the White House residence as Jimmy Carter did, he could do phone-ins to local talk radio programs including those that are not political in nature like sports talk radio as he had during his 2016 effort and he could use his press operation to do themed weeks to sell policies. Mostly, he focused on using Twitter and media scrums to disseminate his brand to the exclusion of everything else. These choices limited his ability to become more than the President of a few segments of the American population.

Trump's use of the sticky branding strategy meant that he did things that were memorable but did not fit the idealized image many Americans have of a President. Trump did not fit the idealized images Americans hold of the President nor did he try to reach out to his opponents. Instead, his strategy stressed dominating specific segments of the electorate. It is why he lost the Electoral College in both 2016 and 2020 but won the Electoral College as a challenger and came close to doing so as an incumbent four years later. Trump kept his political opponents mobilized throughout his Presidency. This strategy produced a sense of chaos and polarization in the country that is beyond what exists on the ground. Trump argued that the rationale for his reelection campaign amounted to two things: an improved economy and increased safety. This was about as personalized and market oriented as it is possible for politics to get. Social media has made it cheaper for campaigns to communicate and has helped them to communicate more precisely with their target audiences thus opening the door to a broader spectrum of viable candidates on the national stage than there has been in a long time. Trump posed such a threat that media outlets invested in "fact checking" much of which was done by people who were more likely to be members of the professional classes that opposed Donald Trump than was the general population.

Further, social media companies modified their terms of service to limit the spread of "disinformation." As the evolving discussion of the origins of COVID-19, the possibility that vaccines for COVID would be available by the end of 2020 and that average Americans in large numbers could have access to them by April 2021 as Donald Trump claimed or the fact that the FBI really was interested in documents on the Hunter Biden laptop months after the election show, the definition of disinformation can be in the eye of the beholder and there may be things going on other than what a "fact checker" knows.[46] In the cases of the origins of COVID Trump had access to US intelligence information and in the case of the vaccine trials, Trump, as President, would have had access to that data if he wished to see it. The "fact checkers" saw neither while they were evaluating Trump's claims. Concerns about disinformation and an emphasis on specific facts served to disadvantage an incumbent President seeking reelection in 2020 because that candidate was using a brand strategy heavy on narrative and emotion, not facts. It can be seen as one of the vehicles through which the professional classes that did not like Donald Trump's story took steps to limit his chances of success.

Trump's brand omnipresence and sticky branding strategies did him no favors when the COVID crisis hit. During this crisis, Trump could have reached out to his opponents and projected leadership in the process but instead he stayed true to his brand. In the process, he inadvertently made himself the face of the crisis and of a response that many Americans thought was inept. Trump did daily briefings that strayed far from their ostensible topic, openly fought with the media, and did not adjust his brand values to fit a rapidly changing marketplace. The steadfastness with which Trump stuck to his core brand persona did him no favors when economic and racial justice crises began unfolding as Spring turned into Summer 2020. Trump could have been an empathetic leader and manager as the worst public health crisis in a century unfolded but instead, he was the same brand personality that he had been throughout his political life. This is one of the biggest reasons why Trump did not win reelection. He did not project an image of managerial competence, nor did he seem like he was fully in touch with the issues and concerns most Americans had leading up to the election. One can see the difference between the way the Trump brand was received in 2020 versus the way in which the Republican brand was received by looking at the difference between the result Trump got versus the result that the Republican Party got in that cycle. Republicans ran on a message that Democrats would defund the police and institute socialist policies. They did at the Congressional and state levels getting satisfactory results at both. The Republican messaging, unlike the Trump messaging, was about policies that would impact the average voter, not personal branding. In 2020 Donald Trump chose to run on the economy and stuck to his core brand but he had targeted so narrowly, alienated so many, and the environment in which he ran was so different than in 2016 that even though he turned out more voters than he had in that cycle, his opponent turned out more meaning Trump lost.

The upside to a sticky brand is that it builds a strong tie, the upside to the brand omnipresence strategy is that keeps people engaged with the brand, but the downsides are that these strategies can combine to repel many people and produce a sense of public weariness as happened in the case of Donald Trump. Trump lost the election at least as much as Joe Biden won it. While his refusal to concede might have been excellent for his purposes of keeping brand engagement and raising money, the loyalty that he had built led to the events of January 6, 2021. Trump told the brand story of elites and Democrats out to stop him at any cost that, when he barely lost the Electoral College, blaming it on corruption by opponents was believable to his target audience. In the current segmented media environment in which most Americans live, it's likely that many Trump supporters only saw his version of events as presented through conservative media outlets and conservative Twitter. Ever the marketer, Trump built a platform brand allegedly to raise money for his legal efforts, but the bulk of the money went to retiring Trump's campaign debt. The "stop the steal" platform brand was believable to its targets because Trump had been telling them that something like this was likely to happen on Election Day for months if not years, because there were a lot of ad hoc electoral rules changes in 2020 in response to a raging pandemic and because the processes through which Americans count votes varies by state with some states being more transparent than others. The latter two charges served to give the cries of theft credibility to the audience and help Trump raise a fortune. That it culminated in chaotic scenes at the United States Capitol Building on January 6th just after one of Trump's emotionally charged rallies shows the power that targeting, segmentation, and emotional branding can have.

NOTES

1. O'Brien (2015, especially Chapter 1).
2. O'Brien, pp. 143–155.
3. O'Brien, pp. 196–198.
4. Zito and Todd (2018) note the direct-to-consumer aspect of Trump's twitter usage but argue he uses it to build a category. Brand omnipresence is unmentioned by them.
5. https://www.politico.com/magazine/story/2019/03/08/trump-jfk-225697.
6. Ibid.
7. Ibid.
8. Cameron Joseph. "Donald Trump Has Apparently Gotten Away with Posing as His Own Publicist 'John Barron' Many Times Before." *New York Daily News.* May 13, 2016. https://www.nydailynews.com/news/politics/donald-trump-posed-john-barron-times-article-1.2636536, accessed January 9, 2019.
9. See Al Reis and Jack Trout. *Positioning: The Battle for Your Mind* (2001) for an in-depth discussion of the uses of positioning and Coca-Cola's use thereof.
10. Woodward (2018, pp. 206–207).

11. Donald. J. Trump. "Remarks by President Trump at the Presidential Social Media Summit." July 12, 2019. https://www.whitehouse.gov/bri efings-statements/remarks-president-trump-presidential-social-media-sum mit/, accessed July 31, 2019. Currently Available at https://trumpwhit ehouse.archives.gov/briefings-statements/remarks-president-trump-presid ential-social-media-summit/
12. Ibid.
13. Ibid.
14. Stefan Wojick and Adam Hughes. "Sizing Up Twitter Users." Pew Research Center Internet and Technology. https://www.pewinternet.org/ 2019/04/24/sizing-up-twitter-users/, accessed July 1, 2019.
15. Ibid.
16. Ibid.
17. Stephanie Sugars. "From Fake News to 'Enemy of the People' An Anatomy of Trump's Tweets." CPJ Blog. https://cpj.org/blog/ 2019/01/trump-twitter-press-fake-news-enemy-people.php, accessed July 5, 2019.
18. Ibid.
19. See David Greenberg. "The End of Neutrality: Society's Shared Middle Ground Is Quickly Turning into a Battlefied. What Will That Do to Democracy?" *Politico Magazine*. September/October 2018. https:// www.politico.com/magazine/story/2018/09/06/common-ground-good-america-society-219616/.
20. Zito and Todd (2018).
21. Priyanka Boghani. "Brad Parscale Trump's 2020 Campaign Manager Calls Facebook Ad Policy: "A Gift"." PBS Frontline. November 28, 2018. https://www.pbs.org/wgbh/frontline/article/brad-parscale-tru mps-2020-campaign-manager-calls-facebook-ad-policy-a-gift/, accessed July 5, 2019.
22. Ibid.
23. Ibid.
24. Antonio Garcia Martinez. "How Trump Conquered Facebook Without Russian Ads: Why Russia's Facebook Ads Were Less Important to Trump's Victory Than His Own Facebook Ads." *Wired*. February 2, 2018. https://www.wired.com/story/how-trump-conquered-facebookw ithout-russian-ads/, accessed July 5, 2019.
25. Ibid.
26. Ibid.
27. Ibid.
28. Priyanka Boghani. "Brad Parscale Trump's 2020 Campaign Manager Calls Facebook Ad Policy: "A Gift"." PBS Frontline. November 28, 2018. https://www.pbs.org/wgbh/frontline/article/brad-parscale-tru mps-2020-campaign-manager-calls-facebook-ad-policy-a-gift/, accessed July 5, 2019.

29. Joshua Green and Sasha Issenberg. "Inside the Trump War Room with 12 Days to Go." Bloomberg, 2016. https://www.bloomberg.com/news/art icles/2016-10-27/inside-the-trump-bunker-with-12-days-to-go.
30. Ibid.
31. Ibid.
32. Priyanka Boghani. "Brad Parscale Trump's 2020 Campaign Manager Calls Facebook Ad Policy: "A Gift"." PBS Frontline. November 28, 2018. https://www.pbs.org/wgbh/frontline/article/brad-parscale-tru mps-2020-campaign-manager-calls-facebook-ad-policy-a-gift/, accessed July 5, 2019.
33. Joshua Green and Sasha Issenberg. "Inside the Trump War Room with 12 Days to Go." Bloomberg, 2016. https://www.bloomberg.com/ news/articles/2016-10-27/inside-the-trump-bunker-with-12-days-to-go and Antonio Garcia Martinez. "How Trump Conquered Facebook Without Russian Ads: Why Russia's Facebook Ads Were Less Important to Trump's Victory Than His Own Facebook Ads." *Wired*. February 2, 2018. https://www.wired.com/story/how-trump-conquered-facebookw ithout-russian-ads/, accessed July 5, 2019.
34. Antonio Garcia Martinez. "How Trump Conquered Facebook Without Russian Ads: Why Russia's Facebook Ads Were Less Important to Trump's Victory Than His Own Facebook Ads." *Wired*. February 2, 2018. https://www.wired.com/story/how-trump-conquered-facebookw ithout-russian-ads/, accessed July 5, 2019.
35. Jacob Gershman. "Trump Campaign's Libel Claims Are Longshots." *Wall Street Journal*. March 6, 2020. https://www.wsj.com/articles/ trump-campaigns-libel-claims-are-longshots-11583498061?mod=search results&page=1&pos=1.
36. Liz Roscher. "Miracle on Ice Team Defends Decision to Appear at Trump Rally." *Yahoo Sports*. February 23, 2020. https://sports.yahoo.com/mir acle-on-ice-team-defends-decision-to-appear-at-trump-rally-200916430. html, accessed March 7, 2020.
37. Ibid.
38. See Cosgrove and Shrader in Moufahim (2021) for a detailed examination of the relative strength of Joe Biden as a challenger to Trump.
39. Ibid.
40. Ibid.
41. President Donald J. Trump as quoted in Bill Scher. "Pocahontas Could Still Be Elizabeth Warren's Biggest Vulnerability." *Politico Magazine*. August 27, 2019. https://www.politico.com/magazine/ story/2019/08/27/pocahontas-elizabeth-warrens-biggest-vulnerability-227912, accessed March 7, 2020.
42. Anthony Terrell, "Trump Out-Campaigned Clinton by 50 Percent in Key Battleground States in Final Stretch." NBC News. November 13, 2016.

https://www.nbcnews.com/politics/2016-election/trump-out-campai
gned-clinton-50-percent-key-battlegrounds-final-100-n683116,   accessed
July 5, 2019.
43. Steven Bertoni. "Exclusive Interview: How Jared Kushner Won Trump
the White House." *Forbes*. December 20, 2016. https://www.forbes.
com/sites/stevenbertoni/2016/11/22/exclusive-interview-how-jared-
kushner-won-trump-the-white-house/#6b670c703af6, accessed July 31,
2019.
44. Ibid.
45. Ibid.
46. Brooke Singman and Jake Gibson. "Laptop Connected to Hunter Biden
Linked to FBI Probe." *Fox News*. October 20, 2021. https://www.
foxnews.com/politics/laptop-hunter-biden-linked-fbi-money-laundering-
probe.

REFERENCES

Cosgrove, Kenneth and Nathan Shrader. "Political Branding in the USA Election
of 2020." In Mona Moufahim (ed.) *Political Branding in Turbulent Times*.
Palgrave-Macmillan, 2021.
Hall-Jamieson, Kathleen. *Packaging the Presidency: A History and Criticism of
Presidential Campaign Advertising* (3rd Edition) Oxford University Press,
1996.
O'Brien, Timothy L. *Trump Nation*. Open Road Media, 2015.
Woodward, Bob. *Fear: Trump in the White House*. New York: Simon and
Schuester, 2018.
Zito, Salena and Brad Todd. *The Great Revolt* Crown Forum, 2018.

CHAPTER 5

Trump: Race and Class

Abstract Donald Trump's political brand shows that race and class matter in American political marketing. The Trump brand is targeted at older, working-class audiences and some of his appeals aim at specific demographic groups. Trump's political brand is consistent with the working-class-focused branding Trump has done throughout his career. Trump has been consistent in presenting his brand as candidate and as President. The messages he distributes, the clothing he wears and even the food he eats all constitute parts of a brand aimed at working-class voters. Cosgrove posits that Donald Trump sought to attract working-class voters to the GOP even if it meant the party lost support from other audiences. Donald Trump's brand can be racially polarizing. Cosgrove argues that Trump's problems with audiences of color mirror the GOP's problems with these audiences that are a result of a long-ago strategic choices to target conservative white voters. Trump targets people of color along age, class, nationality, and religious lines. He targeted African Americans by saying that they had been failed by the Democrats and should consider something new. While observers have been arguing for many years that the Republican position on immigration would hurt the party with Hispanic voters, Trump shows that there are multiple ways to segment that audience and that issues other than immigration of interest to Hispanic audiences.

K. M. Cosgrove, *Donald Trump and the Branding of the American Presidency*, https://doi.org/10.1007/978-3-030-30496-6_5

Keywords Social class · Working class · Race · Brand style · Brand story · Brand emotions · Crooked Hillary · National Football League and Donald Trump · Professional Wrestling and Donald Trump · Sports and Political Marketing · African American voters · Hispanic voters · Segmentation · Republican Party · 2021 Presidential Inauguration

Branding tells a story. That story can include text, logos, colors, language, event settings, the people who appear on stage behind a candidate, buses, airplanes, signs, and digital products like tweets and emails. Trump's brand promises of disrupting the elite, creating economic prosperity, supporting law and order, and building a strong national defense were the core of his brand story during his time on the national stage. Trump personally did not cause everything to become politicized. His brand story tapped into the politicization of every aspect of life. His political messaging riffed on popular culture, music, celebrities, sports, and news stories. Trump would use these topics as examples around which he would tell his core brand story, to position itself in the mind of its audiences and to signal specific audiences that they should be interested in it. He used many aspects of American life to show what he favors and opposes. Political branding and segmentation might have caused polarization because both build the kind of identity and emotive loyalty to a group or candidate that scholars like Norris and Inglehart (2019), Jardina (2019), and Mason (2018) have argued helped people define their place in the world in cultural, racial, and tribal terms. Consider the way in which Trump used the image of the professional athlete as someone who should feel grateful and patriotic to build contrast with African American NFL players who were using the pregame national anthem to heighten awareness of disparate treatment of their community in this country. Trump's depiction of the athlete is more in keeping with the image of athletes several decades ago than the actual behavior of athletes now or then and it is an archetype with which his audiences target audiences were familiar. Some also argue that it is a subtle form of racism and a way to present Trump as upholding white cultural dominance.[1]

Donald Trump built a class-conscious brand. Its working-class elements changed the style, contents, and presentation of the GOP house brand. Implicit in this transformation was a tradeoff between attracting working-class voters and repelling upper-middle-class college-educated professional voters. Given the much larger number of working-class than professional class voters in the electorate, this tradeoff had the potential to pay big dividends. The risks were that working-class voters, especially working-class white voters, had been an underperforming part of the electorate in past several cycles and were not uniformly distributed across the country. Trump won the bet in 2016 but lost it in 2020. His party was shellacked in 2018 when he was not on the ballot himself and it got better results in 2020 at the Congressional and state levels than he did meaning the future of Trump's more class-based branding in GOP political marketing is unresolved as of now.

By combining class with race, Donald Trump produced a brand that had different heritage than that of recent Republican offerings. Trump's brand tapped into sentiments that have been present in this country for much of its history. Donald Trump is the latest in an extensive line of populists to fuse race and class, but he is also the second one in a quarter of a century to fuse business experience with populism (George W. Bush being the other). Donald Trump might have graduated from the University of Pennsylvania, but his branding played up other personal traits and his brand persona was decidedly working class. His election called into question the assumption that the progressives and multiculturalists would inevitably win the culture war and that the more statist economic policies proposed by the Democrats would carry the day.

What was unique about Trump's time on the national stage is that there was another candidate on it simultaneously who also used class in his marketing: Bernie Sanders. Donald Trump's class-based brand differed from the Sanders brand because it was aimed at different segments of the electorate. Sanders aimed at working-class people. He also targeted a young diverse audience because this is a growing share of the Democratic Party's electorate and he had won it overwhelmingly during the initial stages of the 2020 Presidential contest.[2] Donald Trump's class-based brand was aimed at older, whiter audiences. It differed in values, emotions, and the aspects of American life that it presented to its targets from those that Sanders or moderate Democrats like Joe Biden or Hillary Clinton presented in theirs.[3] Donald Trump built narratives in which facts were only important as far as they helped to build the story. His opponents and the media obsessed with his lies and misstatements but missed the point to them: they built a brand narrative. Trump told a brand story and brand stories are often more about emotion and narrative than policy or facts. The Trump brand story fits the sticky brand's need to be simple and clear (Miller 2015). Too many facts could make the brand story less clear and less sticky.

Donald Trump's brand was primarily aimed at his core audiences and presented them with images of "the way things ought to be" as Rush Limbaugh said. Trump's brand-building activities differed from presenting a nuanced discussion on the complexities of American life or public policy. Trump's brand, like all brands, was a marketing tool intended to reach its target audience and help make a complicated world and choices simple for it. Consistent with the sticky branding strategy, Trump's offering targeted a few audiences. His campaign was not afraid to chase away some voters to attract the ones it really wanted to attract. Saying outrageous things and doing outrageous things are not gaffes for a candidate who is trying to build a sticky brand. These kinds of behavior are ways to segment an audience, differentiate the candidate and build omnipresence. Donald Trump did for political branding what commercial producers like Nike did for commercial brands. Trump and Nike took sides, make statements of which their core audiences approve and are willing to drive away customer segments that do not perform well for them.[4] Trump's emotional branding included immoderate statements that differentiated him from the standard Republican offering in the primaries.[5] These helped him to stand out from prior Republican offerings and differentiated him from his Democratic competitors. The strategy worked much better against Hillary Clinton than it did against Joe Biden because Trump could never establish himself as the working-class candidate against Biden as he could against Clinton nor could he depict Biden as the Washington insider while presenting himself as the disrupter versus Biden as he had with Clinton.

Trump's immoderate statements signaled interest to target audiences and attempted to build brand loyalty among them. Trump, like Sanders, sparked disagreement among his core audiences but they were attracted to them because they would say and support their statements unlike establishment politicians who often dealt in bland platitudes and subtle distinctions of policy.[6] Like Sanders, Trump said what his targets would say and did so using language they would use themselves. Thus, his brand style and persona mirrored the audiences he was trying to add to the GOP column and, in that sense, was a form of signaling. At the same time, Trump's messaging appealed to those conservatives who felt that too many of their leaders had substantively become Republicans in name only. Consistent with the principles of sticky branding, Donald Trump's verbiage attracted some audiences, and repelled others but built very deep brand loyalty among his target audiences. His statements signaled his audiences that Trump was like them, was unafraid to speak his mind and would do as he said once in office. As Trump's and Sanders' success show, many voters value this kind of authenticity.[7]

Trump's opponents have fulminated that it was almost impossible to get Trump supporters to change their minds: this is the power a political sticky brand possesses to build loyalty. Trump presented his crassness and pugnaciousness as proof of his working-class disruptor brand promise. Consider the way in which his campaign built a defense against a leaked Access Hollywood tape by attacking Secretary Clinton's ethics, arguing his offense was "locker room talk" while Bill Clinton took actions that were criminal and responded to her assertion that he was unfit to be President and enforce the nation's law: "it's just awfully good that someone with the temperament of Donald Trump is not in charge of the law in our country" to which Trump shot back, "Because you would be in jail."[8] In this exchange, Trump raised questions about the Clintons' behavior by tapping into a long-running conservative theme that the couple was corrupt to the core and did so in a memorable way. Doing this let Trump show that he was unafraid to challenge the elite in ways that had not been done before. In the second debate, he told journalist Tim Alberta that he thought was the one that won the 2016 election for him because he made his brand promise to be a fighter real to his target audiences while restating his positive brand story about himself and his negative brand story about his opponent and the incumbent administration.[9] Trump's pugnacious style in this matter fit his brand promises.

Once in office, Trump made decisions that irritated his opponents to show that campaign promises were being kept and that he was a man of action unlike Barack Obama who he presented as a man of words.[10] During the first week of the Trump Administration, the Administration issued a flurry of executive orders. The most notable of these implemented a travel ban on citizens of a few countries all of which were majority Muslim in religiosity. This showed that Barack Obama was not in charge anymore and that Trump was keeping his word.[11] Trump's branding was anti-establishment and far from that of Barack Obama who had become a darling of the political establishment in both parties. Obama's brand style and personality resonated with much of it and reflected the meritocratic ideal, he shared their cultural assumptions, and professional backgrounds in ways Donald Trump did not. Further, their brand personas resonated with vastly different racial, class, and age cohorts as their behaviors showed. Barack Obama had an organic garden, periodically ate at trendy restaurants in DC, and brewed beer in the White House. Trump eats at McDonald's, steak drenched in ketchup, enjoys Doritos and M&Ms but does not drink alcohol. Barack Obama would vacation in the meritocratic playground of Martha's Vineyard for a month every summer. Donald Trump vacations at his golf resort in Bedminster, New Jersey, annually, leaves Washington frequently to stay at his golf resort in Florida, and has made plenty of time even when in Washington to play golf. Barack Obama issues an annual list of movies, books, and films he enjoyed during the prior year that's invariably erudite and fits with what his various voting groups would enjoy. Trump tweets about the NFL playoffs. Barack Obama attended NBA and college basketball games and his annual March Madness bracket was widely anticipated. Donald Trump attended the World Series, the Super Bowl, and a pro wrestling event. After being booed at the wrestling and the baseball game both of which were held in places that did not vote for him, Trump attended college football games in Alabama and Louisiana where he was popular and the Daytona 500 (something George W. Bush had also done during his 2004 reelection campaign). These games featured teams from those states plus another Trump depends on in his electoral coalition: South Carolina.

Trump and Obama's sporting interests diverged in part because of their personal traits but also in part because they reflected the audiences each of them was trying to reach.

Like his customers, Trump is no policy expert. He follows public affairs through conservative print, broadcast, and media outlets. His brand style fits the channels he consumes and uses in that he responds to the latest progressive outrages and defends tradition. While he dealt with lots of politicians, most of them were in New York, were Democrats, and all these dealings were undertaken for business reasons.[18] Obama was superficially optimistic and presented a cool, hip, diverse brand personality aimed at audiences quite different from those that Donald Trump targeted. Obama epitomized the class that the writer David Brooks (2001) termed the bourgeoisie bohemians. Donald Trump brought a working-class sensibility to the White House in that he eats at McDonalds, watches the Fox News channel, listens to conservative talk radio, does not read, listens to classic rock, and wears the same CEO uniform suits that he wore before becoming President and even his ties are Trump-branded products.[19] Trump's dominant brand emotions are anger, self-righteousness, and pity, a keen sense of humor aimed at his elite opponents who take him seriously and a message of hope that stresses that the country can be restored to its lost greatness out of the mess this elite made of it. His values reflect a respect for established institutions like the church and the police, symbolic patriotism, a sense that mainstream values should predominate, and aspirational about building a better country.

Donald Trump's emphasis of narrative over facts typifies the way in which emotional branding works. His pre-political background in commercial, sports, and celebrity marketing helped him to build a sticky political brand. Trump's political brand differs from those associated with Republicans and, indeed, many Democrats because it is specifically aimed at working-class people. This is clear in the way in which Trump used sports that overlap with his target audiences' interests, the best examples of which are professional wrestling and football. Trump conducted himself in ways that would be familiar to any fan of professional wrestling. Sports provide entertainment and spectacle to be sure. Donald Trump's political brand presentation is very much in keeping with the way sports are presented right down to the venues in which they are presented. Trump was like a sports marketer because he presented his potential customers with coherent, often moralistic, stories in which there are clear winners and losers. Sports are heavily branded and merchandised just like Trump was and sports businesses never stop selling just like Trump never stops selling. Trump combines emotional branding and target marketing with the kind of showmanship one finds in sports game presentation generally and most notably in professional wrestling. Trump, like any sport promoted played up conflict because people are attracted to events that feature it. Trump uses combative language to attract attention. His rallies are, like professional wrestling shows, large-scale spectacles that emotionally engage the audience in terms they can understand.[12]

His 2016 campaign ran on the cheap for a long time by using these techniques and they were also a way for him to circumvent the media gatekeepers. Trump tells stories just like professional wrestlers do by frequently speaking in superlatives, language that engages the audience, and emotions that fit the context in which he is speaking.[13] For example, he was very much the wrestler strutting at the defeat of his opponents when he called out a list of defeated Republicans who had not supported him on the day after the 2018 midterm elections. Just like professional wrestlers, Donald Trump has a stage persona and a stage patter. His events were frequently filled with mentions of the "big, beautiful wall" and his opponents who were often the worst, the most corrupt, far left radicals "Democrats are becoming the Party of late-term abortion, high taxes, Open Borders, and Crime."[14] While he was in a situation in which "No president ever worked harder than me (cleaning up the mess I inherited)!"[15] or in a swipe at all his critics: So great to watch & listen to all these people who write books & talk about my presidential campaign and so many other things related to winning, and how I should be doing 'IT'. As I take it all in, I then sit back, look around, & say "gee, I'm in the White House, & they're not!"[16] This is a commonly used technique in wrestling patter: playing up one's own accomplishments while belittling those of one's critics and showing how one overcame and achieved while they just complained and undermined him. Trump contrasted his vision of the country with those of his opponents by using the kind of differentiation story that is commonly found in sports marketing generally and professional wrestling.[17]

Trump's election and ability to generate earned media show that technology offers a solution to the problem of money in politics. Trump understood how to get attention and how to provide his audiences with a sense of engagement, community, and emotional satisfaction.[18] He held big rallies and spoke bluntly at them, the large events and his blunt statements got media coverage. If that coverage attracted big audiences, he would subsequently get more coverage and got his message out to his target audiences cheaply. Trump built a brand personality that worked with Twitter and did so himself. His staff was useful for building data-driven targeting, media buying, and providing political intelligence. The Trump Presidency was truly the triumph of the political brand. The political brand that triumphed was one that was omnipresent, sticky, highly emotive, and targeted. Such a brand was not developed to produce social consensus, harmony, and happiness. Instead, it was more likely to produce division, emotional conflict, and a sense that the very Republic itself is in some ways threatened especially among the educated elite who had run it for years with little challenge before Trump came along. The vulnerabilities in the strategy were on full display during the 2020 general election. The media outlets that carried Trump's events live in 2016 refused to do so in 2020 and social media platforms that allowed unmediated communication in 2016 imposed strict terms of service in 2020. Some of these policies seemed directly intended to limit Donald Trump's ability to get his brand story out because they emphasized "facts" over narrative and relied on specific arbiters of these concepts few of whom were in the Trump target audiences, to discern one from the other.

Trump's brand story was consistent with the sticky branding strategy because it presented Trump as being proud to serve and speak on behalf of the people who are good, patriotic, and wise. Opponents are presented as being malevolent, self-interested, radically outside the mainstream, and anti-American. The far left of the Democratic Party is presented as the representative of the whole because clear contrasts help produce stickier brands as Miller (2015) notes. Trump's brand story presents him as being totally committed to securing American interests and advocating for his constituents yet willing to make deals if they are good for the country. His reelection campaign sold him as someone who had kept his promises even if he was not the nicest or most polished person in the world. This choice made sense until the COVID-19 pandemic emerged in 2020. After COVID emerged, Trump's performance in managing and narrating the crisis raised fundamental questions about the veracity of that claim.

Trump's brand story presented him as being on the side of absolute right while his opponents had the wrong ideas and were either evil or incompetent. He said things that a normal politician would not and said these things in ways that normal politicians would not say them. The combination gave Trump's brand credibility with his audiences. Candidate Trump contrasted his business acumen against the people who had led the country through a series of high policy public policy failures to argue that he and the people who came into government with him were more talented than those who have run in the country in recent decades. This is the same technique that wrestlers employ to try to show how flawed and how many times their opponents have failed when speaking of them. He likened his political opponents to wrestling heels. He promised to dispense justice to them and win the day for his followers. Donald Trump the politician tries to be like Donald Trump the wrestling participant: always the good guy (the babyface in wrestling terms). Trump negatively brands his opponents by using the personal trait patter that is familiar to any pro wrestling fan. His opponents are opponents by using patter that any wrestling fan would be familiar with. His opponents were branded in negative terms like "lyin'" and "cryin" and for 2020 "Sleepy," "Mini-Mike," and "Crazy Bernie."[19] As Adams (2017) notes these names were sticky, focused the audience on his opponents' undesirable traits, kept the debate on higher conceptual levels that were Trump's strength and out of the specifics of public policy that were not, and Trump would try them out in front of live audiences meaning that he had a good sense of which ones should become part of his messaging.[20] He even went as far as to use the term made famous by wrestling manager Classy Freddie Blassie, who used to use the term "pencil neck geek" to describe the opponents his wrestlers were facing when he called Democratic Representative Adam Schiff "a pencil neck."[21] Blassie recorded a song that was famous during the 1970s and 1980s that elaborates on the meaning of the term and would have been something many in Trump's audiences would know and could easily see as Trump drawing another contrast between himself and his opponents that only his fans would understand.

In 2016, he branded Hillary Clinton as "Crooked Hillary," "Crooked H," or even more simply "Crooked" and often led crowds in a chant of "lock her up." Republican entrepreneurs produced "Hillary for Prison" merchandise. Her choice of the vague brand "stronger together," her extensive messaging about Donald Trump's personal traits instead of what she would do in office, and inefficient resource allocation helped Trump's branding of her stick. Trump's "Crooked" brand tapped into decades of Conservative negative branding campaigns around the Clintons. Trump's effort attracted some disgruntled Bernie Sanders voters, anti-establishment populists, and Republicans. Trump's campaign reminded many Americans about their concerns about the Clintons' ethics. Over the years, the conservative branding efforts produced limited results because of questionable subjects and sourcing. The Trump campaign solved this problem by making use of a sourced book from a reputable think tank, *Clinton Cash*.[22] This was the fruit of advanced scouting and opposition research underwritten by conservative activists who had known for years who their general election opponent would be, researched her extensively, and presented the results in a credible format.[23]

Trump branded her in a way that made her appear to be the embodiment of the Washington establishment against which he was running. His claims could seem valid to voters for several reasons. First, she did not seem to have a good understanding of the day-to-day realities of life for average Americans. Her leaked emails bore that contention out and her opponents pounced on it at every opportunity. Second, she had gotten very wealthy by authoring books and giving speeches to elite organizations like hedge funds that the populists blamed for causing the 2007 financial crisis (Bernie Sanders demanded that she release the transcripts of these talks something she refused to do). Third, she was involved in an email server investigation that came to the kind of conclusion that an insurgent could easily turn into an example of the establishment protecting its own. Such a claim was reinforced by a tarmac meeting that was caught on video between sitting Attorney General Loretta Lynch and Bill Clinton in Phoenix during the 2016 campaign. Fourth, there were the lasting impacts of the conservative branding campaign that had been running since at least her husband's 1992 campaign. These efforts left both Clintons with damaged reputations. Fifth, times had changed since she had helped her husband deal with issues around sexual improprieties. What once had been seen as someone having been a loyal spouse and effective attorney looking after their own could now be spun into a negative and a means for Trump to muddy the waters in the wake of his own issues in these areas being revealed. Even though Trump himself was no man of the people in terms of his income, educational credentials, social circle, or zip code of residence, he used his marketing background to tell a story in which she was the out-of-touch elite heel while he was the people's champion.

A Michigan rally shows how Trump negatively branded Secretary Clinton. After saying she had made the world a more dangerous place he said: "This is the legacy of Hillary Clinton: death, destruction and terrorism."[24] It would be hard to put her service as Secretary of State in more negative terms than those but using negativity to build stark contrasts is the stock in trade of wrestling patter and political campaigns thus making it a key element of the "Crooked Hillary" brand. He presented her as self-interested: "While our country lost badly under Hillary Clinton, she cashed in big time. Bill Clinton's speaking fees surged while Hillary was Secretary of State – Bill was paid almost $50 million for speeches during her tenure, an increase of 44% over the previous 4 years."[25] Even worse, he argued that she was corrupt: "Then there was all the money funneled into the Clinton Foundation from foreign governments and corporations it was pay-for-play."[26] Trump works in the corrupt arrogant elites' riff that is a core part of his branding when he said "Hillary Clinton, who is indifferent to the suffering she has caused, has no remorse. She offers no apologies for selling government favors. No apologies for unleashing ISIS. No apologies for open borders. No apologies for lying about her emails, or about Benghazi."[27] The use of the term remorse implies wrongdoing or criminality thus tapping into a legacy of conservative branding that presented the Clintons as heading the political equivalent of a criminal organization. Trump built on the idea by bringing up the volume of her deleted emails, called her corrupt then issued a call to action that encouraged people to vote in big numbers in order "to get justice in this rigged system."[28] After branding her negatively, Trump made a contrasting affirmative argument for himself by saying that the country deserved better and that he wanted to change while his opponent sought to preserve the current situation.[29] He closed by arguing that he was on the side of the people, would "end the corruption and restore integrity to government service."[30] Further "No one will be above the law. In a Trump Administration, the State Department will work for the country – not for Hillary Clinton's donors. And I will work for you – and for no one else."[31] Trump used these themes to position himself as the babyface and his opponent as the heel in wrestling terms. In marketing terms, he branded himself positively and his opponent negatively.

Branding Joe Biden proved to be a more difficult proposition.[32] Trump was running as the incumbent, not as the insurgent challenger meaning that the try it once strategy wouldn't work again. Trump had to earn repeat business and find new customers given that he had lost some of the voters he had won in 2016. He was also faced with the Democrats' efforts to turn out a much bigger electorate in a belief that doing so would work to their advantage. Biden proved to be an elusive target because he kept a limited public campaign schedule and because his campaign had the good sense to stay out of the way while Trump struggled to manage a series of crises during 2020. Trump ended up in the opposite position in 2020 to the one that he had been in during 2016 because Biden successfully negatively defined him, and his own performance showed that promises of effective management made in 2016 might not have been kept during the COVID crisis.

Trump's commercial and political brands do more than just develop contrasts or work like professional wrestling patter. They tell an aspirational, emotional story. This story was aimed more at whites than minorities unlike Trump's other brands.[33] It replaced some of the more garish elements of his commercial brands with patriotic themes while working in the brand heritages of Ronald Reagan and Richard Nixon, as well as the legacy of Andrew Jackson. Trump's commercial brand heritage remained prominent in the campaign and in his Presidency. Consider the way Trump's air fleet was deployed (as a candidate and as President Trump held rallies in airplane hangars into which his plane would pull. The only difference is that as a candidate Trump used his own plane and as President, he uses Airforce One). He sometimes used the "Theme from Airforce One" during the campaign[34] His campaign was announced in Trump Tower, and he sometimes put displays of Trump-branded products where they were visible to the media and audience. Trappings of and assertions about wealth are key parts of the Trump brand because they make the argument that he entered politics to serve the public not to enrich himself. He presents himself as the CEO as President by always appearing in a dark suit, white shirt, and red or purple tie. Presenting himself in this way and mentioning the successes of his commercial ventures, let Trump exploit a contrast between the efficiencies of the private sector versus the inefficiencies of the government something that sells to conservatives.

As a politician, he retained an ability to appeal with a sense of "downscale luxury" lifestyle branding that empowered his commercial brands.[35] He did not fit the profile of the super-elite because he was not in the elite circles of New York real estate but instead was a wheeler-dealer who presented himself as having worked for what he had earned just like the customers whose votes and purchases he sought had done.[36] Trump talked about the lessons he learned at military school through working for his father's construction company and dealing with average Americans when telling his brand story.[37] Trump knew exactly what his audiences wanted when it came to brand style, story, and emotions. His ability to understand the audience was helped by the fact that his campaign team came from the same background as did his audience. They did not have the high-end educational credentials many national-level campaign operatives do and like his audience targets, were impressed with his downscale luxury commercial brand.[38] Trump's lifestyle and behavior are important parts of the Trump brand and things that this audience would emulate if they could.[39] In keeping with the notion of the way that Trump segments audiences, the people who most loved Trump were people who worked with their hands thus showing why Trump's campaigns made the pitches that they did.[40] Trump's political brand extends his lifestyle brand and appeals to many of the same audiences that bought his commercial brand. His political brand was a sticky brand in that it built deep loyalty, presented the product in a unique way, and positioned it differently from its opponents in the marketplace.

Trump's first opportunity to make good on his brand promises happened during his inaugural address. The controversy around it focused on relative crowd sizes. Crowd size was important because it was a proxy for Trump's (or any new President's) popularity. If Trump really was the leader of a class-based movement then one would have expected huge crowds thus the battle over turnout that took place. His speech tried to build fellowship between Trump and some of his predecessors, restated Trump's election themes and outline how American could be made great again. Trump used this speech to argue again that the interests of Washington and the elite had diverged from the rest of the country in a cataclysmic way. He argued that he had been elected to put a stop to the carnage that had resulted. As one of the leading elites, former President George W. Bush allegedly described the contents of the speech "that was some weird shit."[41] Bush was one of Trump's brand villains, so his reaction is not surprising. Trump, like other American populists, was rhetorically very combative. Like his populist predecessors, Trump's rhetoric was anti-establishment.

> "For too long, a small group in our nation's Capital has reaped the rewards of government while the people have borne the cost".[42] Trump then noted the difference in economic fortunes between the residents of the National Capital area and its denizens then juxtaposed that with what had gone on in much of the interior of the country "Washington flourished – but the people did not share in its wealth. Politicians prospered – but the jobs left, and the factories closed."[43]

Much of this small group was seated before him when he said: "The establishment protected itself, but not the citizens of our country. Their victories have not been your victories; their triumphs have not been your triumphs; and while they celebrated in our nation's Capital, there was little to celebrate for struggling families across our land."[44] Trump rhetorically confronted his opponents and outlining their transgressions just like professional wrestlers do, positioned them as the villains, and himself as the hero while building brand awareness among the public in the process. Trump sold his inaugural as the moment that average Americans took back their government from an elite who had not acted in their interests for years. In classic reality TV show host style he referenced the home audience: "That all changes – starting right here, and right now, because this moment is your moment: it belongs to you. It belongs to everyone gathered here today and everyone watching across America. This is your day. This is your celebration."[45] He went on to argue that his election was a reassertion of the popular will and tried to be non-partisan: "And this, the United States of America, is your country. What truly matters is not which party controls our government, but whether our government is controlled by the people. January 20th, 2017 will be remembered as the day the people became the rulers of this nation again. The forgotten men and women of our country will be forgotten no longer. Everyone is listening to you now." [46] Trump argued that he embodied a popular movement reasserting itself and making the country's institutions work for them again: "at the center of this movement is a crucial conviction: that a nation exists to serve its citizens."[47] His list of demands was short and consisted of things nobody could really be against: "good schools, good jobs and safety."[48] But in Trump's narrative, the Washington establishment was more interested in perpetuating its own position than helping the citizens.

This is stock in trade in the conservative brand because it tries to position liberals as defending special interests in contrast to the conservatives trying to promote the general welfare. A case in point is the battle over education funding and policies in which the Democrats argue for a vastly distinct set of policies than do the Republicans. The Republicans try to present the Democrats as advocating for the interests of teacher unions. Trump used some of this narrative when noted that "for too many of our citizens, a different reality exists: Mothers and children trapped in poverty in our inner cities; rusted-out factories scattered like tombstones across the landscape of our nation; an education system, flush with cash, but which leaves our young and beautiful students deprived of knowledge; and the crime and gangs and drugs that have stolen too many lives and robbed our country of so much unrealized potential."[49] Even though this is standard conservative brand narrative materials, Trump said these things in a way that fit his sticky brand. His message was more vivid and emotionally engaging than the stock-in-trade conservative messaging on these topics. He presented the entirety of it in apocalyptic terms and himself as the corrective by saying "This American carnage stops right here and stops right now."[50] Given that they were the subject of his attacks, the heel in his brand story, and Trump's argument that he represented a challenge to the Bush laden GOP establishment, President Bush's barnyard description of it is understandable.

Race was another area in which Trump's campaign and administration used segmentation to reach an extremely specific part of the audience and sticky branding to build loyalty for Donald Trump. Race is used in two separate ways in Trump's branding. First, there is the obvious way that his opponents are happy to discuss but second is a more subtle niche strategy designed to shift the Electoral College. The latter strategy bore some fruit in both elections. Trump's campaign began with a rant about the ills Mexican immigrants brought to the United States and much of his rhetoric consciously or unconsciously appealed to the archetypes and stereotypes his biggest audience targets had about people of color while defining in and out groups. Trump's team segmented the market in communities of color in search of just enough supporters to win individual states. Donald Trump argued that African Americans had been failed by Democrats for whom they had voted for decades and that Hispanics who were in the country legally had much to gain from the policies his Administration would enact while those who were not here legally would be removed. Doing this, he argued, would make economic conditions better, make everyone play by the same rules, and restore a sense of order to the country. Trump's rhetoric was, as is true across the board of the ascendant populist movements, harsh regarding Muslims whom he often equated with being terrorists and he promised to enact a ban on Muslims entering the country until "we can figure out what the hell is going on."[51] As is typical of Trump he mentioned that he had Muslim friends and used their support for his policy as both a credential for promoting this policy and as a shield against being called anti-Muslim.[52]

Some, like Reny, Collingwood, and Valenzuela argue that race and immigration were the key determinants of vote switching among people who voted for Barack Obama and then changed to Trump.[53] While they do not explain how Trump appealed to these audiences, branding (especially sticky branding) and segmentation provide an answer. This combination let him play to the concerns of whites to bump up their share of the electorate while simultaneously making a niche pitch to African Americans as is consistent with the sticky branding strategy. The combination helped to win just enough votes to flip states in the Electoral College in 2016, a feat he nearly repeated in 2020. Trump could be perceived as a racist because he reached out to constituencies that no mainstream candidate had in years. He made the kinds of class-based appeals around racial themes that had not been heard in decades. Further Trump's audience targets included specifically racialized audiences like white nationalists and supremacists whom his campaign would signal by using some of their verbiage and symbolism as his campaign did when it tweeted out a picture of Pepe the frog (a white nationalist symbol) or retweeted items in which it was included. Trump feigned ignorance of the importance of these symbols and argued that he did not accept support from these groups in public. Regardless of his protestations, there was no way for him to disavow the ballots these audiences cast for him. All that mattered was who turned out to vote and who did not. People would respond to what they would no matter how much it horrified the media and the Washington establishment or how retrograde it seemed to other audiences. In Trump's defense, there certainly is no law against racists voting nor it is a crime to target and mobilize them. It is considered unacceptable to reach out to them by many in Washington, in the media, and in the public. Targeting these audiences was a form of brand style because Trump would welcome people whom the elite shunned.

Trump's problem with attracting minority voters mirrors the GOP problem with attracting minority voters. The GOP's problems with African Americans result from the strategic choice it made in the wake of the Civil Rights movement to focus on white Southern voters and its subsequent decision to pursue a similar strategy elsewhere in the wake of policies like Affirmative Action and desegregation in schools and housing. The GOP's regional messaging on race show how race and class can be fused into a potent political product. It also shows and how parties make strategic decisions based on the probability of winning elections and future potential growth. Donald Trump's marketing problem with African Americans in general is the branding problem facing the Republican brand. Both share a history of at minimum racially aware and at most outright racist messaging and behavior. It is easy to understand why African Americans would see Donald Trump's brand persona and messaging as offering them a return to an America that was not so great for them. He had once publicly called for the death penalty for five young men who, eventually, were cleared in a famous case involving the rape of a jogger in New York's Central Park during the 1980s. Trump ran an ad in the New York Times in the aftermath of the case calling for a restoration of the death penalty and using the kind of emotional branding language that he would later use to win the Presidency when he used the tag line "Bring back our safety" ad "bring back our police".[54] Trump's real estate company was accused of discriminating against African Americans in renting during the 1970s. Trump was one of the leading voices in the country questioning if Barack Obama were native-born and therefore eligible to be President something that could be seen as very racist. Once Obama released his birth certificate, on a morning when Donald Trump was speaking in New Hampshire in advance of the 2012 Presidential contest, ever the marketer he just moved on to the next product:

Making America Great Again and blamed the Clinton 2008 campaign for inciting the entire episode.[55] When Hillary Clinton raised his involvement in the birther movement, he blamed her supporters for starting it: "Well, you owe the president an apology because, as you know very well, your campaign, Sidney Blumenthal, he's another real winner that you have. And he's the one that got this started along with your campaign manager and they were on television just two weeks ago he was saying exactly that. The you really owe him. Or the one who sent the picture to run your campaign -- the pictures around President Obama in a certain garb. That was long before I was ever involved, so you actually owe an apology." [56] Thus, Trump's answer is roughly that he did not start the story meaning nothing that happened afterwards was his fault even though he promoted it for years.

Conservatives have been making anti-elite pitches based around racial policy featuring out-of-touch liberals since the late 1960s. Race is sometimes discussed directly, sometimes not but there is a long history of racialized appeals in Conservative politics even these appeals come wrapped in other issues like rights and taxes as Edsall and Edsall (1991) note, or the Trump-inspired mobilization campaign against the teaching of critical race theory in schools that took place in the early months of the Biden Administration.[57] The longstanding GOP problem with marketing to African Americans is a result of the way in which Republicans have marketed to other audiences including Ronald Reagan's musings about social welfare policy, the Jesse Helms "Hands" ad, and the Willie Horton ad among others plus a series of policy and political initiatives that could be seen as race conscious.

Donald Trump's innovation was to build a sticky brand that could work with multiple audiences simultaneously. It included racial messaging aimed at whites while it simultaneously pitched voters of color that they would be wise to give Republican policies a shot given that they had been failed by Democrats who took them for granted. The messaging aimed at whites included the same anti-elite pitch Conservatives have been making since the 1960s in which rich liberals are happy to impose their agenda on working people but are not subject to its dictates themselves. One of the better examples of this is provided by the exchange between GOP campaign operative Lee Atwater and political scientist Alexander Lamis in which the former outlines how economics and race tie together to build a winning message.[58] The combination of an anti-elite, economic, racial, and cultural message is not new, but Trump built a brand that allowed it to be deployed to some white audiences but not others and audiences of color were given an entirely different message: they give the Trump Republican Party a shot because the Democrats had both taken their votes for granted while not solving their problems. Trump was not the first recent Republican to try to diversify the party's offering. The party itself had commissioned an autopsy after the 2012 election to try to do it and George W. Bush and Karl Rove tried too. Rove, in Bush's service, showed how the Hispanic community could be presented with issues that would make it more receptive to the Republicans' product. John McCain and Mitt Romney tried to do the same thing. On the other hand, voters across racial and ethnic lines showed that there was a good-sized audience for the populist sentiments that Stephen Bannon, other populist activists, and, eventually, Donald Trump figured out and capitalize on.[59]

Trump's problem GOP affiliation, brand personality, and style could easily have been seen by African Americans as racist. Trump's class-based pitch focused on issues and images of African Americans, but his audiences seldom contained big numbers of African Americans. He was invited to HBCU campuses, to the NAACP Convention and to the important community institution of the Church but declined all these invitations.[60] On the other hand, working-class African Americans saw their wages grow during Trump's Presidency and this community is hardly monolithic on social issues. Especially for older working-class African American voters Trump's brand story could have had some appeal especially if the other option was voting for a leftist or elitist candidate. Trump's task was to find enough African American voters who agreed with him that the Democrats were not like them. The kinds of databases that marketers use to segment the population offered Trump the chance to find exactly the right audience. All he needed to do was win just enough votes or convince enough voters to stay home from within these audiences to move states in his direction. Trump's approach to African Americans to try a new product was a niche marketing effort that worked both times. His share of the African American vote was higher in 2020 than it was in 2016 and he showed strength among African American men. Barack Obama, in an interview in *The Atlantic*, opined that this was because Trump's style resonated with this audience because it was close to the image presented by rap music stars.[61] His personal traits and expressions resonated with their own reality in the way that effective branding seeks to do.

Trump's critics pointed out that his language and past positions proved his animus toward people of color. Trump's suggested that many of the

problems facing African Americans were the result of the Democrats' policies. He usually did so by putting this in a try it once pitch based on
the brand promises he was making juxtaposed against the failures of the
Democratic product he was pointing out. The best expression of this pitch
is his ad-lib before a largely white audience at a Michigan rally: "You're
living in poverty, your schools are no good, you have no jobs, 58% of your
youth is unemployed – what the hell do you have to lose?"[62] He attacked
Hillary Clinton when he said nobody had done more to hurt African
Americans than her and the Democrats. He made this case by presenting
the situation facing African Americans in Detroit as an example.[63] He
closed with a classic pitch to switch by arguing that the Democrats had
failed African Americans and that, absent a switch nothing would change:
"To those hurting, I say: what do you have to lose by trying something
new? One thing we know for sure is that if you keep voting for the same
people you will keep getting the same result. My Administration will go
to work for you as no one ever has."[64] Trump emotively argued that
the Democrats' policies kept African Americans in a subservient socio-
economic position something that conservatives have sometimes argued
over the past thirty years.

Trump made a similar what do you have to lose pitch a few days
earlier in Wisconsin, in the wake of a police officer involved shooting in
the region, again before a mostly white audience he asked for "the vote
of every African-American citizen struggling in our society today who
wants a different and much better future."[65] His promised "Jobs, safety,
opportunity, fair and equal representation" things that everyone would
want.[66] Trump argued that African Americans should take a chance and
he promised that he would deliver for them economically. As a reelection candidate, Trump argued that he has delivered based on an increase
in African American wages and employment during his term.[67] Trump
suggested that the Democrats had enacted a system that sought to keep
African Americans loyal to them but that the party had made a series
of bigoted assumptions about them by saying: "We reject the bigotry of
Hillary Clinton which panders to, and talks down to, communities of
color and sees them only as votes – that's all they care about – not as
individual human beings worthy of a better future." [68] Trump's pitch to
African Americans was that the Democrats took them for granted and did
not deliver for them despite decades of lofty rhetoric while, he, Trump
would not do so. This is the same try it and see if you like it approach
often used in commercial marketing in which a prospect is told that

their present company takes their business for granted or has an inferior product to the company chasing their business. Trump presented himself as an insurgent encouraging African American voters to look at making the Democrats compete for their votes.

In the early stage of the 2020 campaign, Trump argued that campaign promises made to African American voters had been kept and that he would do more on their behalf in a second term. Proof of this can be found in the fact that, of the two Super Bowl ads that team Trump bought in 2020, the one that ran first featured an African American woman who had benefitted from the criminal justice reform bill Trump had advocated for and signed into law. Further, Trump made specific pitches toward African American voters in his 2020 State of the Union Address by highlighting the criminal justice reform bill, the overall economy, school choice, and a bill pushed by Senator Tim Scott (R-SC), himself an African American, that created opportunity zones from which African Americans would benefit.[69] Trump was helped in 2020 by Democratic calls to defund the police in the wake of a series of violent encounters in which police either killed or wounded African Americans. On the other hand, he was hurt by his lack of empathy about these events with some African American voters and his lack of empathy also hurt him with a lot of White upper middle class and professional voters.

He spoke to mostly white audiences about the problems of African Americans something that did little to answer the questions being asked about his racial attitudes. His argument that he was seeking to deal with the problems of the "inner city" can be seen as a form of racially coded language and his presentation of African American life was often the archetype of what his largely white audiences were accustomed to hearing. Indeed Trump's 2020 pitch to African Americans can be seen as being as much about reassuring white voters as it was about attracting African American support.[70] Trump, like many conservatives, focused on incidents in which African Americans commit crimes against each other and sometimes trots out crime statistics from specific neighborhoods in Chicago, many of which have high percentages of people of color living in them, as evidence that his points are accurate. An example is provided in a speech to the international association of police chiefs in which Trump discussed crime in Chicago, attacked the ACLU, and defended the broken windows theory of policing tactics that his confidant and lawyer Rudy Giuliani used in New York:

I have directed the Attorney General's office to immediately go to the great city of Chicago to help straighten out the terrible shooting wave. We want to straighten it out. We want to straighten it out fast. There's no reason for what's going on there. (Applause.) I've told them to work with local authorities to try to change the terrible deal the city of Chicago entered into with ACLU, which ties law enforcement's hands; and to strongly consider stop-and-frisk. It works, and it was meant for problems like Chicago. (Applause.) It was meant for it. Stop-and-frisk. And Rudy Giuliani, when he was mayor of New York City, had a very strong program of stop-and-frisk. And it went from an unacceptably dangerous city to one of the safest cities in the country – and, I think, the safest big city in the country. So, it works. It's got to be properly applied but stop-and-frisk works. The crime spree is a terrible blight on that city, and we'll do everything possible to get it done. I know the law enforcement people in Chicago, and I know how good they are. They could solve the problem if they were simply allowed to do their job and do their job properly. And that's what they want to do. So, Chicago, we're going to start working with you, as of today (Applause.)[71]

These passages contain a series of controversial statements including the standard conservative law and order messaging but go further to mention policies that many Americans feel were racist in their application. It is easy to see why some people of color and upper-middle-class whites placed Trump in an extensive line of Republicans using racist brand aspects. On the other hand, it is also easy to see how working-class voters could have seen Trump as a truth-teller mirroring their daily reality. He argued for supporting the police and the importance of having them in order. It's easy to argue against these things from a leftist ideological position or the safety of a swanky suburb or exurb. Further in cases of controversial shootings by police, Trump ordinarily sided with the police something that had not been a given during the Obama years. Obama's Administration brought questions of police treatment of African Americans to public view in a way that was congruent with the experiences of many African Americans and with a rising social movement questioning police tactics. This Presidential approach was not something that many white Americans were accustomed to experiencing. Trump's approach restored the messaging that white Americans were used to hearing regarding these issues and did so as part of his overall brand promise of making America Safe Again. In Trump's construction, the police were honest and if someone was shot committing a crime, that was their fault. This was miles away from what Americans had seen under Obama or the experience of many African Americans. It found a ready audience among working-class white voters who were concerned with their physical and property safety and may well have had an extant mental of what a criminal looked like. The series of incidents that happened in 2020 and the mobilization around them were really part of a much longer, much broader battle over policing and criminal justice policy in the United States that Trump's messaging put him squarely on one side of.

Trump used high-profile figures as credentials or navigators to enhance his credibility with communities of color.[72] These were persons whom a broad swath of the electorate would be comfortable and with whom they would be familiar.[73] Trump's navigators of color were people that white conservatives would feel comfortable with too. For example, Sheriff David Clarke who was a determined opponent of Black Lives Matter and strong law and order advocate and boxing promoter Don King. King has a personal redemption story and was a successful entrepreneur, sporting figure, and frequent user of nationalist themes, former Presidential candidate Herman Cain who is a successful entrepreneur. In 2020, Trump made much of his working relationship with South Carolina Senator Tim Scott. They are navigators because their endorsement and word can help people make buying decisions.

Trump's campaign had two very prominent women who embodied his message to African Americans: Linda "Diamond" Hardaway and Rochelle "Silk" Richardson acting as. These two women are social media brand evangelists for Donald Trump who argued that they became Republicans specifically so they could vote for Donald Trump.[74] They started a "ditch and switch now movement" to encourage other African Americans to follow their example and argue that they represent the silent majority.[75] They then started the "Women United for Trump" movement, spoke as the opening act at Trump rallies.[76] They base their support for President Trump on the premise that his "non-traditional approach is exactly what this country needs. President Trump inspires hope in the American Dream, because unlike modern day politicians who dance to the tune of lobbyist, he's a successful businessman who has the ability to dictate strategies without the interference of special interest groups whose money often play a role in creating disadvantages for Americans."[77]

Another of Trump's navigators, Candace Owens, has had this quote on her Twitter feed "black people don't have to be Democrats" and is a frequent promoter of the hashtag #blexit obviously modeled after the term Brexit. Owens hints at one conceivable way candidates can segment that African American population by looking at them in terms of the length of their time in the country when she tweeted:

> Today I am studying why Caribbean immigrants far surpass Black Americans in terms of economic success.
> If America awards success based on skin color, this wouldn't be possible.
> All researchers conclude that they are simply more driven!
> I'm of St. Thomas descent. VERY PROUD!.[78]

Ms. Owens shows how segmentation can work to help marketers find their target audience in any community. The number of Black immigrants to the United States has increased from about 800,000 in 1980 to over 4 million in 2016, these immigrants are more likely to be US citizens and speak English than other immigrants and only slightly less likely to have a college degree than the general population and have a rate of increase in college education that is higher than that for white Americans.[79] This is an audience that has a different set of experiences in this country than do native-born African Americans whose ancestors experienced the horrors of slavery or the children of long-established immigrant families. Socioeconomic status, marital status, education level, and religious engagement afford campaigns opportunities to segment the African American audience so that a candidate, like Donald Trump, could win just enough votes from it to gain electoral victory. Just as is the case with Hispanic voters as we will see in the next section the Trump team did not need to win a majority, it needed to win just enough of these audiences while racking up big margins among its primary working-class white audiences.

Donald Trump made immigration in general and illegal immigration especially into a focus issue for his campaign. Given the substantial number of people who have come to the United States since 1965 from Mexico, his choice to focus on anti-Mexican immigrant rhetoric fits a need among his white audience targets but also leaves open the possibility that he could talk about other issues with more acculturated Hispanic voters. For example, he discussed criminal gangs like MS-13 and international drug and human trafficking organizations to argue for his proposed border wall and immigration policies, he did not just argue that these would stop population flows and sometimes argued that his crackdown will make life better for Hispanics because the places they live will be more secure.[80] Republicans have articulated restrictive immigration positions for years that many people assume damage them with Hispanic voters across the board. As with the above-noted African American community, members of this community too behave differently from each other depending on several other things. For example, the acculturation level of Hispanic voters is important. Alvarez, Dickson, and Hunter found four different clusters of Hispanic consumers based on acculturation level.[81] Trump could target at least three of the four clusters (biculturals, assimilators, and non-identifiers) with his standard marketing with some hope of success.

Trump could also segment Hispanics by race because the Hispanic experience differs in the United States between white Hispanic and Black Hispanics in the United States.[82] Trump could segment these markets by race as subunits meaning that some Hispanics well could be Trump targets. Trump's anti-Mexican immigrant rhetoric is rooted in decades of Republican marketing around immigration and population migration. Given the way in which Conservatives have invested heavily in the fast-growing states of the South and West. Given that these regions are home to large numbers of recent Mexican immigrants and Mexican Americans, this is no surprise. Conservatives often claim to be welcoming to legal immigrants. They also argue that the 1965 Immigration Act changed the country's population much more than its sponsors said it would at the time. Republicans further see this as a law, order, and security issue. These two appeals have been stock in trade for Republican messaging for decades. Donald Trump simply applied a sticky branding technique to them and presented them to non-traditional audiences for the Republican Party. Donald Trump took advantage of decades of successful relationship building between the party and Cuban Americans many of whom came to this country fleeing communism. Given that Barack Obama had normalized relations between the US and Cuba during his term, Trump had an issue that he could use to engage these voters just as events in Venezuela gave him a chance to gain support in that community.

One thing that was often overlooked in understanding Trump's pitch to Hispanic voters is the fact that there have been Mexican Americans, Puerto Ricans, and other populations that could be understood as being Hispanic who have been in the United States for longer than many of the working-class white audiences that Trump targets ancestors have been meaning immigration would not be a high salience issue for them or for those whose families had immigrated decades ago.[83] While first-generation immigrants and their children might blanche at Trump's statements, second, third, and fourth-generation Hispanics might not. Trump was able to pitch Cuban Americans based on the policy changes that Barack Obama had made toward Cuba. He could do the same by talking about his objections to the Venezuelan socialist model in that community. Trump pitched Hispanic voters around moral and economic policies as the George W. Bush campaign had done in the 2000s. The Bush campaigns noted the differences between its candidate and his Democratic opponents and then discussed those with Hispanic voters.

Given the large advantage Democrats enjoy among Hispanic voters but also their low voter numbers, the Trump effort can be seen as an effort to both shear off some votes and depress turnout among the voter categories he did not wish to attract. If Trump could reduce the level of some Mexican American voters have in politics while increasing turnout among Hispanics who were more favorably disposed toward him that could go a long way toward shaping an electoral outcome.[83] Texas provides an example of how Trump's strategy worked. In 2020, Trump won the state in part because he won a lot of votes from Hispanic voters whose families have been in Texas for an exceedingly long time and who had much more in common politically with conservative White voters than they did with naturalized Mexican immigrants or their children.[84] This could be seen as central to his microtargeting strategy but analyzed through the prism of class, age, religiosity, and education level, race becomes more one of a host of variables than a determinative one.

One of the striking things about the messaging American politicians use is how little of it is aimed at Asian-Americans. Such targeting and messaging are common right next door in Canada in which specific Asian-Canadian groups are targeted by different parties and some communities see their votes as being coveted by all three major parties. Donald Trump did nothing to buck the trend of American politicians not specifically targeting Asian-American votes. The Asian-American market offers an opportunity for both parties because it is comprised of different nationality groups who have different psychographic and demographic makeups. Canadian political marketers are fully aware of these differences and battle over specific portions of the different nationality groupings that makeup this population.

When COVID-19 broke out, Donald Trump tried to blame it on China. While he might have been engaging in blame shifting for a poor US Government response, trying to increase American soft power around the globe or simply stating what he believed to be the truth, many of his political and media opponents were quick to label his construction racist. One wonders what the response would have been to Trump using the phrase Communist flu instead of just using a nation's name that overlapped with a domestic ethnic community's name. It was easy to see a racial motive in Trump's phrasing that would have been much more difficult to see had he used the more ideological phrase. His parallel argument that the virus escaped from a lab could have been used to buttress the more ideological phrasing. Communist regimes have a long history of trying to cover up their failures and mishaps. There were many nuclear accidents in the Soviet Union, including the Chernobyl disaster, that the regime only disclosed after its effects had been detected in Sweden, and China's communist government has historically had its own problems that it did not rush to disclose. Trump could have built on that history to tell this story but instead opted for a form of nation branding that his opponents could and did dismiss as racist.

Presenting responsibility for COVID through an ideological rather than a racial or a nationalistic frame could have made Trump into a unifying figure as the pandemic raged on. Instead, it allowed the idea that he was a racist to retain currency. This episode shows one of the key issues with Trump's sticky branding strategy: it lets people see and feel whatever they were predisposed to see and feel. Trump was everywhere but that allowed supporters and opponents alike to impute their own meaning to his statements and behavior. As a result, their predispositions about him became reinforced. Between his birtherism, his statements about young Black men accused of crimes, his description of the countries people left to come to the United States and their behavior once in the country, it is easy to see why many people thought that Donald Trump's depiction of them was racialized at best and racist at worst.

The combination of Trump's omnipresence strategy and his opponent's relentless negative branding campaign kept the interest in politics high during his campaigns, time in office, and beyond. While Trump's brand promised a return to an older, better, America, his opponents pointed out that this country has never been more diverse than it is presently, and has not always been supportive of diverse lifestyles or welcoming to immigrants. They argued that the country that Trump sought to restore had a racial hierarchy that put his key white constituency at the top of the heap. They successfully used elements of his personal and business traits, his policy positions, his alleged involvement with the Russian Federation and President Vladimir Putin, his failed business ventures in the 1990s and his subsequent comeback, and, most especially, his ventures that had been the subject of legal action like his university and his foundation against him. They argued that he is a racist and a sexist, accusations that have some credibility given his behavior or lack thereof at times. His opponents saw him as "a con man" as Tom Steyer put it in a 2020 Democratic Primary TV ad entitled "Economy."[84] They tried to diminish the size of his wealth, demanded copies of his tax returns, and suggested he is not fit to be President. They impeached him twice, launched state-level investigations of his business, and tried to use the emoluments clause of the Constitution against him. Prior to Trump trying to overturn an Electoral College win by his opponents in 2020, some Democrats tried to do the same to him via the same kinds of court and legislative challenges that Trump tried to initiate. They launched the same kind of campaign to overturn state electoral outcomes in the Electoral College via their "Hamilton Elector" effort and in state court and recount challenges like the ones that Trump launched in 2020.

His opponents in the bureaucracy continuously leaked negative information about him and tried to defy his authority. Trump generated such staunch opposition because sticky brands can repel as much as they attract, because he threatened to disrupt several established policies and policy networks, because he won in an upset even most of his own campaign team did not see coming meaning that they had done little transition planning, because he was not well versed in policy, often not Presidential in his behavior and did not fit the image of the modern President that many Americans hold.[85] His was a class-based sticky brand that told a story that resonated with working-class voters more than any other. Having such a tight focus on a few audiences and intentionally setting out to alienate others might be an effective way to sell consumer products and might even win an election but the problem comes once in office. All those interests, political opponents, media outlets and figures, and the voters who opposed him and who he used as fodder for his marketing campaigns had no reason to try to find common ground with him nor he with them.

It is easy to see why Trump's attitudes generated so much pushback. Even if Trump was not a racist or a sexist operationally, he certainly sounded like he could be based on some of his rhetoric. Sometimes his opponents would distort what he said to make it worse than it was as was true in the case of Trump's statements about "very fine people" in the wake of civil disorder in Charlottesville, VA in 2017 or about the possibility of disinfecting people with COVID, like surfaces sometimes are disinfected for viruses, in 2020. The Democrats choice of Joe Biden as a nominee and a promise of a return to something more normal after four years of Trump was a smart strategy. There was little exciting about Joe Biden and that was much more of a selling feature than a defect after four contentious years of Trump's brand omnipresence. He seldom appeared at public events or engaged the press in the way that Trump or Obama did, he spends most of his time in the White House or at Camp David. While he brought back the President's Weekly Radio Address, one must wonder in the age of Tik Tok and YouTube how valuable that exercise is in a marketing sense. Biden took a page from Trump's book and issued more executive orders than any modern President in short order after taking office but beyond that has been placid in brand style and persona and seldom directly available to the press and public in the way that Donald Trump was. Biden leaves the marketing of his Administration to the professionals. Much like the protagonist in the film "Bob Roberts," Donald Trump's election indicated that the times might be changing but not in the direction that many people had anticipated. Joe Biden's marketing strategy shows that this trend might be more pronounced than anyone anticipated because Biden is much closer stylistically to a nineteenth century President than any President we have had since Woodrow Wilson. This is because Biden is the representative of a party in the White House, not an individual trying to control the Executive Branch as Trump and Obama often tried to be.

NOTES

1. See for example Kevin Powell. "Donald Trump and the Black Athlete." *New York Times*. August 5, 2018. https://www.nytimes.com/2018/08/05/sports/trump-lebron-james.html, accessed February 25, 2020.
2. Eric Levitz. "The Bernie Campaign Is Fortified by a Human Shield of Millennials." *New York Magazine*. January 29, 2020, https://nymag.com/intelligencer/2020/01/anyone-but-bernie-sanders-biden-age-gap-millennials-gen-z.html, accessed February 25, 2020.
3. Pew Research Center: US Politics and Policy. "An Examination of the 2016 Electorate Based on Validated Voters." *Pew Research Center*. August 9, 2018. https://www.people-press.org/2018/08/09/an-examination-of-the-2016-electorate-based-on-validated-voters/, accessed February 25, 2020.

4. Bill Snyder. "Phil Knight on the Controversial Kaepernick Ad and Nike's Never Give Up Attitude." *Insights By Stanford Business.* February 14, 2019. https://www.gsb.stanford.edu/insights/phil-knight-controversial-kaepernick-ad-nikes-never-give-attitude
5. Zito and Todd (2018, pp. 12–17).
6. Ibid.
7. Terry Sullivan "Sanders Isn't So Much Trump's Challenger as He Is His Sequel." *Wall Street Journal.* February 23, 2020. https://www.wsj.com/articles/sanders-isnt-trumps-challenger-so-much-as-his-sequel-11582477250?emailToken=fdc0d8bde88f9df81abddc5459e5f5548yV5/uswAUQW8EclGPh67CC9OvhsHP50W1a6GUKKPVX05pNjVUy+azikVxMYkjYzmlg29P/txpIUx98qC5co6kGJ8m14qGaMJ005W01Gapb EKHtrzVoxNdExQkqXdeXJ&reflink=article_copyURL_share, accessed February 24, 2020.
8. Presidential Commission on Debates. "Second Debate Transcript." October 9, 2016. https://www.debates.org/voter-education/debate-transcripts/october-9-2016-debate-transcript/, accessed March 8, 2020.
9. Tim Alberta. ""Mother Is Not Going to Like This": The 48 hours That Almost Brought Down Trump: The Exclusive Story of How Trump Survived the Access Hollywood Tape." *Politico Magazine.* July 10, 2019. https://www.politico.com/magazine/story/2019/07/10/american-carnage-excerpt-access-hollywood-tape-227269, accessed July 10, 2019.
10. During Patrice Taddino. "Watch: How Steve Bannon Engineered President Trump's Travel Ban." *PBS Frontline.* May 22, 2017. https://www.pbs.org/wgbh/frontline/article/watch-how-steve-bannon-engineered-president-trumps-travel-ban/, accessed February 25, 2020.
11. Ibid.
12. Hans Fiene. "Pro Wrestling Explains Why Trump Wins Every Battle with the Media." *The Federalist.* https://thefederalist.com/2018/11/05/pro-wrestling-explains-trump-wins-every-battle-media/, accessed February 26, 2020.
13. Harris Fiene. "Pro Wrestling Explains Why Donald Trump Wins Every Battle with the Media." *The Federalist.* November 5, 2018. https://thefederalist.com/2018/11/05/pro-wrestling-explains-trump-wins-every-battle-media/, accessed February 26, 2020.
14. @realdonaldtrump tweet January 31, 2019, for more on Trump and wrestling imagery, see Stephen Miller. "How Professional Wrestling Explains Donald Trump's Political Persona." *National Review Online.* April 4, 2016, and *The Wilderness* April 12, 2016. http://thewilderness.me/wwt-how-professional-wrestling-created-trumps-political-persona/, accessed February 24, 2020.
15. Trump tweet, February 11, 2019.

16. Trump tweet, January 31, 2019.
17. Hans Fiene. "Pro Wrestling Explains Why Donald Trump Wins Every Battle with the Media." *The Federalist.com*. November 5, 2018. https://thefederalist.com/2018/11/05/pro-wrestling-explains-trump-wins-every-battle-media/, accessed February 26, 2020.
18. Kalryn Borysenko. "After Attending a Trump Rally I Realized Democrats Are Not Ready for 2020." *Medium*. February 11, 2020. https://gen.med ium.com/ive-been-a-democrat-for-20-years-here-s-what-i-experienced-at-trump-s-rally-in-new-hampshire-c69ddaaf6d07, accessed February 11, 2020.
19. For an explanation of the way Trump's use of nicknames resembles wrestling patter see Stephen Miller. "How Professional Wrestling Created Donald Trump's Political Persona." *National Review Online*. April 4, 2016, and *The Wilderness* April 12, 2016. http://thewilderness.me/wwt-how-professional-wrestling-created-trumps-political-persona/, accessed February 26, 2020.
20. pp. 129-135.
21. Ian Schwartz. "Trump Mocks Pencil Neck Schiff at a Rally." Real Clear Politics. March 19, 2019. https://www.realclearpolitics.com/video/2019/03/28/trump_mocks_pencil-neck_schiff_at_rally_has_the_sma llest_thinnest_neck_ive_ever_seen.html, accessed February 24, 2020.
22. Green (2017) especially on p. 152 makes the point that the sourcing used in this book was very important in giving it credibility with mainstream journalists.
23. Ibid.
24. "Full Transcript: Donald Trump Speaks in Michigan." August 19, 2016. https://www.politico.com/story/2016/08/donald-trump-mic higan-speech-transcript-227221, accessed July 31, 2019.
25. Ibid.
26. Ibid.
27. Ibid.
28. Ibid.
29. Ibid.
30. Ibid.
31. Ibid.
32. see Cosgrove and Shrader (2021) for an in-depth discussion of the Trump-Biden Contest.
33. Joshua Green.
34. See for example Pollack and Schweikart (2017 p. 28).
35. Mackay Coppins. "Meet Donald Trump's Proud Bullies, Goons, and Thugs." *Buzzfeed*. July 28, 2015. https://www.buzzfeednews.com/art icle/mckaycoppins/meet-the-proud-bullies-goons-and-thugs-in-donald-trumps-inne#.op35nP118, accessed August 1, 2019.

36. Ibid.
37. Ibid.
38. Mckay Coppins. "Meet Donald Trump's Proud Bullies, Goons, and Thugs." *Buzzfeed*. July 28, 2015. https://www.buzzfeednews.com/art icle/mckaycoppins/meet-the-proud-bullies-goons-and-thugs-in-donald-trumps-inne#.op35nP118, accessed August 1, 2019.
39. Ibid.
40. Ibid.
41. Yashar Ali. "What George W. Bush Really Thought of Donald Trump's Inauguration." *NY New York*. March 29, 2017. https://nymag.com/int elligencer/2017/03/what-george-w-bush-really-thought-of-trumps-ina uguration.html.
42. President Donald J. Trump. "The Inaugural Address." January 20, 2017. https://www.whitehouse.gov/briefings-statements/the-inaugural-address/, accessed July 2, 2019.
43. Ibid.
44. Ibid.
45. Ibid.
46. Ibid.
47. Ibid.
48. Ibid.
49. Ibid.
50. Ibid.
51. Jenna Johnson. "Trump Calls for Total and Complete Shutdown of Muslims Entering the United States." *Washington Post*. December 7, 2015. https://www.washingtonpost.com/news/post-politics/wp/2015/12/07/donald-trump-calls-for-total-and-complete-shutdown-of-muslims-entering-the-united-states/, accessed January 10, 2020.
52. Ibid.
53. Reny, Tyler R. Loren Collingwood and Ali A. Valenzuela. "Vote Switching in the 2016 Election: How Racial and Immigration Attitudes, Not Economics, Explain Shifts in White Voting." *Public Opinion Quarterly*. Spring 2019 83(1):91–113. https://doi.org/10.1093/poq/nfz011, accessed January 15, 2019.
54. See the full ad at http://apps.frontline.org/clinton-trump-keys-to-their-characters/pdf/trump-newspaper.pdf, accessed August 4, 2019.
55. NPR Staff. "Fact Check: Clinton and Trump Debate for the Second Time." https://www.npr.org/2016/10/09/497056227/fact-check-clinton-and-trump-debate-for-the-second-time, accessed July 30, 2019.
56. Ibid.
57. Theodoric Meyer, Maggie Severns and Meredith McGraw. "'The Tea Party to the 10th Power': Trumpworld Bets Big on Critical Race Theory." *Politico*. June 23, 2021.

58. Rick Perlstein. "Exclusive: Lee Atwater's Infamous 1981 Interview with Lee Atwater on the Southern Strategy." *The Nation*. November 13, 2012. https://www.thenation.com/article/archive/exclusive-lee-atw aters-infamous-1981-interview-southern-strategy/.

59. PBS Frontline "Zero Tolerance." October 22, 2019. https://www.pbs. org/wgbh/frontline/watch/, accessed October 22, 2019.

60. Reid Epstein and Michael Bender. "Donald Trump Courts Black Vote While Avoiding African-American Communities: Supporters Have Asked Candidate to Speak at Black Colleges, Churches and to NAACP." *Wall Street Journal*. August 23, 2016. https://www.wsj.com/articles/donald-trump-courts-black-vote-while-avoiding-african-american-communities-1471944606, accessed July 6, 2019.

61. Jeffery Goldberg. "Why Obama Fears for Our Democracy." *The Atlantic*. November 15, 2020.

62. Tom Lobianco and Ashley Killough. "Trump Pitches African-American Voters: "What the Hell Do You Have to Lose?"" CNN. August 29, 2016. https://www.cnn.com/2016/08/19/politics/donald-trump-african-american-voters/index.html, accessed July 6, 2019.

63. Ibid.

64. Tom Lobianco and Ashley Killough. "Trump Pitches African-American Voters: "What the Hell Do You Have to Lose?"" CNN. August 29, 2016. https://www.cnn.com/2016/08/19/politics/donald-trump-african-american-voters/index.html, accessed July 6, 2019.

65. Ginger Gibson. "Trump, in Law-and-Order Speech, Calls for African-American Support." Reuters. August 16, 2016. https://www.reuters. com/article/us-usa-election-trump-idUSKCN10R1P0, accessed July 6, 2019.

66. Ibid.

67. Eric Morath and Soo Ooh. "As Wages Rise, Black Workers See the Smallest Gains." *Wall Street Journal*. April 16, 2019. https://www. nytimes.com/2019/05/02/business/economy/wage-growth-economy. html, accessed January 18, 2020.

68. Ginger Gibson. "Trump, in Law-and-Order Speech, Calls for African-American Support." *Reuters*. August 16, 2016. https://www.reuters. com/article/us-usa-election-trump-idUSKCN10R1P0, accessed July 6, 2019.

69. Eugene Scott. "During State of the Union Trump Makes His Most Direct Appeal to Black Voters Yet." *Washington Post*. February 5, 2020. https:// onedrive.live.com/edit.aspx?cid=77f030235b4a5a8e&page=view&resid= 77F030235B4A5A8E!2629&parId=77F030235B4A5A8E!101&app= Word&wacqt=mru, accessed February 26, 2020.

70. Eugene Scott. "During State of the Union Trump Makes His Most Direct Appeal to Black Voters Yet." *Washington Post*. February 5, 2020. https://onedrive.live.com/edit.aspx?cid=77f030235b4a5a8e&page=view&resid=77F030235B4A5A8E!2629&parId=77F030235B4A5A8E!101&app=Word&wacqt=mru, accessed February 26, 2020.
71. Remarks by President Trump at International Association of Chiefs of Police October 8, 2018. https://www.whitehouse.gov/briefings-statem ents/remarks-president-trump-international-association-chiefs-police/, accessed July 6, 2019.
72. Doug Sosnik, brown and Fournier Applebee's America.
73. Sosnik et al. (2007).
74. Lynette "Diamond" Hardaway and Rochelle "Silk" Richardson "DIAMOND AND SILK CHIT CHAT: About Diamond and Silk." https://www.diamondandsilkinc.com/about-us, accessed July 5, 2019.
75. Ibid.
76. Ibid.
77. Ibid.
78. @realcandaceowens July 5, 2019.
79. Monica Anderson and Gustavo Lopez. "Key Facts About Black Immigrants in the United States." *Pew Research Fact Tank*. January 24, 2018. https://www.pewresearch.org/fact-tank/2018/01/24/key-facts-about-black-immigrants-in-the-u-s/, accessed February 27, 2020.
80. See for example: John Bowden. "Trump Rips Democrats for Allowing MS-13 'Animals' into Country." https://thehill.com/latino/392608-trump-rips-democrats-over-ms-13-slaughter-in-weekly-address, accessed August 4, 2019.
81. Cecilia Alvarez, Peter Dickson and Gary Hunter. "The Four Faces of the Hispanic Consumer: An Acculturation-Based Segmentation." *Journal of Business Research*. February 2014 67(2):108–115. Accessed August 4, 2019.
82. For details on the racial makeup of the Hispanic population, see John R. Logqn. "How Race Counts for Hispanic Americans." Lewis R. Mumford Center, SUNY Albany July 14, 2003. http://mumford.albany.edu/cen sus/BlackLatinoReport/BlackLatinoReport.pdf, accessed August 4, 2019.
83. See Kristian Ramos. "Latino Support for President Trump Is Real and That's a Problem for Democrats." *The Atlantic*. February 20, 2020. https://www.theatlantic.com/ideas/archive/2020/02/latino-sup port-trump-problem-democrats/606613/ and Mark Hugo Lopez, Ana Gonzalez Barrerea and Gustavo Lopez. "Hispanic Identity Fades Across Generations as Immigrant Connections Fall Away." *Pew Research Center Hispanic Trends*. https://www.pewresearch.org/hispanic/2017/12/20/hispanic-identity-fades-across-generations-as-immigrant-connections-fall-away/, both accessed February 27, 2020.

84. Tom Steyer. "Economy." https://www.youtube.com/watch?v=HRTxOn
ABVqg, accessed March 8, 2020.
85. On the Trump transition see Michael Lewis "This Guy Doesn't Know
Anything: The Inside Story of Trump's Shambolic Transition Team."
The Guardian. September 27, 2018, https://www.theguardian.com/
news/2018/sep/27/this-guy-doesnt-know-anything-the-inside-story-of-
trumps-shambolic-transition-team, accessed June 28, 2021.

References

Adams, Scott. *Win Bigly: Persuasion in a World Where Facts Don't Matter.*
Penguin, 2017.
Brooks, David. *Bobos in Paradise: The New Upper Class and How They Got There.*
Simon and Schuster, 2001.
Cosgrove, Kenneth and Nathan Shrader. "Political Branding in the USA Election
of 2020." In Mona Moufahim (ed.) *Political Branding in Turbulent Times.*
Palgrave-Macmillan, 2021.
Edsall, Thomas and Mary Byrne Edsall. *Chain Reaction: The Impact of Race,
Rights and Taxes on American Politcs.* W.W. Norton, 1991.
Green, Joshua. *Devil's Bargain: Steve Bannon, Donald Trump and the Storming
of the US Presidency.* Penguin, 2017.
Jardina, Ashley. *White Identity Politics.* Cambridge University Press, 2019.
Mason, Liliana. *Uncivil Agreement: How Politics Became Our Identity.* Chicago.
University of Chicago Press, 2018.
Miller, Jeremy. *Sticky Branding: 12.5 Principles to Stand Out, Attract Customers
and Grow an Incredible Brand.* Page Two Books, 2015.
Norris, Pippa and Ronald Inglehart. *Cultural Backlash: Trump, Brexit and
Authoritarian Populism.* Cambridge University Press, 2019.
Pollack, Joel B. and Larry Schweikart. *How Trump Won: The Inside Story of A
Revolution.* Regnery Publishing, 2017.
Sosnik, Douglas, Matthew B. Dowd and Ron Fournier. *Applebee's America:
How Successful Political, Business and Religious Leaders Connect With the New
American Community.* Simon and Schuster, 2007.
Zito, Salena and Brad Todd. *The Great Revolt.* Crown Forum, 2018.

CHAPTER 6

The Trump Brand Story: Attract and Repel

Abstract Trump's omnipresent brand thrills and attracts some audiences while simultaneously terrifying, angering, and repelling others. The Trump Administration has been a constant brand faceoff between a Trump seeking to keep promises and opponents determined to stop him. Conservative Christians, blue-collar workers impacted by globalization and American nationalists love the Trump branded political products but Americans who benefit from the cultural and economic changes that have taken place in the United States since the 1960s or an advocate for globalization, Trump's branded products are anathema. Cosgrove's overall argument is that Trump's omnipresent political brand has great power to attract and repel.

Keywords Culture wars · Class · Materialist values · Post-materialist values · Economic transformation · 1960s · COVID-19 · Brand emotions · Brand personality · Brand differentiation · 2020 Presidential election · Barack Obama · Populism · Deep state · 2016 Presidential election

© The Author(s), under exclusive license to Springer Nature Switzerland AG 2022
K. M. Cosgrove, *Donald Trump and the Branding of the American Presidency*, https://doi.org/10.1007/978-3-030-30496-6_6

Donald Trump's election, administration, and subsequent defeat show the strengths and weaknesses of political marketing and branding. Trump's sticky branding and omnipresence strategies produced two close electoral outcomes. They also produced incessant conflict during his time in the Presidency. This brand, and the products it supported, repelled many people at the same time it built deep loyalty among his target audiences. Trump was never particularly popular by Presidential standards even though many of the policies that his Administration promoted were. He had little political capital or goodwill to draw on when the COVID crisis hit. Trump wasn't reelected in 2020 because his performance during the COVID-19 pandemic undermined some of his original brand promises but he also lost because he didn't add the key brand value of empathy as the pandemic unfolded, a series of crises arose, and public uncertainty grew.[1] He didn't adjust to a rapidly changing marketplace in terms of product offering or brand style and emotions.[2] Instead, he stuck to his brand, questioned the experts, and held COVID briefings in lieu of campaign rallies that included plenty of jousting with the national media.[3] His approach was consistent because he stuck to his brand story and focused on his core products, but it might not have been the best way for a President to publicly lead during a crisis.

Trump's reelection team stuck to its course of selling Trump to a few audience targets even during the COVID crisis. Trump barely lost the Electoral College votes of a few states and barely lost the Presidency in 2020 just as he had barely won it in 2016. Trump and his team used a combination of market research, segmentation, and branding to reach specific audiences with targeted stories instead of doing broad public outreach. This is an excellent formula for selling consumer products but might not be an effective governing strategy especially during a crisis. In his campaign and term in office, he worked with themes and issues that had the potential to be society building but as he deployed them, they were segment reinforcing because they resonated with their targets in a positive way but with others not at all or extremely negatively. This is consistent with the way in which sticky brands, like the Trump brand, build awareness and loyalty within their targeted audiences. Trump's broad theme of restoration appealed to specific audiences, that benefitted from the good old days meaning that he had deep but narrow support. This is consistent with the sticky brand's emphasis on specialized products and audiences to create a lasting advantage.[4] Trump's constant emphasis on conflict was useful for marketing purposes. It created an authentic difference between him and his competitors. This is something that makes a sticky brand effective in any application.[5] It was much less useful for governing purposes because it reduced the probability that he could build a working relationship with Congress, especially not with a Congress controlled by the opposite party, or state governors during the COVID crisis. Electing a President who had a marketing and sales, not a political background, before taking office has consequences for the things that do and do not get emphasized. In the Trump Administration, safeguarding the brand's power appears to have taken precedence over dealing with Congress or solving the COVID crisis. Mr. Trump's narrow win in 2016 and narrow Electoral College defeat in 2020 represented the triumph of segmentation, emotion, and sticky branding in political marketing.

His election, administration, and the response to it showed the power that archetypes have in political marketing.[6] Trump is an effective story-teller and salesperson who works in themes and narratives but is often wrong on the facts of the matters he is discussing. Trump's lack of knowl-edge about facts is part of what Scott Adams (2017) has termed the high ground maneuver that takes a discussion from a specific to a very conceptual thematic level and, as Adams notes, Trump has repeatedly used this technique.[7] He timed the market for his offering perfectly in 2016 because, while Barack Obama was broadly popular, his Adminis-tration had taken decisions that irritated and activated deep audiences among conservatives, his brand style left Trump's target audiences cold because it was aimed at upper-class professionals and young people more than them, and because Obama's race represented a threat to some of Trump's audiences. Trump promised conservatives that he would cut taxes and regulations thus reviving the economy, repeal and replace Obamacare, restore order at the border, and respect for the police thus making America Safe Again, and appointing social conservatives to the federal judiciary. All these policies fit comfortably with the platform on which Republicans had run for decades. The problem his campaign faced in 2020 was that he was running as an incumbent in a time of crisis to which his response seemed tepid. Trump was not telling the story that the key audiences he was trying to reach wanted to hear. His economic and disruptive story was popular but not popular enough to win the election. As Brad Parscale noted, a key to being an effec-tive President is "good storytelling" and if Trump had adopted a more empathetic, inclusive tone, he "would have been the hero" and possibly done better in the segments he performed worse in 2020 with than he had in 2016.[8] Instead, he offered Americans the same tightly targeted chaotic, confrontational story that placed him at the center of everything and valued economic recovery more than anything else including public health. Trump lost in 2020 partly because he failed to adjust his branding to meet the circumstances in which the race was conducted and the branding of the opponent with whom he was faced. Joe Biden stressed his personal empathy and respect for the seriousness of the situation COVID had presented the country and the world with.[9]

Donald Trump presented himself as the anti-Obama in 2016. If Barack Obama represented multicultural internationalist urban America, Donald Trump represented working-class nationalistic America. Trump's brand promise was that, if he elected, he would disrupt a self-serving, corrupt order that looked down on average Americans, and then restore a lost American Eden in which hard work was valued, people followed the rules, respected authority, attended church, and lived according to its tenets. This was a vision of a country that might have existed before the cultural upheavals of the late 1950s through early 1970s that kicked off a culture war that resulted in meaningful change. Trump presented the Democrats as defenders of a disorderly, dystopian country in which sloth and cheating were rewarded, police officers were the criminals, borders did not matter, productive workers were heavily taxed or saw their jobs shipped abroad because of corporate greed or unfair trade deals, and the undeserving got ever more benefits. Meanwhile, veterans went uncared for and unappreciated, the average American was forgotten, and the country was being taken advantage of by its so-called allies and threatened by its numerous opponents, abused by the rest of the world. Trump's restoration story said that the elite would be swept away, and average Americans would find their values, patriotism, and hard work rewarded.[10] In 2020, Trump played up his accomplishments in office, hinted that COVID vaccines were on the way, and argued that a vote for Biden was really a vote for the restoration of the Obama Administration.

An America for the average American might sound theoretically fabulous but Trump's election and administration show how difficult it is to determine who the average American is exactly. In Trump's depiction, the average American was straight, most likely white, more likely than not to be religious, and live in a rural or suburban area. Trump depicted a country that was closer to the one that existed before the beat poets, free love, free expression, minority rights, and the rampant individual choice and freedom that had developed since the 1960s. It's easy to understand how this construction could alarm those who did not fit into it. Trump's rise was facilitated by the Great Recession and its long aftermath. Donald Trump, with his promise to restore a lost better America, tapped into feelings of economic dislocation caused by the Great Recession, dizzying demographic change in the country, endless conflict abroad, and high-profile incidents of foreign and domestic terrorism. Instead of a disorderly America at home and a weak America at the mercy of global trends abroad he promised a strong, orderly America across the board and optimized Warren G. Harding's promise to bring normalcy to the country for the age of emotional branding. Ironically, Joe Biden would make use of a promise to bring normalcy back against Trump in 2020. Trump's "Make America Safe" brand encompasses more support for law enforcement and thus is one of the ways that it makes a pitch for order in the country. As Mr. Trump said in a speech to the international association of chiefs of police in October 2018 "In order to keep every American safe, we are also making officer safety a top priority. (Applause.) In 2016, an officer was assaulted in America on an average of every 9 min. Is this even believable?"[11] His law-and-order pitch fit with long-standing conservative branding while playing up the strong, safe America aspects of the Trump brand. While some Trump audiences agreed with this pitch, other Americans saw the way in which the police behaved toward them as a threat that government should act upon, and the Obama Administration had pushed police accountability and improved police sensitivity. Trump represented the backlash to these efforts and, not shockingly, when civil unrest broke out across the country in the Spring of 2020 in response to the killings of African Americans at the hands of the police, Trump stuck with his law-and-order branding rather than adopting a more empathetic tone.

Trump's brand story is a tale of fighter who took on an elite that looked down on and exploited average Americans. Trump presented himself as a class traitor, an entrepreneur, and a disruptor. His message was well timed in 2016 to fit a country in which many voters were unhappy economically, culturally, or both. The strife he generated in his campaign continued in office and, on some level, continues to this day. Generating strife and conflict became a way of showing that he was keeping his promises. Even impeachment did not hurt him with his core audiences because they could interpret it as Trump keeping his brand promise to drain a resistant swamp. Trump's team wisely played up the immoderate statements made by Democrats as part of the Impeachment and 2020 primary processes. They especially highlighted the words of Texas Congressman Al Green who in 2019 said "I'm concerned if we don't impeach this President, he will get re-elected."[12] Trump's team tried to emphasize more moderate aspects of the Administration especially around the promises he has kept in office. The net result was a rise in Trump's job approval ratings.

The impeachment proceedings raised the question of who was responsible for making and implementing policy. As Skowronek et al. (2021) note, Trump's "drain the swamp" pitch produced a great deal of resistance from the permanent bureaucracy and the elite media.

Trump's argument to his supporters that the Deep State and its minions were targeting him could seem plausible to the casual observer who happened to tune into one of these hearings. They featured a parade of bureaucrats talking about "our policy" and "the interagency" and how displeased they were that Donald Trump did not listen to their expertise and deviated from their policy choices.[13] Add to this the relentlessly negative media coverage of his campaigns and administration, the public disdain from some leading Republican figures (and Trump's rejoinders) way in which leading Republican figures publicly disdain him and the scorched earth tactics of the Democrats and it is easy to understand why all of it reinforced Trump's core narrative among his target audiences. He may have been fighting the swamp, but the swamp was fighting back. There would be no chance for domestic tranquility in such an environment.

Trump showed how branding can reduce the nuances of governance to promises and themes that resonate with specific audiences. Branding makes this possible because it packages a product or policy emotionally and thematically. Including the nuances of policy and complicated nature of the process are not important when it comes to building a political brand. His brand narrative and themes might not have resonated strongly outside of his core audiences, but they only need to resonate just well enough that Trump could win by razor-thin margins. Throughout the 2016 campaign and the bulk of his Administration, Trump made appeals that resonated with specific audiences not the general population. Contrary to his opponents' assertions, Trump's themes were nothing new in American politics. Trump's appeals echoed those of George Wallace, Richard Nixon, and Huey Long.[14] He differed from these earlier populists because Trump wove these themes into a highly emotive brand.

In the process of doing so, he rekindled the culture wars of the 1960s in which a populist "silent majority" faced off against the Democratic liberals. Culture, race, and class were bound up in those battles just as they are in Trump's culture war, the brand that supports it, and the way in which his supporters and opponents react to the brand. Trump's brand story sold because many people on the right feared that the Obama years definitively proved conservatives had lost the culture wars and because of issues of white racial or cultural identity as Jardina (2019) and Norris and Inglehart (2019) show in the context of attitudinal behavior. Trump built a brand that tapped into these conceptions and his promise to take on the liberals solidified his support with cultural conservatives who might not like him but did share his policy vision and supported his proposed list of judicial nominees.[15]

Trump raised questions about the elite and the role it played in shaping policy across areas. Trump rejected the liberal internationalist world order that the United States had built during the twentieth century in favor of pursuing the nation's own interests and built a marketing campaign against the multilateral, internationalist worldview that America had built from World War II onward. The rationale for America's role in the world was alternatively to fight the Red Menace or prevent another global conflagration but once the USSR dissolved in 1991, the rationale for these arrangements became fuzzier. The United States was the only remaining superpower. It did not draw down its military or reduce its security state in any significant way. Instead, it was drawn into conflicts in the Balkans and Somalia that were not vital to American national interests in the same way as fighting the Cold War had been. The rationale for American power and involvement abroad gained steam with the 9/11/01 terrorist attacks that led the country into two long-running wars and deepened the security state. Two of Trump's populist predecessors, Ross Perot and Pat Buchanon had raised questions about these arrangements during their campaigns.[16] By large, elites in both parties saw the country as the essential nation without which the world could not function peacefully.

Trump articulated nationalist themes in reaction to 9/11 and the two subsequent long wars. Trump linked crime and terrorism with border and immigration problems to show that the establishment's border policies were putting average Americans at risk. He was critical of the country's inability to develop a mutually beneficial relationship with China, he was a determined critic of the Iran Nuclear deal, Obama's approach to the Russian Federation and the bipartisan policy failure toward North

Korea. Trump's brand story amounted to a critique that these policies either failed or provided concentrated benefits but broader costs. As President he would put these situations right. Donald Trump was not the first recent candidate to raise questions about and promise changes to America's approach to the world. It was the way that he did it and to whom he presented the critique that made the strategic difference at the ballot box. Presaging the rise of a targeted emotionally branded candidate like Mr. Trump the costs of these economic and military policies were not evenly distributed socially. Americans were asked to support the troops after 9/11 but few of them became the troops. Because of the shift in recruiting, the personal costs of these conflicts were borne by small segments of the American population. Unlike in World War II, Korea and Vietnam, the United States fought these wars with volunteers. These volunteers were younger, more male, more diverse and had a much higher percentage of working and middle-class people in their ranks than did the general population.[17] Instead of mass mobilizations like those that took place when both World Wars were launched, these wars were fought by specific subsets of the population that had volunteered for military service. The elite in both parties could easily downplay what was happening in these two wars because their family and friends were not serving them. The costs and policy failures were experienced indirectly at best by the elite while they were experienced very directly by some of the audiences Donald Trump targeted. This was one of the things that set Joe Biden apart from Trump's other potential 2020 rivals. Mr. Biden's late son, Beau, had served in Kosovo and Iraq, winning a Bronze Star for his service in the latter. Trump could not claim that Biden was out of touch when it came to the realities of the suffering borne by service families during the last two decades. He and his family had experienced it first-hand.

In 2016, Donald Trump's campaign found people who had paid those costs and presented them with an engaging brand story. Trump's foreign policy brand story fused elements of leftist and rightist critiques of America's role in the world. It borrowed from the right by tapping into an America first notion that, along with the desire to avoid entangling foreign alliances, has always been present in the country's political culture. In this construction, the United States is the global patsy doing the heavy lifting of providing international security while getting bad trade deals, allies cheating on NATO contribution agreements, currency cheating, and a stream of bad folks crossing its borders in return. Trump's approach to the world could be described as sticky branded nationalist realism. For example, despite critics presenting his advocacy for a different relationship with Russia nefariously, several of his recent predecessors had sought the same thing. One of the biggest differences between Trump and them was his famous request for help in finding dirt on his 2016 election opponent. Trump echoed leftist criticisms of American foreign policy by moralizing about the bad things that the United States had done on the world stage. One difference between Trump and the leftists was that Trump used past sins as a rationale for not intervening in contemporary events or to try to minimize other countries' present transgressions by mentioning similar past American transgressions.

Trump's criticism of NATO tapped into a long-running sense among some on the right that Americans were being taken advantage of by a global community that was happy to have access to American defense dollars and its huge market but disdained the country overall. Throughout the post-Cold War period, there developed a sense that Americans were part of a global community and that their troops would do much of the heavy lifting, their basic manufacturing would be outsourced to developing economies, and that the nature of work Americans would do involved knowledge not physical labor. Given that most of the people developing these policies had been to college and a lot of them were the product of very elite institutions, there appeared to be a consensus that these were good things even though, as Trump's political success showed, such was not the case. Post-Cold War America sought to preserve and expand the global trading system based on the notion that the theory of comparative advantage was correct as was the idea that stable middle-class nations would not go to war with each other. These arrangements had always faced criticism but usually from the left or labor unions.[18] Trump adopted this criticism as his own. Simultaneously with the free trade push, a series of technological revolutions changed the way work was done, how many people it took to do it, and where work was located. While these things produced many benefits and winners, they also produced costs and losers. Trump targeted the latter in his marketing campaigns and many of them happened to be in swing states with large numbers of Electoral College votes.

As a candidate, Trump ran on the idea that his negotiating skills were superior to those of the government bureaucrats and Washington insiders who had negotiated these bad deals and he would put these superior skills to work to make life better for average Americans. Trump's self-interested America is a direct rebuttal to the idea that the United States is the essential nation and leader of the free world that it has dominated for three quarters of a century. Trump pointed out aspects of free trade deals that did not serve specific sectors of the economy. For example, his critique about Canadian dairy protectionism is justified. There were other elements of the US–Canada free trade deal that Canadians complained about, like softwood timber harvesting rules, as well. Overall, the deal provided great benefits to people in both countries, but Trump pointed out specific aspects that did not to audiences that cared about those. Trump sought to change deals in ways that would deliver benefits to the people who voted for him. In the Canadian dairy case? His voters in New York, Pennsylvania, and Wisconsin could meet all of Canada's dairy needs at a cheaper price than what the Canadian domestic dairy industry could meet.[19] This is typical of the Trump approach to renegotiating these deals: always looking for a good deal for his customers and trying to keep his brand promises. Trump's reelection campaign could credibly argue that the Administration secured a better deal for American labor in the case of the renegotiated NAFTA arrangement meaning this treaty could be used as another example of a brand promise kept.[20]

Trump's immigration position was consistent with his "Make America Safe Again" brand aspect. He promised to crack down on those in the country out of status, to secure the border to make such entries more difficult, and to make it more difficult to legally immigration to the United States. There are economic, racial, and cultural reasons why Trump made this pitch. He singled out Mexican migrants because from 1965 to 2015, over 16 million Mexican nationals came to the United States, constituting half of the total migration to the country from Latin America and double the migration to the United States from Europe.[21] By the time Trump raised this issue, Mexicans had been replaced by Central Americans as the biggest group of people migrating to the United States. Trump's story and his proposed solution tapped into a sense of public frustration about the substantial number of people who had come into the United States outside of the normal process from 1965 forward. The number of people coming in this immigration wave was double that of the one that dramatically changed the United States in the middle nineteenth century. That wave too produced a strong popular reaction.[22] The immigration issue taps directly into questions of race because without so much immigration from Latin America and Asia, the United States would have a population that was 75 percent white instead of 62 percent white and 8 percent Hispanic instead of 18 percent Hispanic.[23] Trump tapped into a sense among whites that their culture, national identity, and race were under siege by elites in both parties who favored more cosmopolitan policies.[24] This appeal resonated as Trump's targets saw clusters of immigrants transforming their communities and felt culturally uncomfortable, because they saw the newcomers as economic competition and a drain on the public purse. His eventual immigration proposal to Congress fit with the conservative position that immigration should be based on skills not family reunification or humanitarian considerations. Trump gave voice to these concerns in his campaign marketing and actions in office. In his famous 2015 campaign announcement (itself a form of bringing the brand to life) he said:

> "When Mexico sends its people, they're not sending their best. They're not sending you. They're not sending you. They're sending people that have lots of problems, and they're bringing those problems with us. They're bringing drugs. They're bringing crime. They're rapists. And some, I assume, are good people. But I speak to border guards, and they tell us what we're getting. And it only makes common sense. It only makes common sense. They're sending us not the right people. It's coming from more than Mexico. It's coming from all over South and Latin America, and it's coming probably— probably— from the Middle East. But we don't know. Because we have no protection and we have no competence, we don't know what's happening. And it's got to stop and it's got to stop fast".[25]

Consistent with the sticky brand approach that Miller (2015) outlined, Trump's emotive pitch positioned him distinctly from his competitors and let him own the strongest anti-immigration position in the marketplace. Trump's sticky brand gained credibility when the Border Patrol's union endorsed him and because he had appeared on a Border Patrol talk radio show meaning that he was familiar with the agents' worldview and concerns from talking with them.[26] Because of this, when he talked, he could claim distinctiveness, authority, and credibility on the topic with his target audiences.[27] Commercial product marketers often brag about the awards their products win or survey results that show them to be favored for in a specific aspect. Trump's lament about the impact immigration has had on the country, as a candidate and as President is consistent with the conservative narrative about the impact that the Immigration and Nationality Act of 1965 had on the country as Cadava has noted.[28] The difference is that Trump expressed this lament using a sticky brand aimed at mobilizing and emotionally engaging specific audiences rather than general ones.

Trump's nationalistic branding and policies directly challenged the globalist, internationalist, multicultural worldview dominant in both parties. Trump was the vehicle for a group of conservatives who strongly disagreed with the party's moderating stance on immigration policy and instead promoted the ideas that Trump popularized.[29] While the elite might have seen him as a crank and a racist, his target audiences saw him as a truth teller speaking their language. For example, his criticism mirrored the way that Trump supporter and conservative media figure Michael Savage's messaging to his audiences on nationalism themes.[30] Savage has promoted the importance of borders, language, culture, and religion in maintaining a strong national identity and country. Trump's argument on these topics is remarkably similar because it focuses on the dangers of human and drug smuggling on the Southern border. He sometimes mentioned the possibility that a terror group could exploit this vulnerability to launch attacks in the United States and often talked about his desire to remove the gang MS-13 from the country. His solution to the problem kept with the brand strategy, promoting a wall is an excellent sticky branding strategy because it's a simple, clear concept and it provided a unique visual identity for Trump. Having such an identity is a key principle of sticky branding.[31] The wall visually defined the nation's space and membership in a national community.

Globalists would have been much more comfortable with Hillary Clinton's suggestion of allowing goods and people to move freely in the Americas than they would have been with a wall. Trump's nationalistic position was exactly the opposite: a wall will secure the border and take away a pull factor that lures people toward the United States. The Wall with its strong visual and emotive responses on both sides dominated policy discussions for extended periods of time and, at a minimum, gave Trump and the Republicans an immigration position people could see in their mind's eye thus it helped build the Trump sticky brand. The wall was a way for Trump to show that he sided with working-class Americans who sought order, safety, and a common culture. Simultaneously, it fits with his economic restoration story because a tighter labor market might drive-up working-class wages. Thus, his wall, immigration, and economic narrative were holistic sticky branding. The wall demonstrates the law of the visual in marketing.[32] So did his Administration's rules changes that made it much harder for people to claim asylum at the border and requiring them to remain in Mexico while applying to do so. Trump's insistence that the wall was being built and his reprogramming of federal funds to do so are both examples of how branding requires that promises made are being kept and the fact that he can do so visually increases the strength of his claims.

Consistent with the brand's emphasis on delivery, Trump tried to visually show how he kept promises in this and other areas. Like the European populists, Trump targeted Muslims for exclusion but did so in a way that was consistent with his "Make America Safe Again" brand aspect. He presented Muslims as a terrorist threat and argued that they needed to be subjected to stricter scrutiny when entering the country or be banned entirely. The European themes of Islam and culture did not sell as well in the United States as the theme of Islam as a source of terrorism, so Trump built on work done by the Bush and Obama Administrations to scrutinize people coming from Islamic countries to argue for full exclusion. The factual basis for excluding these countries was that they did not share information with the United States and the Trump team argued that these were failed states meaning there was no government to coordinate with or they were America's enemies. Trump's list of countries fit with his brand promises to shift the country's foreign policy to a more aggressive, more pro-Israel, and anti-Iran footing. Trump promised that he would pull out the Iran nuclear deal because he thought it was too much for too little, questioned the Obama Administration's response to the Syrian Civil War, a terrorist attack on a US diplomatic facility in Benghazi, Libya and questioned the patriotism of Muslims by telling dubious tales of them cheering on September 11, 2001. All of this could and was seen by his opponents as being racist, sectarian, and discriminatory.

The approaches to foreign policy and the world that Donald Trump sought to alter had well-established support networks in Washington, DC and in the country that were fully capable of opposing him. These include government agencies with deep intellectual and financial investments in specific policies, interest groups dedicated to the promotion of specific issues, and a Washington politics that had become ossified under "norms" that served specific class and career interests. They include people who had built careers based around specific policies or who were products of specific career tracks that either had or seemed poised to put them in positions of responsibility for implementing American policy until

Donald Trump got elected. Washington can be seen as a place in which elite networks vie for influence and the ins and outs change depending on which party wins control of the White House. Trump's election was a direct challenge to the elite networks in both parties given that he came from the New York real estate world. Trump looked for loyalty to and support for him in deciding who was hired in his Administration something that intensified once he was in office partly because he was concerned that many of the people around him were more loyal to the Republican Party than they were to him.

Trump's 2016 victory brought people from backgrounds and networks to Washington that differed from the networks and types of people one usually encountered in government service. He did not bring many of them either. One of the biggest changes Trump attempted to implement as President was to apply the principles of lean management meaning that many fewer people were hired. Further, the principles of a selling business that suggest churning through staff quickly was a net positive. This was quite different than the ethos of long-serving civil servants or the in and out world of Washington. Trump came to a city filled with disappointed people in both parties. They had spent years networking, campaigning, and making the right contributions only to be confronted with the spectacle of a real estate mogul turned reality tv star moving into the White House. Trump disdained the entire culture of which they were a part and had gotten elected in part by promising to "drain the swamp" in which they resided. Thus, he posed a direct threat to the institutions and patrons in which they had invested their lives. Instead of seeing themselves as swamp creatures most of these people saw themselves as dedicated public servants, high skilled conduits between government and industry, or committed advocates for a given cause. It's easy to see why Trump's rhetoric around them caused offense.

Many of the people whom Trump defined as swamp critters availed themselves of twitter as he did to build their own brands and get their message out. Some served as media commentators and built their own brands because of doing so. Trump churned through staff as he had in his other businesses but not all of those who left did so voluntarily or happily. The disgruntled Democrats, Republicans, and ex-Trumpers availed themselves of social media just as the President does, authored books, or became media commentators. Their media positions illustrate a transparency problem with the news analysis-driven format of cable television news in the United States. Often these folks will be accurately introduced as having held a high-level position in the American Government but, unlike in the financial news media in which conflicts are often disclosed at their introduction, cable news shows seldom disclosed the conflicts of the people they were presenting as analysts of Trump meaning that their true orientation was seldom obvious at the outset of their appearances. Having a panel composed of people who served in the Obama Administration, who lost their jobs when Trump came to town or mainstream Republicans who Trump refused to hire or former staffers who were not happy to be part of the Administration's churn, presents the viewer with a different metric to assess credibility than having a panel composed of the former undersecretary for something in an undisclosed White House does. The latter sounds much more impartial and credible than the former. Given the way Trump disrupted the status quo in Washington elite networks, refused to play along in the social rituals of the city and is all about confrontation? It is not surprising that he has taken a relentless pound during his term from most of the media.

Trump's election raised the exceptionally good question of who has the right to make policy in this country: the elected officials or the unelected civil servants and judiciary? Trump's policy proposals were consistently blocked by federal judges in more liberal-leaning federal circuits like the San Francisco-based 9th Circuit, that issued nationwide injunctions. These tied his executive orders and agency rule changes up in legal battles for months if not years. Further, as the impeachment hearing showed, there were well-established policy networks composed of career civil servants who were heavily invested in specific policy choices.[33] For example, some outlets have argued that the whistleblower in Trump's first impeachment was a partisan with ties to Joe Biden, a deep stater tied to John Brennan, strongly favored a specific policy toward Ukraine and was unhappy that Trump wanted a different policy.[34] During the Impeachment hearings there were frequent references to "our policy" but little reference to who exactly had the right to make said policy and the way in which "the interagency" coordinated and implemented said policy but not as much mention about the people to whom they were accountable.[35] This is a serious question regarding the way in which bureaucracy, the separation of powers and representative government intersect. These significant questions have, as Ginsberg and Shefter (1999) suggested often happened, become subsumed into fodder for a short-term oriented political battle. Trump used the first Impeachment, the Mueller Inquiry, and a slew of lawsuits at the federal and state levels, to show that he was keeping his promise of draining the swamp and that its denizens will fight his doing so with everything they had at their disposal to do so. For example, Trump responded to the dismissal of the emolument's lawsuit against him in July 2019 by tweeting "Word just out that I won a big part of the Deep State and Democrat induced Witch Hunt. Unanimous decision in my favor from The United States Court of Appeals for The Fourth Circuit on the ridiculous Emoluments Case. I don't make money, but lose a fortune for the honor of..."(second tweet "serving and doing a great job as your President (including accepting Zero salary!)."[36] In these tweets, Trump presented himself as both a Patriot and a victim of these nefarious forces. When dealing with the Mueller investigation and FBI director James Comey, he branded him and Deputy Directory Andrew McCabe as a "dirty cop" and "known scoundrels."[37] After the release of the Mueller Report, Trump told the media that: "there are a lot of people out there that have done some very, very evil things, very bad things—I would say treasonous things—against our country, And hopefully people that have done such harm to our country—we've gone through a period of really bad things happening—those people will certainly be looked at. I've been looking at them for a long time."[38] Trump in this case, likened the kinds of activities by political opponents that Presidents have had to deal with since Watergate to "treason." Regardless of the veracity of his claim, making it worked to build omnipresence for the Trump brand while building his authority with his core audiences.

Trump's opponents were not just Democrats. Not all elements of the Washington-based conservative establishment liked him either. They represent a part of the Republican Party that some media entrepreneurs, like Rush Limbaugh and a lot of the more conservative elements of the audience, have had questions about regarding their ideological commitment. They are the embodiment of the complaint that many in the Tea Party had that these people have either become comfortable in Washington and just wanted to go along to get along as Sam Rayburn once put it or were just cartoon conservatives who were in it for the money not the movement. Trump took on the Washington establishment when he went after the Bushes and John McCain. Trump most famously went after the latter by diminishing his service to the country on the campaign trail in 2015 by saying "He's not a war hero," said Trump. "He was a war hero because he was captured. I like people who weren't captured."[39] People had gone after John McCain before based on his temper, judgment, or involvement with corrupt Savings and Loan owner Charles Keating, but nobody had ever done anything like this before. Most in Washington thought Trump would eventually apologize for breaking the norms of behavior but he did not. For Trump going after McCain in this way was another means through which he could show that he was different from the standard Republican and part of the way he achieved brand omnipresence something that is one of the goals of the sticky branding strategy in all its applications.[40] Trump's constant activity, much of it controversial, was a way of showing his brand promises made were being kept, a way to maintain brand omnipresence by keeping his message dominant daily in the media and Trump at the center of everything. All of which helped to build a community of supporters around Trump's sticky brand as it does around any sticky brand.[41]

Brand omnipresence was a key tool that Donald Trump used to define opponents and control public perceptions of him and his opponents. Three cases that prove the point are the branding of Hillary Clinton as "Crooked Hillary" the way in which he used a government shutdown in the aftermath of the 2018 midterm elections and his decision to hold a campaign-style rally in South Carolina on the day that Special Counsel Robert Mueller testified before the House of Representatives. One can argue that the Crooked Hillary brand was partly aimed at showing that there were different rules for different people in the country and partly aimed at defining both Clintons as ethically and morally dubious thus building on decades of Conservative marketing. Given that President Bill Clinton had been branded by Conservatives as "Slick Willie" during his term in office, it is consistent with the brand strategy and a form of brand fellowship that Donald Trump branded his spouse as "Crooked Hillary" during her quest for the White House. Further, when questions about Trump's own virtue surfaced in the form of a leaked audio track made while shooting the tv program "Access Hollywood" emerged near the end of the 2016 campaign, the Trump campaign both sent out a video of the candidate apologizing and held a press conference featuring several women Bill Clinton was accused of sexually harassing who raised questions about the role that Hillary Clinton had played in silencing them and enabling her husband's behavior. This strategy of "muddying the waters" is common in political campaign communication. Trump both moved to blunt the damage to himself by apologizing and flipped the script by trotting out people who accused his opponent of covering up and therefore enabling similar things in her own marriage. In the case of the Government Shutdown, Trump sought to distract from the 2018 midterm debacle while trying to secure one of his key promises, building a wall on the Mexican border, and when the shutdown started to prove to be unpopular, he began floating the possibility of withdrawing the United States from NATO to switch the subject and show that Trump was still trying to shake up the establishment. Constant activity and brand omnipresence were used as techniques aimed at showing that Trump is different and is trying to keep his brand promises.

As a candidate and as President, Trump consistently updated his offerings and added new elements to his brand story. Doing has helped him build brand omnipresence despite the nation's fragmented media universe. The downside to this was that is that Trump has seemed at least as interested in building up his own brand as he has been in promoting the GOP brand. For example, in declaring a national emergency to build a wall along the Mexican border, Donald Trump attempted to make good on a brand promise that he made but he did it using a process that makes well to make it easier for the next liberal Democrat who occupies the White House to implement their administration's plans without dealing with Congress. One of the limiting factors to the Trump brand's ability to expand was the uncertainty around his beliefs in these areas based on his behavior. Donald Trump was personally nobody's idea of a champion of women, even though he pointed to the number of women he has hired for key roles in his organizations over the years.[42] Some of the policies for which he advocated appeared to be exclusionary and were segment making not society making. Especially for communities that benefited from the Obama years and policies, Trump's promise of restoration and winning the culture wars was something to be fought against. An example is provided by the presence of Mike Pence in the Vice Presidency. Trump targeted Christians by putting Indiana Governor Mike Pence on the ticket. Pence is strongly pro-life and an advocate for Christian Conservatism thus appealing to a core Republican constituency. This constituency might not have liked Mr. Trump's personal traits. Trump further appealed to this audience by circulating a list of potential conservative appointees to the federal judiciary. True to the brand strategy, he kept this promise by filling three Supreme Court seats and 226 other judges in four years including one less appellate judge than Barack Obama nominated in eight years.[43]

Ever the marketer, once in office Trump focused on judicial nominees and issues relevant to trans-people first because those were far less institutionalized than something like same-sex marriage, that had come to involve majority support, was. Trump took actions to undo transgender friendly policies something conservatives have repeatedly done in office and sought to do through subnational referendum campaigns. LGBTQ2A communities saw Trump as an existential threat and fought accordingly. Trump affirmed his support for gay rights and marriage during the campaign but his choice of Mike Pence as Vice President, his judicial appointments, and several of his actions in office indicate that he prioritized pleasing his cultural conservative and Christian audiences and was willing to trade off support from the LGBTQ2A communities to accomplish this. He linked a cultural and a political complaint when he raised questions about the ways in which LGBTQ2A friendly policies had come about during the Obama years. These he sold to Christian and small government conservatives. During the Obama years, gay marriage became legal nationwide because of a court case (Obergefell versus Hodges) gay and transgender people could openly serve in the military and gender confirmation surgery was covered by Medicare. A particularly potent example that became fodder for Trump's and a lot of other conservative marketing is provided by the Masterpiece Cakeshop case. This case involved the question of a state requiring a baker, who had raised a religious freedom question, to make a wedding cake for a same-sex couple. This case generated a great deal of energy among Conservative Christians for Donald Trump's 2016 campaign. The Conservative argument was that the evidence in the case showed that the state of Colorado was hostile to Christians and some who opposed expanded rights for LGBTQ2A community members. On the other side of the equation, the LGBTQ2A community was concerned about equal treatment in public accommodations and a couple who wanted the same kind of quality work done for their wedding, by a provider whose work they appreciated, as any straight couple could get.

It's easy to see why the Trump restoration brand story delighted Conservative Christians while it terrified LGBTQ2A community members especially those in the transgender community. Based on history, they fear that the America Trump seeks to restore his no place for them, would again criminalize or stigmatize them as being mentally ill. Trump's sticky brand worked in a similar fashion across issues and across audiences. It's part of the reason the Trump years were so fraught and polarized. His brand resonated with his target audience at the same time it repulsed and scared many other Americans based on the historical experiences people like them had endured in this country. While his themes, images, and emotions engaged many people during the campaign and during his Presidency, they terrify and activate many others. He shows the power and pitfalls of emotional branding and segmentation in political marketing.

NOTES

1. Annie Karni. "In a Fox News interview, Parscale Blame Trump's Lack of Coronavirus Empathy for His Election Loss." *New York Times*. December 1, 2020. https://www.nytimes.com/2020/12/01/us/politics/in-a-fox-news-interview-parscale-blames-trumps-lack-of-coronavirus-empathy-for-his-election-loss.html.
2. Ibid.
3. Annie Karni. "In Daily Coronavirus Briefing Trump Tries to Redefine Himself." *New York Times*. March 23, 2020. https://www.nytimes.com/2020/03/23/us/politics/coronavirus-trump-briefing.html?searchResult Position=20, accessed June 28, 2020.
4. Miller (2015, p. 20).
5. Miller (2015, p. 20).
6. See Mark and Pearson (2001) for a book length discussion of the power of archetypes in marketing.
7. Adams (2017, p. 96).
8. As quoted in Katherine Doyle. "He would have been the hero": Brad Parscale says Trump need to show more empathy." *Washington Examiner*, December 2, 2020. https://www.washingtonexaminer.com/news/he-would-have-been-the-hero-brad-parscale-says-trump-needed-to-show-more-empathy.
9. See Cosgrove and Shrader in Moufahim (2021) for an in-depth discussion.
10. For a good example see either Green pp. 49–67 that discusses Trump advisor Stephen Bannon's background and how it is consistent with the Trump campaign's brand promises or Michael Kirk "First Interview with Stephen K. Bannon. PBS Frontline. interview conducted on March 17, 2019. https://www.pbs.org/wgbh/frontline/interview/steve-bannon-3/, accessed February 27, 2020.
11. Remarks by President Trump at International Association of Chiefs of Police. Orange County Convention CenterOrlando, Florida. October 8, 2018. https://www.whitehouse.gov/briefings-statements/remarks-president-trump-international-association-chiefs-police/, accessed July 13, 2019.
12. Tim Haines. "Rep. Al Green:" I'm Concerned If We Don't Impeach This President, He Will Get Reelected." Real Clear Politics. May 6, 2019. https://www.realclearpolitics.com/video/2019/05/06/al_green_im_concerned_if_we_dont_impeach_this_president_he_will_get_re-elected.html, accessed February 27, 2020.

13. For a good example of this point see Carl J. Schramm. "The Inter-agency Isn't Supposed to Rule." *The Wall Street Journal*. December 4, 2019. https://www.wsj.com/articles/the-interagency-isnt-supposed-to-rule-11575505183, accessed December 4, 2019.

14. Something Jon Blistein notes in "This Is Normal: The Enduring, Knotty Relevance of Randy Newman and Drive-By Truckers45 and 15 years after their releases, Good Old Boys and The Dirty South still speak to the best and worse impulses in America." *Rolling Stone*. September 6, 2019. Accessed September 6, 2019.

15. For example, Zito and Todd, 2018 call the Christian segment of these audiences King Cyrus Christians in their Chapter 8.

16. see for example Jeet Heer. "Donald Trump's Foreign Policy Revolution." *The New Republic*. March 25, 2016. https://newrepublic.com/article/132044/donald-trumps-foreign-policy-revolution, accessed February 27, 2020.

17. George M. Reynolds and Amanda Shendru. "Demographics of the United States Military." Council on Foreign Relations, April 24, 2018. https://www.cfr.org/article/demographics-us-military, accessed October 11, 2019.

18. Edward Alden. "In the NAFTA Deal Trump Got What Democrats Couldn't." *Politico*. October 2, 2018. https://www.politico.com/magazine/story/2018/10/02/trump-nafta-deal-democrats-220813, accessed February 27, 2020.

19. John Barber. "Why Canadian Milk Infuriates Donald Trump: Trump's Latest Trade War Target Is Canada's Protected Dairy Industry. But Cana-dians Have No Intention of Abandoning It—Because It Works." *The Guardian*. Sat June 9, 2018 07.00 EDT. https://www.theguardian.com/world/commentisfree/2018/jun/09/milk-canada-us-trade-wa, accessed July 12, 2019.

20. Edward Alden. "In the NAFTA Deal, Trump Got What Democrats Couldn't." *Politico*. October 2, 2018. https://www.politico.com/magazine/story/2018/10/02/trump-nafta-deal-democrats-220813, accessed February 27, 2020.

21. Pew Research Center on Hispanic Trends. Modern Immigration Wave Brings 59 million to U.S., Driving Population Growth and Change Through 2065: Views of Immigration's Impact on U.S. Society Mixed. https://www.pewhispanic.org/2015/09/28/modern-immigration-wave-brings-59-million-to-u-s-driving-population-growth-and-change-through-2065/, accessed July 12, 2019.

22. Ibid.

23. Ibid.

24. Judis (2018, pp. 43–46).

25. Time Staff. "Here's Donald Trump's Announcement Speech". *Time*. June 16, 2015. https://time.com/3923128/donald-trump-announcement-spe ech/, accessed July 12, 2019.
26. Garett M.Graff. "Donald Trump's Army on the Border." *Politico Maga- zine*. July 2016. https://www.politico.com/magazine/story/2016/ 07/2016-donald-trump-mexico-us-border-patrol-immigration-undocu mented-illegal-customs-texas-rio-grande-214060, accessed February 27, 2020.
27. Eric Bradner. "Border Patrol Union Endorses Donald Trump." CNN. March 26, 2016. https://www.cnn.com/2016/03/30/politics/ border-patrol-union-endorses-donald-trump/index.html, accessed August 5, 2019.
28. Geraldo Cadava. "How Should Historians Remember the 1965 Immigra- tion and Nationality Act?" The American Historian (undated). https:// tah.oah.org/issue-5/how-should-historians-remember-the-1965-immigr ation-and-nationality-act/_.
29. PBS Frontline "Zero Tolerance". October 22, 2019. https://www.pbs. org/video/zero-tolerance-en2plm/, accessed October 22, 2019.
30. Jeremy W. Peters. "Michael Savage has his doubts about Donald Trump. His Conservative audience does not." *New York Times*. June 18, 2018. https://www.nytimes.com/2019/06/18/us/politics/michael- savage-trump.html, accessed February 27, 2020.
31. Miler (2015, p. 21).
32. For more on the law of the visual see Ries and Ries (2009).
33. This topic is explored in depth by Bachner and Ginsburg in their 2019 work What Washington Gets Wrong (Prometheus).
34. Paul Sperry. "The Beltway's 'Whistleblower' Furor Obsesses Over One Name." Real Clear Investigations. October 30, 2019.
35. Daniel Drezner "Who Should Be Running US Foreign Policy: Trump vs. The Interagency Process vs. The Better Way to Frame All This." *Wash- ington Post*. November 3, 2019. https://www.washingtonpost.com/out look/2019/11/03/who-should-be-running-us-foreign-policy/ and Carl J. Schram. "The Interagency Isn't Supposed to Rule." *The Wall Street Journal*. December 4, 2019. https://www.wsj.com/articles/the-intera gency-isnt-supposed-to-rule-11575505183.
36. @realdonaldtrump tweet July 10, 2019, accessed July 12, 2019.
37. Melissa Quinn. 'Dirty cops:' Trump hits ex-FBI officials, Comey." Wash- inton Times January 14, 2019. https://www.washingtonexaminer.com/ news/dirty-cops-trump-hits-ex-fbi-officials-comey, accessed July 12.
38. Alex Newman. "Trump Calls Coup Attempt "Treasonous." Deep State in Panic Mode." New American. March 30, 2019. https://www.thenew american.com/usnews/crime/item/31885-trump-says-deep-state-coup- attempt-was-treasonous, accessed July 12, 2019.

39. BEN SCHRECKINGER. Trump attacks McCain: 'I like people who weren't captured.' He takes his feud with the Arizona senator to a new level. Politico. July 18, 2015. https://www.politico.com/story/2015/07/trump-attacks-mccain-i-like-people-who-werent-captured-120317, accessed July 12, 2018.
40. Miller (2015, pp.121–135).
41. Ibid.
42. Donald Trump. The Art of the Deal p. 173 and Crippled America pp. 132–134 and 166.
43. John Gramlich "How Trump Compares with Other Recent Presidents in Nominating Federal Judges." Pew Research Center. January 13, 2021. Accessed June 30, 2020. https://www.pewresearch.org/fact-tank/2021/01/13/how-trump-compares-with-other-recent-presidents-in-appointing-federal-judges/.

References

Adams, Scott. Win Bigly: Persuasion in a World Where Facts Don't Matter. Penguin, 2017.
Ginsberg, Benjamin and Martin Shefter. Politics by Other Means: Politicians, Prosecutors and the Press from Watergate to Whitewater. W.W. Norton, 1999.
Jardina, Ashley. White Identity Politics. Cambridge University Press, 2019.
Miller, Jeremy. Sticky Branding: 12.5 Principles To Stand Out, Attract Customers and Grow an Incredible Brand. Page Two Books, 2015.
Norris, Pippa and Ronald Inglehart. Cultural Backlash: Trump, Brexit and Authoritarian Populism. Cambridge University Press, 2019.
Skowronek, Stephen, John Dearborn, and Desmond King Phantoms of a Beleagured Republic. Oxford University Press, 2021.

CHAPTER 7

Brand Battle: Omnipresent Trump in Office and Beyond

Abstract This chapter argues that Trump focused on issues that are popular with his core audiences but unpopular with many other segments. This situation limited his ability to succeed in office. President Trump acts more like a candidate and brand manager focused on keeping his best customers happy not on uniting and leading the country. The Trump years have been a brand battle between Trump and his opponents that has left many Americans exhausted by them all. Trump's experience as a marketer has not translated into leadership skills or an understanding of how the federal government really works thus empowering the denizens of the swamp that he promised to drain to oppose or coopt him.

Keywords Permanent campaign · Presidency · Political Parties · Political Coalitions · Joe Biden · 2020 Presidential Election · US Conservatism · Populism · Donald Trump · Mueller Investigation and Report · Trump communicative strategy and style · Presidential transitions · Obamacare repeal effort · Political branding · 2020 Presidential election

The arc of the Trump experience on the national stage shows that political marketing and branding can help a candidate win an election, but it might not provide a road map to govern. While Trump talked of substantial change and rapid action on the campaign trail, he had no

© The Author(s), under exclusive license to Springer Nature   167
Switzerland AG 2022
K. M. Cosgrove, *Donald Trump and the Branding of the American Presidency*, https://doi.org/10.1007/978-3-030-30496-6_7

public sector experience and had a steep on the job learning curve.[1] His campaign brand story did not include ways he would work with Congress or the bureaucracy but instead focused building omnipresence for its sticky brand. Consistent with the sticky brand strategy Trump built omnipresence by constantly moving, being omnipresent, being visually engaging, and telling an emotive story just as Miller (2015) notes sticky brands do. Trump's branding fit the image Americans have come to hold about the omnipotence and omnipresence of the Presidency because it promised that he would be able to do deal with all sorts of problems as Americans assume Presidents will attempt to do.[2] Donald Trump's personality was nothing like the image most Americans usually hold about Presidents. His personal traits formed the basis around which his opponents tried to negatively brand him. Trump played on the widely shared public assumption that Presidents can solve all problems, but his opponents pointed out that Trump's ability to do so might be far less than he claimed it to be, and his personal traits made him unfit for office. Trump and his opponents have spent his entire public life engaged in a brand battle regarding these topics.

As President, Donald Trump was at the center of everything all the time as brands seeking to build omnipresence are. The actions his Administration took, the way in which he used social media and continually battled his opponents produced an omnipresent political brand. Trump did not inspire public confidence in a crisis as the Iran and coronavirus episodes showed. While Trump's use of a drone strike to wipe out the architect of Iran's anti-US strategy in early 2020 could have been an action that other Presidents were cheered for doing, the episode simply offered another opportunity for his opponents to raise questions about his judgment. They were able to do so in part because Donald Trump did not reach outside of his segments to try to build support very often, because his Administration's daily management style was chaotic to the outsider and because he did not take the time to build public support taking such an action as past Presidents had before making such a decision. This was starkly different from the ways in which other modern Presidents, including the current one, have been presented to the public.

While Trump generated a lot of attention by using these marketing strategies, he did not get a lot done with Congress. These strategies built deep loyalty in a few segments; he also drove enough others away in just the wrong places that his branding campaign failed in 2020. He reduced the office of the President from something magisterial to just another product being marketed via social media. He sometimes used the trappings of office like the White House, the military, and the Air Force one to present himself as President but these efforts were inconsistent and paled in comparison to what the Biden Administration has tried to do and what other Presidents have done. His failure hampered his Administration's ability to promote its legislative agenda and empowered his opponents in Congress, the interest group and think tank universe, the media, the bureaucracy, and other levels of government to fight against him.

Donald Trump excelled as a brand builder and promoter. He struggled as a public President because he did not build the broad support for his ideas that could have translated into the kind of leverage with Congress that can lead to lasting policy changes. Consider Trump's failure to repeal Obamacare, secure consistent funding for a border wall and the difficulty his Administration had in passing a tax bill or communicating about what was in it for example. Reliance on building brand that is omnipresent but not widely popular is hardly the stuff on which successful Presidents have built relationships with Congress or the public. In Trump's defense, he was faced with difficult structural, strategic, and symbolic issues even before COVID-19 broke out. He said things in memorable ways and tried to keep his campaign promises and generated significant opposition in the process of doing so.

His focus on the brand was part of his effort to change the Republican Party by adding a working-class base to it to preserve the Reagan coalition. Trump can be seen as a sign that this GOP conservative coalition is changing by either becoming more conservative or falling apart.[3] Trump was trying to hold conservatism together just as Jimmy Carter tried to hold liberalism together long ago.[4] The Reagan coalition is fraying because of generational replacement and because the problems it was empowered to solve have been solved, those solutions have produced their own problems and the world changed in ways that produced other issues for which Reaganism had no answer.[5] One notable example is the way in which the policies that Ronald Reagan pursued helped to end the Cold War but that, by ending it, these policies produced other problems for which Reaganism had no answer. The end of the Cold War turned the United States into the global hegemon meaning that it sometimes was pulled into conflicts abroad that were not in its immediate national interest. Its global involvement sometimes made it the target of terrorists as was the case with Al Qaeda and ISIS. The country responded to the events of September 11, 2001, with military force but the nature of the American military meant that most Americans did not have to fight in these wars. The logic of the Cold War world unleashed a wave of economic globalization and modern technologies that advantaged some elements of American society while disadvantaging others, produced domestic economic dislocation, and fueled globalization. The policies conservatives used to restore order have produced disquiet among liberals and some people of color who argue that the government has established a regime of mass incarceration that has economically devastated their communities. Issues like income inequality, what to do about the large population of undocumented people in the country, housing policy, foreign policy, and climate change have all risen in salience since 1980.

Just like Carter tried to expand the Democrats' base by becoming more conservative in response to market changes, Trump made the GOP coalition friendlier to working-class audiences in response to market changes.[6] The opportunity to do so arose given that the Democrats have bet heavily on a coalition of upper income well-educated whites, visible minority voters, and young people to win in the future but assembling this coalition entailed giving up working-class support to attract these other segments.[7] Trump's working-class appeal cut across racial and ethnic lines. Trump did better in 2020 with African American and Hispanic voters than Republicans had in quite some time.[8] In the case of African American men, President Obama raised a point about Trump's brand style and its equivalence to the public personas of rap music artists.[9]

Trump and his team identified an underserved market and pitched it using populist and nationalist themes. While Trump might have been correct in asserting that the GOP needed to add more working-class voters just based on the sheer size of their population alone, driving away the college educated population that votes in big numbers and controls most of the country's cultural institutions came with significant downsides. Trump received extraordinarily little favorable media coverage outside of conservative circles and his opponents were continually mobilized against him. He stuck to his brand in a way that has made him more akin to a national brand manager than what Americans usually envision from Presidents. On the other hand, he sought to expand the role that Presidents play in the political system, and this produced a backlash from his many opponents who depicted him as either a putative dictator or a naïve rube unsuited for high office.

One can see how Trump's audience targets differed from those of his Democratic opponents in the stark differences in the age distribution between Trump's voters and those that supported Hillary Clinton in 2016 but also in the age differential in the 2020 Democratic primary process in which younger voters overwhelmingly supported Bernie Sanders while older voters chose other candidates. A January 2020 Suffolk University poll bears this out because when asked who they would support in the primary process for President, 27% of 18–34-year-old responded that they would support Bernie Sanders while only 12% of those aged 50–64 and only 4% of those aged 65 and over said the same. On the other hand, only 12% of 18–34-year-old respondents said they would support Joe Biden while 27% of 50–64-year-old respondents said they would and an even higher 37% of aged 65 plus voters said that they would do so. In a choice between Trump and Sanders, the same pattern appears with 52% of 18–34-year-old voters said that they supported Sanders, but 52% of 50–64-year-old respondents said they supported Trump.[10] Trump's voter profile was older than Sanders's. This shows how different voters bring quite different experiences to the political marketplace meaning that the brand that works with one set of voters will not have the same resonance with other voters.

Older voters were more supportive of Trump because they are more affluent, and some supported him because they grew up in an America with a distinct cultural and racial composition from the one it has now. Younger voters, obviously, are much more familiar with this America than the one that their parents and grandparents knew. The issues younger voters care about differ significantly from those older voters care about. As Galston notes, younger voters are more diverse, have been negatively affected by the residue of the 2000s economic crisis, have different attitudes toward diversity than do older voters and care about issues like climate change that do not resonate with older voters thus a different kind of branding resonates with them than the one with which Donald Trump scored big points with older voters.[11] Trump's 2016 branding was effective because it told a story of a successful America that had been pushed into decline by bad management but could be restored to greatness and, given the Administration's emphasis on keeping promises, Trump unsurprisingly ran on a platform that the country has been restored thus a vote to reelect Trump is a vote to "Keep America Great." Trump's reelection branding was not in lockstep with what a lot of the public was feeling as the pandemic unfolded.

Trump tried to add populist and nationalist elements to Conservatism. He criticized President Obama before some audiences as having been too liberal while simultaneously criticizing him for having not done enough before other audiences. This is how emotionally branded, segmented politics works. Trump engaged intermittent voters but some of those voters held positions that were not considered mainstream, and Trump did things, like tweet out pictures of Pepe the Frog (some that has been used by Trump media ally Alex Jones and white nationalist groups as their symbol even though its creator has taken legal action to stop them from doing so) that alarmed some segments who opposed him.[12] In office, Trump used segmented emotional branding, targeting, and some populist tweaks on trade and economic policies in 2016 but he struggled to get anything through Congress and relied on Executive Orders to make policy changes. He stuck to the brand strategy because his Administration focused on keeping the brand promises that kept his base happy. He focused on culture war issues and on fiscal and monetary policies that fit within the traditional Republican economic offering (low taxes, low interest rates, and lessened regulatory burdens on business). The biggest detriment to Trump's economic policy was, until COVID and in some ways, Trump's trade war with China because it caused slower growth, more farm bankruptcies, and limited hiring and investment.[13] This policy might well have long-term broad benefits for the US economy but, like many of Trump's policies, he was so focused on keeping his core audiences happy and so interested in building brand omnipresence through constant motion and conflict, he did not spend the kind of time advocating for this policy agenda to the public that Presidents usually do.[14]

Trump's brand omnipresence meant that people were aware of him and might have had some idea of what his proposals were but not necessarily how they or the country could benefit from them. Instead, his focus on the personal Trump brand made it easy for his opponents to define him and his policies in terms that presented him as an advocate for discrimination. Two of the things that he accomplished legislatively were things on which Republicans agree: tax cuts and conservative appointments. He has enacted a pro-business regulatory program. His other big legislative accomplishment was a criminal justice reform package of which many on the left and in the African American community approve (as mentioned this was the focus of the first ad that team Trump ran during the Super Bowl). He negotiated changes to trade agreements, given notice to leave international treaties, kept promises about travel bans, and trying to build the border wall through executive orders (and budget reprogramming). Many of these policy choices have spawned litigation but they also provided the kind of news coverage that showed Trump's audiences that he was trying to keep his brand promises. He deviated from American orthodoxy by engaging North Korea's leader personally and setting foot in that country, made good on the rhetoric of his predecessors by moving the US Embassy in Israel to Jerusalem and launching a trade war against China instead of just complaining about its trade practices.

He was very defensive about Russia, the Mueller Investigation and report because these things crowded out space, he could have used to define why his agenda was the correct one for the moment and for most Americans. Instead of telling an engaging story as President, Trump drove people to distraction with the kind of back and forth that he has engaged in during his entire New York career. Thus, his political persona was consistent with the other uses of the Trump brand from its creation.[15] A March 2017 Suffolk University poll found that voters were divided about Trump's policies but understood the leadership aspect of branding that he was promoting.[16] The same survey showed that 60% disapproved of his temperament and only 28% thought that his tweeting was an effective way to communicate with the people.[17] Repealing Obamacare, a touchstone of Trump's 2016 campaign and GOP marketing since its passage, was only supported by 17% of respondents but the number rose to 50% when the idea of improving it was broached meaning that Trump's promise to repeal and replace was not outside the realm of possibility.[18] Trump's policies split the above noted poll with 46% of respondents stating that they approved of them and 46% stating that they disapproved but consistent with the argument that targeting, and segment marketing are especially important in contemporary American politics, there were significant variations in support level based on demography and geography.[19] Donald Trump built brand omnipresence but did not expand much outside of his core targets because his brand story, emotions, and products were focused and consistent. Even though the world changed dramatically in the early Spring of 2020, Trump did not. While continuing to sell a product that is one's customers like makes sense, it is entirely possible that a bigger market could be grown by selling other products that applied to broader audiences as the GOP's electoral success at the Congressional and state levels showed in 2020.

Trump had a different kind of message discipline in contrast to that every President who has used the brand model since Reagan has had. His branded predecessors used weekly or daily thematicization to sell their policy preferences and personalities. Unlike these administrations, the Trump Administration operated in a constant, fast, social media-driven news universe. Trump's emphasis on building an omnipresent brand through constant motion and conflict suited this environment just as the way in which his predecessors built their brands suited the media environments in which they governed. Trump was unique as a President because he was fully capable of doing his own marketing and messaging given his professional background. Further, the Trump Administration was confronted from day one by branded media outlets operating in the same competitive environment that Trump he was, and they sought to generate attention for their platforms by reporting on his every move usually in a sensational fashion. The emphasis on conflict and constant motion that built the Trump brand could do the same for their brands. Trump's communications team tried to do as White House communications shops had done for decades and his successor Joe Biden is doing now. Trump personally stepped on their scripted messaging with his own and the combination regularly created an image of a White House in chaos. Trump's focus on building brand omnipresence is different from keeping the kinds of message discipline that politicians have come to practice in recent decades. While Trump may be a very disciplined communicator, his discipline lies in reiterating themes and specific points in highly emotive ways. Trump's put a lot of spontaneity into his persona, policies, and branding. This explains why it is difficult to explain what Trump did while in office beyond some very high-profile issues (most of which have generated a great deal of strife in the country like his Administration's policy of separating migrant families at the border did) but people had a keen sense of attachment to or disdain for his Administration.

Trump built a brand that told an emotive story. It was built out of individual messages but those joined together into a coherent story of disruption. Trump did this himself meaning that he often strayed from the messages his White House press operation had developed for a given circumstance. While Trump would often step over those, he usually did so in a way that was consistent with the Trump brand narrative and values. Thus, President Trump showed a unique way that a politician could use branding aside from daily messaging. Pursuing this strategy built deep brand loyalty for Trump at the same time it built deep antipathy toward him from audiences whose business he was not chasing and his limited his ability to act as the symbolic uniting figure that the President has traditionally been. He became bogged down in arguments about the size of his inauguration crowd or the legitimacy of the Mueller Investigation. Getting into these kinds of scraps, limited his ability to take advantage of the persuasive platform that the Presidency provides meaning that he limited his ability to serve as a symbolic leader for all Americans or build broader support for his brand and his policies.

Mr. Trump's missteps on his first day in office are a case in point. He spoke at the Central Intelligence Agency and his first mistake was to speak in front of the CIA Memorial Wall something that, while excellent branding, was bad form given that he used the speech to attack the media.[20] Trump started out by noting the importance of his visit to the Agency and could have used the event to promote that message alone but instead deviated into an attack on the media using one of the intelligence community's hallowed sites as a backdrop:

> And the reason you're my first stop is that, as you know, I have a running war with the media. They are among the most dishonest human beings on Earth. (Laughter and applause.) And they sort of made it sound like I had a feud with the intelligence community. And I just want to let you know, the reason you're the number-one stop is exactly the opposite — exactly. And they understand that, too.[21]

To compound matters, he then complained about the controversy over the number of people who attended his inauguration and sounded like the entertainment figure he was with his focus on reviews:

> And I was explaining about the numbers. We did a thing yesterday at the speech. Did everybody like the speech? (Applause.) I've been given good reviews. But we had a massive field of people. You saw them. Packed. I get up this morning, I turn on one of the networks, and they show an empty field. I say, wait a minute, I made a speech. I looked out, the field was — it looked like a million, million and a half people. They showed a field where there were practically nobody standing there. And they said, Donald Trump did not drbidenw well. I said, it was almost raining, the rain should have scared them away, but God looked down and he said, we're not going to let it rain on your speech.
> In fact, when I first started, I said, oh, no. The first line, I got hit by a couple of drops. And I said, oh, this is too bad, but we'll go right through

it. But the truth is that it stopped immediately. It was amazing. And then it became really sunny. And then I walked off and it poured right after I left. It poured. But, you know, we have something that's amazing because we had — it looked — honestly, it looked like a million and a half people. Whatever it was, it was. But it went all the way back to the Washington Monument. And I turn on — and by mistake I get this network, and it showed an empty field. And it said we drew 250,000 people. Now, that's not bad, but it's a lie. We had 250,000 people literally around — you know, in the little bowl that we constructed. That was 250,000 people. The rest of the 20-block area, all the way back to the Washington Monument, was packed. So we caught them, and we caught them in a beauty. And I think they're going to pay a big price.[22]

In this example, Americans saw their President complaining about media and mentioning them paying a big price. All of this was on brand for Donald Trump in general and his campaign brand but was like nothing Americans have seen from other Presidents. In the case of the CIA appearance, this seemed like a breach of Presidential protocol that violated the Agency's etiquette because this very political speech was delivered before a memorial to its fallen heroes. It could be seen benevolently as a sign of inexperience because it is like a campaign speech and shows a failure to transition from the role of candidate to the role of President or more menacingly as a declaration of disrespect to the Agency and the media. This kind of behavior fits with the Trump brand promise of disruption even if it does not fit with the image modern Americans have of the way Presidents should behave and it violated the etiquette of the agency in whose building he was speaking. He moved onto discussing who had been on the cover of Time magazine more: he or Tom Brady then followed that up by complaining about a quickly corrected error about the Martin Luther King Statue in the Oval Office.[23]

The same day the President's Press Secretary, Sean Spicer, repeated the sentiments Trump laid out at the CIA as is consistent with the brand strategy. He said that the media had acted in ways that undermined national unity by saying "yesterday, at a time when our nation and the world was watching the peaceful transition of power and, as the President said, the transition and the balance of power from Washington to the citizens of the United States, some members of the media were engaged in deliberately false reporting."[24] Note the way in which Spicer argued that power had been transferred "from Washington to the citizens of the

United States" as if the prior Administration and the Washington establishment had been occupying forces that Trump had driven out. He then tweaked the media for its complaints about Trump's social media use: "For all the talk about the proper use of Twitter, two instances yesterday standout".[25] His first example was "a particular egregious example in which a reporter falsely tweeted out that the bust of Martin Luther King, Jr. had been removed from the Oval Office. After it was pointed out that this was just plain wrong, the reporter casually reported and tweeted out and tried to claim that a Secret Service agent must have just been standing in front of it. This was irresponsible and reckless."[26] Spicer's construction emphasized the boss's fake news pitch because the reporter "falsely tweeted" then when caught "casually reporting(ed)"[27] the mistake. This was very much on brand with the Trump fake news brand aspect.

The second example was a complaint about the coverage of the inaugural crowd. Spicer argued that "photographs of the inaugural proceedings were intentionally framed in a way, in one particular tweet, to minimize the enormous support that had gathered on the National Mall."[28] Spicer provided a technical explanation based around the way in which security limited the crowd from entering the Mall. This shows that the Administration's real concern was visual branding and the bad pictures that the Mall's empty spaces provided: "This was the first time in our nation's history that floor coverings have been used to protect the grass on the Mall. That had the effect of highlighting any areas where people were not standing, while in years past the grass eliminated this visual. This was also the first time that fencing, and magnetometers went as far back on the National Mall, preventing hundreds of thousands of people from being able to access the Mall as quickly as they had in inaugurations past.[29]" He concluded by implying that any crowd size estimates the media had mentioned were either wrong or faked "Inaccurate numbers involving crowd size were also tweeted. No one had numbers, because the National Park Service, which controls the National Mall, does not put any out. By the way, this applies to any attempts to try to count the number of protestors today in the same fashion."[30] As Trump assistant Cliff Sims noted and Spicer himself confirmed in interviews to PBS Frontline, Trump motivated this effort and his staff executed it to please him.[31] Ever the marketer, the fight over crowd size was important for two reasons for Trump. First, it was a way to reiterate the point that the "fake news" was up to its old tricks minimizing his accomplishments again. Second, having a bigger crowd was an important way to show popularity and generate support for the Trump brand. On the other hand, it detracted from whatever momentum the Administration hoped to generate from the Inauguration and did little to generate goodwill from or build a productive relationship with the media. Consistent with the way Trump used branding to control the national agenda, it did distract from the massive "Women's March" that took place in Washington and in cities around the world in opposition to Trump and his policies because it kept the Trump brand at centerstage.

A second example is provided by Trump's responses to the events in Charlottesville, Virginia in 2017. Instead of specifically condemning the right-wing nationalists who instigated a situation that led to a young woman's death, Mr. Trump tried to muddy the waters by saying "We condemn in the strongest possible terms this egregious display of hatred, bigotry and violence on many sides, on many sides. It's been going on for a long time in our country."[32]

Trump's statements indicate that he understood there were strong feelings on both sides about Confederate Memorials. His initial statement drew an equivalence between loud protests and low-level physical confrontations on the one hand with fatal violence on the other. This is a clear example of Trump not using the bully pulpit of the Presidency in the way that Americans have come to expect or in a way that produced national unity. Given the violence at Trump's inauguration perpetrated by ANTIFA activists and the fixation among some of his supporters about those groups, as well as the support Trump received from some who favored keeping the memorials, Trump's response was aimed at furthering his brand narrative and pleasing his best customers thus showing a problem with having a brand manager in the White House. Had he not been President, Trump's words would have gone unnoticed on talk radio or reality television but as President he was expected to be a unifying symbol, promoter of broadly shared values, and national narrator.

Americans have become accustomed to their Presidents calling for toleration and mutual respect but, even if this was what Trump was trying to do, his initial statement missed the mark. He had to make two subsequent statements to try to clean this up, the second of which was much more in keeping with a traditional Presidential tone. A President who was not a one-man marketing operation would have made more use of the experts in their communications shop to make the initial statement than might up with a structured speech. This incident showed Trump, despite his branding chops, had a long learning curve in understanding the way in which the President is expected to serve as unifying national symbol and that the context in which a President operates can sometimes be quite different from the context in which a commercial marketer operates. There have many times when Trump chose to achieve brand omnipresence and serve the needs of his customers rather than fill the symbolic role associated with the Presidency with the Charlottesville incident being just one obvious example. This has built deep loyalty within his target groups but limited the extent to which he could quiet the concerns of others or act as the national leader we have seen the President be for most of the last century.

Trump's campaign team did not focus on a transition plan something that made him dependent on holdover appointments thus giving his opponents an opportunity to restate their concerns about him.[33] Add this to his personal lack of experience in government and the Trump team was not ready to hit the ground running on day one. It was dependent on some of the very same GOP establishment and Obama Administration staffers that he had attacked to keep the government working. Because Trump had run as an outsider, he was bringing a cadre of people into government with him who either lacked experience at all or were considered fringe characters in Washington. Three examples of the former include Trump's daughter Ivanka and her husband Jared Kushner, General Michael Flynn, and Commerce Secretary Wilbur Ross each of whom caused ideological problems, ethics problems, or both. His appointees were the kinds of out of the mainstream picks that have difficulty navigating the Senate approval or security clearance background check processes and, for some of them, being under the kind of scrutiny that comes with being in the public eye was a new thing. Especially in the social media age, things that elected officials to do and say can rocket around the world quickly, a situation that is quite different than life in a commercial business setting. Things that Donald Trump and his staff might have been able to get away with doing in the private sector became the subject of the kinds of ethics complaints that have become common in Washington since Watergate. Things that private sector business can do are things that can be the basis for criminal or ethics complaints and even an impeachment once in government (there is a compelling case that the things for which Donald Trump was impeached would not have been a problem for him if had done them in the private sector). Even if they had good intent in trying to enter government, their actions made it easy for their opponents to cast their intentions malevolently to score political points and strengthen their own brands.

Trump's dependence on Obama holdovers and GOP establishment types did not help build momentum for his proposals or build goodwill outside his target audiences. Some GOP establishment types, who Trump trusted, like Sean Spicer had no experience in government either but knew something of how Washington worked. Putting Spicer in the press secretary role was a misstep because he had little experience in deal with the media in this capacity even though he had run the RNC and worked on several campaigns.[34] Other GOP establishment types had much more loyalty to the party than to Donald Trump and behaved accordingly.[35] Obama holdovers caused more issues for Trump as Sally Yates' refusal to enforce Trump's immigration order showed. While Trump was left with little recourse but to fire her for insubordination, his doing so sparked further outrages among his political opponents. The same was true of the firing of Preet Braha in the Southern District of New York. Trump first asked him to stay on then later decided to ask 46 US Attorneys to leave, among whom was Braha, who refused thus instigating his firing. He said that his motivation was that he sought a confrontation with Trump on the way out to highlight Trump's dithering and possible illegal activities.[36] A third example is provided by the firing of then FBI Director James Comey. A savvier political operator might have fired Comey as part of a transition plan instead of delaying for months then giving multiple explanations for why this action was taken.[37] Further, a seasoned bureaucrat like James Comey knew how to shape public perception just like Donald Trump did. Trump's lack of understanding of how the bureaucracy functions and how federal agencies have their own interests, cultures, and traditions was another downside to putting someone so inexperienced in government without really having people who understood Washington and were loyal to him around him from the outset. This is a problem faced by other outsider Presidents including Clinton, Reagan, Carter, Johnson, and Eisenhower. Truman argued that Iike would expect the Presidency and the government to work like the military in which Eisenhower would issue orders and subordinates would implement them but that is not how the American Government works.[38]

In addition to not getting what he wanted to be accomplished immediately, Trump antagonized some agencies, like the FBI and the intelligence community, with whom he battled throughout his term. Trump's constant tweeting about these matters did nothing to lessen the sense of alienation that many in government felt toward him and produced an environment of almost continuous confrontation between the Trump Administration and the bureaucracy of which he was nominally in charge. They also obscured the serious issues at the bottom of the way in which the FBI surveilled the 2016 Trump campaign in general, Trump aide Carter Page and the way in which the agency behaved in its pursuit of FISA warrants. These are serious matters that Americans of all political leanings should be concerned about, but Trump's branding limited their resonance. Instead, he focused on presenting himself as the victim rather than raising the more serious issues around the behavior of a law enforcement agency in seeking surveillance authority over American citizens engaged in political activity as other Presidents might have done. Chaos and confrontation worked for the disruptor aspect of the Trump brand and the constant coverage of these battles has helped him achieve brand omnipresence, but they kept his opponents constantly engaged, limited discussion of policy issues, and exhausted a great deal of the public. That Trump became the subject of all sorts of inquiries should not come as a surprise given his lack of experience with public sector ethics rules because of his unorthodox background and because of his polarizing personality. Trump brought people into government who were either inexperienced or from whom other administrations had shield away. Trump had beaten the establishment in both parties making him more dependent on unusual hires and holdovers, Trump had defied norms like not putting his assets into a blind trust and not releasing his tax returns, he had egged the Russians on to dig up dirt on Hillary Clinton and was as much a consumer of conspiracy theories like pizzagate as were many of his customers.

His upset win meant that, once in office, he had to take on both party organizations along with a slew of interest groups and issue networks that perceived themselves as the targets of Trump's disruption. Trump's proposed disruption could easily be interpreted as a threat to their accomplishments and positions. He was faced with a bureaucracy that he felt was staffed with his political opponents within which each agency had its own culture, goals, and objectives that have proven resilient in the face of many Presidents' promises to change them as Bachner and Ginsburg (2016) have noted. Add into this toxic brew a media whose credibility he called into question while playing favorites with his access and endorsements (to wit: the shifting relationship between Trump and the Fox News Channel but the constant favorability he showed to Sean Hannity) and the potential for President Trump to become the stationary target for his opponents that candidate Trump was not is clear.[39] Trump's election and administration raised the possibility that the era of dominance of the bureaucracy and the media might be ending thus directly threatening careers. One of the tools that those who lose the Presidency still have is the ability to point out activities that might become scandals or lead to ethics investigations thus bogging down a politically opposite Administration.[40] Trump's Administration was attacked by his opponents using the stock in trade tools of Washington ethics wars and scandals. It was his own inexperience and lack of preparation to govern that laid the groundwork for it to happen. Trump seemed unaware that things that would seem innocuous or subject to little scrutiny in the business world, like asking subordinates for loyalty, could turn out to be fodder for criminal investigations in government.[41]

Trump compounded the problem by modeling his response to these events after the response the Clintons had to the ethics problems faced with in 1990s.[42] While putting one's head down and bulldozing forward made sense in terms of political survival, it opened Trump up to the same kind of branding campaign that Republicans had used against Clinton in the 1990s.[43] It became an article of faith among Democrats and part of their branding that the Trump campaign had actively engaged with a foreign government to subvert an election. Mueller himself became a Democratic icon with a merchandise line devoted to him based on the premise that he would certainly find that Trump's team actively engaged with the Russians. That is until the Mueller Report was released, and the Trump team sprang into action.

There are advantages to having a brand manager in the White House and the Mueller Report episode shows how understanding what the customers want can shape an Administration's approach to a problem before it. Trump's team moved quickly to shape public understanding of the Mueller Report. Attorney General William Barr issued a statement about it before Congress saw it that argued that the Russians had attempted to impact the election but nobody from the Trump campaign was involved in this effort.[44] Trump has consistently argued that the report exonerates him and his Administration as part of the effort to shape public perception. Just after Barr's statement Trump tweeted "No Collusion, No Obstruction, Complete and Total EXONERATION. KEEP AMERICA GREAT!".[45] Trump's opponents and, indeed Mueller himself were placed on the defensive from by this effort. While Mueller tried to push back by releasing a letter to the AG arguing that "The summary letter the Department sent to Congress and released to the public late in the afternoon of March 24 did not fully capture the context, nature, and substance of this Office's work and conclusions. We communicated that concern to the Department on the morning of March 25. There is new public confusion about critical aspects of the results of our investigation. This threatens to undermine a central purpose for which the Department appointed the Special Counsel: to assure full public confidence in the outcome of the investigations. See Department of Justice, Press Release (May 17, 2017)."[46] Shaping public perceptions by going quickly, going first, and being definitive was good for the Trump brand, it limited the damage that it would suffer while allowing team Trump to raise questions about its opponents' credibility and motives. The way that team Trump defined the Mueller Report caused cable tv talk show ratings to drop, some media outlets to reframe the way in which they covered the administration and pushed Trump's accusers to shift their accusations from collusion with a foreign power to more vague claims about obstruction of justice. Cable tv ratings dropped and Trump's accusers had to move from claiming that Trump's team worked with the Russians themselves to murkier claims about obstruction of justice. Had Trump's team been shown to have worked knowingly and directly with Russian operatives that would have been a stronger case for impeachment than are process crimes. Many of them began overtly campaigning for the House of Representatives to begin the impeachment process.

This pattern of behavior replicates what happened during the Clinton years, but it should be recalled that none of those scandals gained traction until after Clinton was reelected and only after he was clearly shown to be lying about easily understood personal behavior. Part of this is the difference between a President who was in office during a time when the direct communication Donald Trump routinely uses did not exist and one who both was and said what other Presidents might have said to their staffs in public on twitter. Both behaviors have helped Trump achieve brand omnipresence in a way that his predecessors could not have imagined. Given that his goal is to constantly keep the Trump brand dominant in the public mind and always available to his users, there is no reason for him to try to avoid this subject as Ronald Reagan routinely did nor is there any reason to simply hunker down in the White House and avoid the media entirely. Instead, Trump embraced the Mueller Report and the way his team shaped the narrative around it with gusto because they keep his

184 K. M. COSGROVE

core audience engaged and provide a ready explanation for why Trump has not delivered on some of his major promises to his core audience.

A similar pattern emerged in the first impeachment episode. Once the Democrats began raising questions about Trump's Ukraine phone call, he released a version of it and described it as "perfect." The Democrats' credibility suffered because there was no obvious quid quo pro or bribery, because Trump had not acted like the mafioso they had originally asserted, and because they would not produce their star witness. Instead, they tried to argue that he was covered by the whistle-blower statues. Some have suggested that the Democrats chose to hide the whistleblower because his ties to prominent Democrats would raise serious credibility issues regarding the entire case.[47] While Trump was impeached by the House, the Articles of Impeachment were voted down by the Senate along a party line vote. Trump branded his chief opponent in this episode, Representative Adam Schiff (D-CA) as "Shifty" something that some saw as being an anti-Semitic reference while others saw it as simply branding him in a way that summed up Trump's relationship with him. He and his supporters termed the Impeachment hearings and trial as part of "Shifty Schiff's Shift Show" to show that this episode was about politics and that the California Representative had used his position as Chair of the House Intelligence Committee to bounce from one anti-Trump investigation to another and was so blinded by what Trump and his supporters call "Trump Derangement Syndrome" that he had no credibility, and his accusations should not be taken seriously. Only the defection of Utah Republican and Trump opponent Mitt Romney denied Trump the opportunity to tell a story in which only Democrats had voted for his impeachment, and they had only done so because they were still sore about their 2016 loss and saw something similar coming up in 2020.

Many observers have noted how Trump's small family business management model was not suited to running the federal government nor did it equip him to understand how the Executive effectively inter-acted with Congress to get things done.[48] Trump's appointments process is atypical for a modern Presidential Administration. It was more well suited to a small family firm.[49] The Administration relied on temporary and recess appointments. From the Trump perspective, the problem with giving permanent appointments to people is that once they secured Senate confirmation, they would have latitude to do as they wished and could be converted to become an advocate for the agency that they were heading. Either thing could reduce the amount of input President Trump might have on their actions and/or their loyalty to him. While this may have created uncertainty in the way in which federal agencies work, it is keeping with the way in which Donald Trump has run some of his other businesses and his brand persona from the Apprentice tv series. The Trump Organization was small and unstructured something the federal government and a modern Administration are not.[50] Trump's lack of public sector experience and steep learning curve limited his ability to get things that were not executive orders done. He knew how to bargain in real estate and how to build then license a brand, but those activities are different from understanding how to deal with members of Congress in either party. Not so different from what was the case when a younger Donald Trump choose to try to do what was good for himself instead of the entire United States Football League, Trump engaged in activities that keep Trump brand promise regardless of what their consequences were for the Congressional GOP.[51] For example, in shutting down the government, Trump sought to keep one of his brand promises, building the wall, not a general GOP brand promise. Making good on this central promise or at least being seen as fighting to do so was vital to Trump's reelection effort because it was a way to show that his product worked as advertised. The Trump White House repeatedly touted the progress on construction that was been made during his term because this promise was vital to the Trump reelection effort regardless of what it did to Republicans in general. Thus, Trump's position shows the problem with having a President who focused on a personal, not a party brand: that person is incentivized to mostly care about how things impact their popularity during their time in office rather than worrying about what is good for the party overall. Trump's marketing instincts encouraged him to focus on visually showing action be accomplished thus explaining his emphasis on executive orders. Implementing these allowed the Trump brand to be omnipresent.

Trump pushed multiple efforts to get Republicans to vote to repeal Obamacare (something they had done many times when they knew President Obama would veto their bill) and he had promised to do himself. Trump encountered the problem of finding an alternative policy that would work, that would provide more access at a better price, that would provide political cover, and could pass the Senate. He wasted much of his early Presidency seeking to keep this core campaign promise, alienated his own party's House of Representatives caucus when he first pushed them to vote on repealing Obamacare then trashed the piece of legislation that they did pass and eventually Senate majority leader Mitch McConnell eventually grew frustrated enough to announce that the Senate was moving onto tax reform and would not be taking up healthcare again. This showed McConnell's orientation toward governing and protecting the interests of his caucus versus Trump's orientation toward building brand omnipresence. The Obamacare and tax repeal issues showed how Trump's expertise as a marketer but inexperience as a politician were simultaneously a blessing and a curse. A President more oriented toward politics and less focused on building an omnipresent political brand could have prioritized an infrastructure program, passed tax reform, and built political capital with Congress before moving onto a difficult battle over Obamacare. This kind of momentum theory of Presidential power would have been but, because Trump was a marketer first and a politician second, his Administration opted to do things that were good for the Trump brand even if other choices that might have been more traditional and better for Trump's ability to govern in the long term had been available. Given the glacial pace of an infrastructure programs and the way in which tax cuts can be not noticed, Trump picking the higher profile Obamacare battle is smart marketing because a long-running fight like that kept the Trump brand relevant and drove the media and public narratives in ways that building literal bridges and small increases in weekly paychecks cannot.

Even after then Majority Leader Mitch McConnell got a tax bill through the Senate, the legislation's benefits were not widely explained to the public, and popular visible middle-class tax deductions disappeared meaning that far from being a marketing boom for the GOP, it can be argued that anger over the way in which the bill raised taxes on upper income suburbanites in expensive blue state real estate markets was the reason the House flipped to the Democrats in 2018.[52] The decision to cap the state and local tax property tax deduction can be seen as a form of market segmentation because Republicans chose to reward their best performing segments in the South and West regions of the country in which such taxes are either unknown or much lower at the expense of ratepayers in the Northeast and Midwest. While this decision made overall marketing sense, it put Northeastern and Midwestern Republicans in a vulnerable electoral position and their vulnerability put the Republican House majority in jeopardy. A more politically oriented, less marketing focused President could have pointed this out as could an Administration with more of a background in public policy because it is not clear that the federal government was subsidizing Northeastern and Midwestern state governments indirectly with this tax write-off given the places from which most federal tax revenue comes.

The Trump Presidency showed that the incentives of political branding and governing do not always align. Thus, the orientation, background knowledge, and preferences of the actual President are important determinants of which focus predominates: political, policy, or marketing? For example, Trump's lack of expertise in governing made it difficult for his Administration to secure a tax cut vote from Republicans, something that should not have been difficult or controversial given the party's anti-tax position is well established. This vote was more difficult than it could have been because of things done and undone during the battle over Obamacare repeal. The tax cut vote too could have been an opening salvo from the Trump Administration because tax cuts are less controversial than was trying to gut Barack Obama's signature domestic and foreign policy accomplishments. The Republican Party held the majority in both houses of Congress and, could pass a tax bill that the Democrats could not stop via the majoritarian budget reconciliation process. The same was not true on the Obamacare repeal thus the decision to prioritize that shows that marketing and brand building objectives took priority in the Trump Administration. This priority reflected Trump's experience in one area and lack of it in the other. Republicans agree on cutting taxes, it's not as controversial a vote as eliminating health insurance subsidies and gutting his predecessor's signature domestic policy initiative was. Tax cuts could be passed in ways that the Democrats could not stop. Inexplicably, team Trump did not develop a platform brand to show individuals how they had benefitted from the cuts or push Congress to insert a provision into the bill that would have required a check in the amount of the tax cut for that year be sent to each taxpayer as the George W. Bush Administration had done. Instead, the Trump team argued that they spurred economic growth and were an example of the "Make America Great Again" brand promise having been kept. His Democratic opponents took advantage of this emphasis on the house brand over the specific policy by branding these as tax cuts for the rich meaning fewer Americans were aware that they had gotten a tax cut than could have been the case had the Trump team chosen to build a platform brand around this instead of trying to build omnipresence for the house brand.[53]

The emphasis on keeping overall Trump brand promises and building omnipresence for it ran through everything the administration did.

Consider the record pace at which Trump appointed jurists.[54] Judicial appointments differ from tax cuts because people can be shown what the impact a tax cut had on their bottom line while jurists tend to go onto the federal bench and rule on common law notions that themselves can be difficult to build a marketing campaign out of even if their overall rulings can be fodder for marketing as the debate over what to call the privacy rights-based ruling that made abortion legal in this country. Democrats discuss abortion in terms like "reproductive rights," "choice," and "reproductive health services" while Republicans have either worked with the bland term "life" or employed more visceral terminology to make their points like "baby killing." Trump has made marketing campaigns out of the bottom line of judicial rulings but has also engaged in the kinds of rhetoric about individual judges and federal circuits making rulings that have stifled his policy initiatives. Conservatives have used similar rhetoric for decades right down to spotlighting individual judges as Donald Trump did during his 2016 primary campaign when he questioned the ability of federal judge Gonzalo Curiel to decide a case involving him fairly because the judge, who had been born in Indiana is "a Mexican national. We're building a wall between here and Mexico."[55] The difference between Trump and the others who have done this was Trump's explicitly racial and nationalist rhetoric. Instead of calling the judge a liberal or a judicial activist, both terms conservatives regularly when speaking in opposition to court rulings, Trump homed in on national identity and used it in a way that both promoted his wall proposal and sought to recast what could be a political liability about his business ethics into evidence that he was being victimized by a jurist allied with a foreign power.

In office, the Trump Administration prioritized actions that showed that promises made in 2016 had been kept. Trump filed for reelection on the day on which he was inaugurated in 2016 something that American Presidents do not usually do but doing it set a marketing goal to be met by the Administration. Taking this decisive step so early on showed how Trump fully intended to market his personal brand first and the GOP brand later. This reflects Trump's insurgent status. He won the GOP nomination, but he had not followed a traditional path to it. A good contrast is provided by his predecessor, Barack Obama, who, while running as an insurgent, was very much a product of Democratic Party politics having served as a US Senator and in the Illinois legislature, spoken at its convention and worked with many allied groups during his time as a community organizer in Chicago. Because Obama had extensive government experience and had served in two legislatures before becoming President, he focused on doing the job to which he had been elected while promoting the party and himself. Like most Presidents, Obama struck a balance between his personal political incentives, those of the party and passing policies that would benefit its electoral fortunes. Donald Trump kept a selling focus in office and that focus has been on selling the Trump not the GOP brand.

While President he continued to do the same kinds of campaign-style rallies that he did as a candidate. The obvious campaigning in office and the volume of these rallies set Trump apart from other American Presidents. Other Presidents might have done events, like George Bush did, with the infamous "Mission Accomplished" appearance on the USS Abraham Lincoln off San Diego on May 1, 2003. As Bush noted placing the banner behind him while he spoke "was a mistake. It sent the wrong message. We were trying to say something differently but nevertheless it conveyed a different message.[56]" In that circumstance, the Bush team was trying to merge politics with Presidential symbolism with Bush playing the role of President welcoming the troops home. Like most Presidents, Bush would sometimes serve as the national narrator in chief. Donald Trump, on the other hand, advocated for the Trump brand, his administration, his staff, and his core constituents always. Even in the middle of a pandemic, an economic crisis, and a racial justice movement, Trump remained focused on making himself the center of all events. The Trump brand was omnipresent in politics and in many aspects of American life.

Trump's rallies while he was in office represented an opportunity to show that the brand promises made have been kept. Trump, from the earliest rallies he held as President, appeared in front of signage reading "Promises Made, Promises Kept" and crowd signs saying the same were prominent at each rally he held. Trump held rallies outside Washington after major events in the life of his Administration such as during and just after his impeachment trial, Senate approval of Brett Kavanaugh's nomination to the Supreme Court and on the night before primary contests are held in states like New Hampshire during the 2020 cycle. These rallies offered Trump a way to speak directly to the faithful in their home areas, to show that he had not become enmeshed in the trappings of power or forgotten for whom he is working. Even though he was unopposed in the 2020 GOP primary, Trump still held rallies. For example, Donald Trump spoke in Manchester, New Hampshire the night before that state's primary and the next day received more votes in that state's primary than anyone other than Ronald Reagan in his reelection bid ever had despite facing minimal opposition.[57] In some areas, Donald Trump even received twice as many votes as Democratic primary winner Bernie Sanders did thus showing the power Trump's omnipresent brand developed during his term in office.[58] The rallies fired up the faithful, allowed Trump to road test material, and were an important source of accurate data and mobile phone numbers through which direct-to-consumer communication was made. It should not be surprising that once COVID-related restrictions on large gatherings were implemented nationwide, Trump's messaging became less innovative and more focused on the themes that he had worked with throughout his time in the public eye. His campaign did not have the data or the test bed to do anything new. This also explains why Trump was so eager to get back on the campaign trail.

In office, Trump focused on doing things that show the Trump brand promises made during the campaign have been kept. Visually showing that brand promises have been kept as a way to increase the probability that Trump was reelected because keeping promises engages audiences and generates enthusiasm.[59] The actual Trump Administration might have operated in a more meritocratic fashion than its brand would indicate given that Trump seeks out young staffers who have Ivy League credentials and high-profile judicial clerkships but the way in which Trump himself presents the brand to his audiences keeps the focus off that and on him as the populist insurgent found in the brand story.[60] The emphasis on keeping brand promises runs through everything that the Trump Administration did because this is a key part of branding.

Donald Trump's 2016 success was the result of a well-designed sticky brand that gradually became omnipresent. His struggles in office, his defeat in 2020, and the aftermath of that election show the potential downsides to this strategy. Trump did not adjust to become the President of all Americans even during a serious public health crisis. While a Presidential candidate might well benefit from being sold like a commercial product and a President in office might benefit from the use of commercial marketing techniques, Donald Trump's single-minded focus on them meant that he never managed to fill the symbolic or most of the substantive roles that Presidents have in recent years. He built an omnipresent sticky brand and stuck with it despite changing market conditions that supported changing the brand's tone and emotions. It can be argued that if Trump had become more empathetic as Americans struggled with a pandemic, an economic crisis, and a series of racially charged incidents, he might have been well positioned to win reelection. Instead, he focused on the same brand and issues that made him successful in the first place. This was a problematic choice given that he was running as an incumbent meaning he was trying to earn repeat business rather than just trying to get the consumer to try something just once and because the public marketplace had changed significantly because of the pandemic.

Trump's hope of the Democrats having a drawn-out 2020 primary contest that produced a weakened winner who would then be immediately buried in Trump funded negative advertising went by the boards when Joe Biden wrapped up the Democratic nomination early in the primary season. Trump's plan of talking about his economic record and the positive impact his Administration had for all Americans but especially for Americans of color went by the boards as COVID took hold. Instead, Trump was stuck in the White House for months focusing on a pandemic for which the United States was ill-prepared and a governmental response that was mixed at best for which Trump became the face. Given these circumstances, he reverted to the same messaging he used in 2016, stressed the need for economic growth, and minimized the danger posed by COVID. It is difficult to know what would have happened in 2020 had COVID not emerged as the year's dominant feature, but we do know that Trump's effort to change the composition of the Republican coalition bore fruit.[61]

Further, he was not running against Hillary Clinton in 2020. Joe Biden was a formidable opponent because he could play the working-class everyman role that Trump played but could do it in a way that appealed to more audiences than Trump did.[62] Trump's decision to remain the same in the face of a distinct set of market conditions and different kind of opponent shows the need for politicians who use the brand strategy to be willing to adjust in the face of changing circumstances. Trump lost because he was too targeted, because his sticky branding developed a strong negative response from those that did not like it, because his management of a series of serious crises raised the salience of attributes beyond disruption and emotions other than anger and because he did not react to a changing political marketplace. Despite these failures, he still almost won and got more votes in 2020 than he did in 2016. The 2020 outcome shows the importance of adjusting the political brand and product to fit changing circumstances not that Trump's brand strategy absolutely failed. It barely won in 2016 and it barely lost in 2020. With just a slight set of adjustments, Donald Trump could have easily won in 2020.

Even after losing the 2020 election, Trump launched a platform brand intended to raise money, change the election results, and delegitimate the Biden Administration. While he accomplished two of these goals, he did not overturn the election but instead became partly responsible for a violent attack on the US Capitol on January 6, 2021. Trump's sticky branded language on that day riled up the crowd that had attended his Mall rally and the rest really is history. People died and were injured, the Electoral College count stopped for a time, but Trump still lost when it resumed, and the Republicans cut their objections to the process short meaning that much of potential marketing benefit that would have been gained by raising said objections were squandered. Instead, Trump became a polarizing, perplexing figure in the Republican Party as he had been in a lot of the rest of the country for quite some time. Trump was impeached again, and the Democrats got an opportunity to try to damage Trump and the Republicans by positioning them as either insurrectionists or obstructionists—a trend that continued when it came time for Congress to investigate the episode. Trump's omnipresence and sticky branding strategies had serious downsides as the 2020 election and its aftermath showed. A less branded candidate might have focused more on playing the long game and either plotting a 2024 comeback or playing the role of kingmaker in Republican politics. Instead, Trump became a pariah for a time. He was banned from social media and has only been heard through press releases or appearances on Fox News and other friendly conservative outlets. Trump made his own problems in these areas, and they are a further sign of his devotion to the brand omnipresence and sticky branding strategies. Given that he had placed so much emphasis on winning and being the hero, there was little chance of his making a graceful exit after he had been defeated by the swamp, the mainstream media, and the liberals in the guise of Joe Biden. On the other hand, these strategies cannot be called a failure. He remains a leading figure in the populist wing of the Republican Party, and it is a source of continual speculation as to his future. His branding strategies built a deep reservoir of loyalty among his audience targets so much so that some of them participated in the disorder of January 6th while many others continue to support him despite it. While his instincts and an extensive data-analytics operation built a winning formula in 2016 that combined society making themes with segment reinforcing issues. This strategy depended on its user being able to adjust to changing market conditions and to attract more people using it to his cause than he was driving away. By 2020 none of this was the case. Trump was so focused, so divisive, and so out of step with the concerns of many Americans during a pandemic that even though his vote total was higher than it was in 2016, his opponent's vote total was even higher than that meaning that Trump had driven away some audiences that traditionally voted for Republicans and did not make those up with voters from other segments in the geographically useful places needed to win. Given that Trump's vote total was higher in 2020 than it was in 2016, his strategy cannot be called a failure but the segments that he lost to Joe Biden who traditionally voted Republican up until the Trump years indicate that there may be profound consequences to doing as Trump did as a public figure.

NOTES

1. Schier and Eberly (2017).
2. Suri (2017) talks extensively about the development of these notions during the twentieth century.
3. Richard Kreitner. "What Time Is It? Here's What the 2016 Election Tells Us About Obama, Trump, and What Comes Next:" https://www.the nation.com/article/what-time-is-it-heres-what-the-2016-election-tells-us-about-obama-trump-and-what-comes-next/, accessed July 18, 2019.
4. Ibid and Cosgrove (2020) outlines the way in which this applied to the Trump political brand.
5. This process is outlined by Skowronek (2011).
6. Ibid.
7. See for example Eric Levitz. "David Shor on Why Trump was Good for the Republican Party." *New York Magazine.* March 3, 2021. https://nymag.com/intelligencer/2021/03/david-shor-2020-democrats-autopsy-hispanic-vote-midterms-trump-gop.html.
8. Jack Herrera. "Trump didn't win the Latino Vote in Texas, He Won the Tejano Vote." *Politico Magazine* November 17, 2020. https://www.politico.com/news/magazine/2020/11/17/trump-latinos-south-texas-tejanos-437027.
9. Jeffery Goldberg. "Why Obama Fears for Our Democracy." *The Atlantic.* November 16, 2020. https://www.theatlantic.com/ideas/archive/2020/11/why-obama-fears-for-our-democracy/617087/.
10. Ibid.

11. William Galston. "Why the Young Back Bernie Sanders." *Wall Street Journal*. February 18, 2020. https://www.wsj.com/articles/why-the-young-back-bernie-sanders-11582071616?mod=searchresults&page=1& pos=3, accessed February 18, 2020.
12. Scott Neuman. "Alex Jones To Pay $15,000 In Pepe the Frog Copyright Infringement Case". NPR. June 11, 2019 (https://www.npr.org/2019/06/11/731520403/alex-jones-to-pay-15-000-in-pepe-the-frog-copyri ght-infringement-casel).
13. Heather Long. "Was Trump's China Trade War Worth It?" *Washington Post*. January 15, 2020. https://www.washingtonpost.com/business/2020/01/15/was-trumps-china-trade-war-worth-it/, accessed February 29, 2020.
14. Ibid regarding the potential benefits for the US economy.
15. O'Brien (2015, pp. 76–79, 81, 94, 121, 194, 214, 216, 236).
16. Suffolk University Polling Center "POLL: VOTERS SAY TRUMP SHOWS LEADERSHIP BUT ARE LESS SURE OF ITS DIREC-TION." March 2017. https://www.suffolk.edu/news-features/news/2018/05/21/20/04/poll-voters-say-trump-shows-leadership-but-are-less-sure-of-its-direction.
17. Ibid.
18. Ibid.
19. Ibid.
20. Ira Winkler. "Why Trump's CIA Speech Was Simply Inappropriate." *The Hil* January 23, 2017. https://thehill.com/blogs/pundits-blog/def ense/315605-why-trumps-cia-speech-was-simply-inappropriate.
21. "Remarks by President Trump and Vice President Pence at CIA Head-quarters Langley, VA." January 21, 2017 (www.whitehouse.gov/briefi ngs-statements/remarks-president-trump-vice-president-pence-cia-headqu arters/, accessed July 1, 2019).
22. Ibid.
23. Ibid.
24. Statement by Press Secretary Sean Spicer Issued on: January 21, 2017. https://www.whitehouse.gov/briefings-statements/statement-press-secretary-sean-spicer/, accessed 14 July 2019.
25. Ibid.
26. Ibid.
27. Ibid.
28. Ibid.
29. Ibid.
30. Ibid.
31. Patrice Taddonio. "How a Fight Over Crowd Size Would Define Trump's Approach to the Presidency and the Truth. *PBS Frontline*, January 13,

2020   https://www.pbs.org/wgbh/frontline/article/how-a-fight-over-crowd-size-would-define-trumps-approach-to-the-presidency-and-the-truth/, accessed February 29, 2020.

32. Carly Sitrin. "Read: President Trump's Remarks Condemning Violence on "Many Sides" in Charlottesville." Vox. August 12, 2017. https://www.vox.com/2017/8/12/16138906/president-trump-remarks-condemning-violence-on-many-sides-charlottesville-rally, accessed August 1, 2019.

33. For a detailed discussion of the Trump transition see Michael Lewis." This Guy Doesn't Know Anything: "The Inside Story of Trump's Shambolic Transition". *The Guardian.* September 27, 2018. https://www.theguardian.com/news/2018/sep/27/this-guy-doesnt-know-anything-the-inside-story-of-trumps-shambolic-transition-team, accessed February 29, 2020.

34. For example, see Schier and Eberly (2017).

35. Sims (2019) provides a host of examples of Trump and RNC infighting. See for example pages 34 and 54.

36. Jackie Wattles. "Preet Bharara Reveals Why He Made President Trump Fire Him." CNN Money. April 6, 2017 (https://money.cnn.com/2017/04/06/news/preet-bharara-donald-trump-cooper-union/, accessed July 1, 2017.

37. Wolff (2018, p. 242).

38. Paul Brandus. "Donald Trump Is About to Learn the Same Lesson Eisenhower Did." CBS MarketWatch (https://www.marketwatch.com/story/donald-trump-is-about-to-learn-the-same-lesson-president-eisenhower-did-2016-11-10, accessed July 15 2019.

39. Thus, positioning Trump in a similarly negative way to the corporations Mannheim (2015) wrote about in *The Death of a Thousand Cuts.*

40. Ginsberg and Shefter (1999).

41. Wolff (2018, p. 99).

42. Wolff (2018, p. 99).

43. Cosgrove (2007) outlines it in detail.

44. Heather Timmons. "Read William Barr's Full Remarks on the Robert Mueller Report." Ozy April 18, 2019 (https://qz.com/1598817/william-barrs-full-remarks-on-the-robert-mueller-report/).

45. @realdonaldtrump tweet March 24, 2019, https://twitter.com/realdonaldtrump/status/1109918388133023744?lang=en, accessed July 13, 2019.

46. Robert Mueller. "Read: Letter from special counsel Robert Mueller to Attorney General William Barr." CNN May 1, 2019, accessed July 15, 2019 (https://www.cnn.com/2019/05/01/politics/mueller-letter-to-barr/index.html).

47. Ian Schwartz. "Rand Paul: Alleged Whistleblower, Friend Plotted for Over a Year to Bring Down Trump." *Real Clear Politics.* January 31,

2020. https://www.realclearpolitics.com/video/2020/01/31/rand_p aul_alleged_whistleblower_friend_plotted_for_over_a_year_to_bring_d own_trump.html, accessed February 29, 2020.
48. Schier and Eberly (2017) for example.
49. Ibid.
50. O'Brien (2015, pp. 18, 35, 83, 89, 99).
51. See Pearlman (2018, pp. 139–141 and 178–184).
52. Ben Casselman and Jim Tankersley. "Face It: You (probably) Got a Tax Cut." *New York Times*, April 14 2019 (https://www.nytimes.com/2019/04/14/business/economy/income-tax-cut.html, accessed July 4, 2019).
53. Ibid.
54. Carrie Johnson. "Trump's Judicial Appointments Were Confirmed at Historic Pace In 2018." NPR. January 2, 2019.
    https://www.npr.org/2019/01/02/681208228/trumps-judicial-app ointments-were-confirmed-at-historic-pace-in-2018
55. Nina Totenberg. "Trump Presses Case That 'Mexican' Judge Curiel is Biased Against Him." *NPR*. June 4, 2016. https://www.npr.org/2016/06/04/480714972/trump-presses-case-that-mexican-judge-curiel-is-bia sed-against-him, accessed March 1, 2020.
56. As quoted in Seth Cline." The Other Symbol of George W. Bush's Legacy." *US News and World Report*. May 1, 2013. https://www.usn ews.com/news/blogs/press-past/2013/05/01/the-other-symbol-of-geo rge-w-bushs-legacy, accessed March 1, 2020.
57. David Brooks. "Trump's N.H. Primary Win Was Historic in Size." *Concord Monitor.* February 12, 2020. https://www.concordmonitor. com/TRUMP-PRESIDENT-DONALD-PRIMARY-2020-WIN-326 40312 accessed March 1, 2020.
58. Ibid.
59. Nancy Cook and Marianne Levine. "Trump Team Convinced Court Overhaul Will Drive 2020 Win." *Politico.* May 19, 2019, accessed July 15, 2019 (https://www.politico.com/story/2019/05/19/trump-judges-2020-1332932).
60. Ibid.
61. Cosgrove and Shrader (2021) discuss the Trump and Biden branding strategies in depth.
62. See Cosgrove and Shrader in Moufahim (2021) for an in-depth discussion of the problem Biden presented for Trump in 2020 and how Trump failed to adjust to changing market conditions.

Bibliography

Bachner, Jennifer and Benjamin Ginsberg. *What Washington Gets Wrong: The Unelected Officials Who Actually Run the Government and Their Misconceptions about the American People.* Prometheus, 2016.

Cosgrove, Kenneth. *Branded Conservatives.* New York: Peter Lang, 2007.

Cosgrove, Kenneth M. "Donald Trump, the Brand, the Disjunctive Leader and Brand Ethics." In Jaime Gilles (ed.). *Political Marketing in the 2020 U.S. Presidential Election.* Palgrave, 2020.

Cosgrove, Kenneth and Nathan Shrader. "Political Branding in the USA Election of 2020." In Mona Moufahim (ed.), *Political Branding in Turbulent Times.* Palgrave-Macmillan, 2021.

Ginsberg, Benjamin and Martin Shefter. *Politics by Other Means: Politicians, Prosecutors and the Press from Watergate to Whitewater.* W.W. Norton 1999.

O'Brien, Timothy L. *Trump Nation.* Open Road Media, 2015.

Pearlman, Jeff. *Football for a Buck: The Crazy Rise and Even Crazier Demise of the USFL.* Mariner Books, 2018.

Schier, Steven E. and Todd E. Eberly. *The Trump Presidency: Outsider in the Oval Office.* Rowman and Littlefield, 2017.

Sims, Cliff. *Team of Vipers: My 500 Extraordinary Days Inside the Trump White House.* St. Martin's Press, 2019.

Skowronek, Stephen. *Presidential Leadership in Political Time: Reprise and Reappraisal* (2nd edition). University Press of Kansas, 2011.

Suri, Jermi. *The Impossible Presidency.* Hachette Book Group, 2017.

Wolff, Michael. *Fire and Fury: Inside the Trump White House.* Henry Holt and Company, 2018.

CHAPTER 8

The President of Segments

Abstract The book concludes by arguing that as a candidate and as President, Trump shows the power and limits of political marketing. Branding, segmentation, and narrowcasting can win elections, but their use does not automatically lead to domestic tranquility but instead can generate significant polarization. Trump's election and behavior seem counter to the zeitgeist of the moment when it seemed to many that the Democrats would replace the first President of color with the first female President, the idea that Donald Trump won using a brand promise of restoration seemed shocking, but it illustrates the potency of political marketing.

Keywords Political Marketing · 2020 Presidential election, January 6 2021 · Congress · Congressional oversight · Brett Kavanaugh nomination and hearings · Richard Nixon · Bill Clinton · Impeachment · Polarization · Covid 19 and Donald Trump · Basket of deplorables · Border wall · Niche marketing · Interest groups · Republican Party · Democratic Party · Political branding · Personal branding · Media branding · Brand promise

Donald Trump as a candidate, as a President, and as an ex-President is both a cause and a reflection of our national discontents. His campaigns and administration used branding, consumer data, and market research to

K. M. Cosgrove, *Donald Trump and the Branding of the American Presidency*, https://doi.org/10.1007/978-3-030-30496-6_8

target messages at specific audiences. They used social media platforms, the campaign website, the White House website, and friendly media to build a direct-to-consumer marketing operation unparalleled in American political history. He used social media to build a direct marketing and earned media operation that got Trump's brand out in an unmediated manner. At the same time, he took direct aim at the stature that elite institutions of all sorts have come to occupy in American life. His most obvious targets were the media and government bureaucrats. He termed the media as "the enemy of the people." In challenging CNN and the New York Times as "fake news," Mr. Trump sought to enhance his brand while tapping into common conservative sentiments about media bias. Trump's style and tone limited his appeal as much as his substantive agenda did. The comments of former New York City Mayor and Democratic Presidential candidate Michael Bloomberg are instructive regarding the problems Trump has had in expanding his support: "a lot of my criticism of Donald Trump are not the policies -it's the way he's doing it."[1] Trump's brand and management styles only appealed to a few audiences, and this made him into more of a President of segments than a President for all Americans. Further, Americans were presented with a brand persona and management style that were vastly different from the norms of the modern Presidency. Many disapproved.

Donald Trump is a devotee of niche marketing. Niche marketing is one of the core elements of the sticky brand strategy that his campaigns and administration employed. Focusing on an issue like a border wall exemplifies a narrowcasting strategy because the audiences that care about that issue care about it deeply and hardly anyone else does. While Mr. Trump's niche strategy did not win the popular vote in 2016, it won the Electoral College and that is all the Trump team claimed it sought to do.[2] It barely worked the first time and barely failed the second, but it was never a strategy that could make Trump broadly popular. Trump's brand story, emotions, and issues were very targeted and aimed at disruption. This was never a strategy aimed at building social harmony or unity and when the COVID crisis broke out its flaws were on display for all to see. Mr. Trump stuck with his brand personality, style, and story throughout his time on the national stage including during the worst public health emergency in a century. He was able to build deep loyalty among some audiences and do better than Republicans have within some of them, but he built deep antipathy among other segments and drove audiences that Republicans used to win into the arms of the Democrats. Given that Mr.

Trump polled at under 50% approval throughout his term, there was no possibility of him winning a majority in 2020. And his weak poll numbers meant Trump did not have the kind of leverage to encourage Congress to pass most of his legislative proposals meaning that he did not have a long record of legislative accomplishments on which to run. Instead, he promoted his executive orders, his economic success, and all the battles with the elite in which he had engaged during his term.

One of the promises Donald Trump kept was that of appointing reliable conservatives to the federal judiciary. This was an important promise to make and keep because much of the most controversial policy decisions the US Government has implemented in recent decades have been promulgated by Courts or bureaucratic agencies. As Bachner and Ginsberg (2016) note, in recent years the amount of policy made by the unelected portions of the federal government has significantly exceeded that made by the elected portions of it. Trump promised to take on the unelected in general. He paid particular attention to the judiciary. His primary method of doing so was through judicial appointments. A second one was by leaving bureaucratic positions vacant. A third one was via the issuance of executive orders. Trump got into fights with the bureaucracy. He then employed these fights to show his audiences the extent to which his opponents would go to defeat him. All three strategies were music to the ears of conservatives. Trump ran against liberal judges and bureaucrats as conservatives do but took the effort one step further than his predecessors by circulating a list of judicial appointments he would make once in office to audiences like evangelical Christians for whom court cases involving social policy were a high priority. Consistent with the brand strategy, Trump kept his word and followed the list that his campaign had circulated.

At the start of 2020, Trump's campaign was built around his economic policy, the border wall, criminal justice reform, the ways in which he had disrupted the Washington Establishment and the ways in which they had fought back to stifle him. The theme of the 2020 campaign was to have been that promises made in 2016 had been kept. Trump was to have been presented as a symbolic leader to the audiences he is targeting (hence his trip to key sporting events like the Daytona 500) and in trying to depict his opponents as an unacceptable alternative. Trump's tacit encouragement of Bernie Sanders' candidacy illustrates this extent to which Trump wanted a clear contrast and an opponent that he could present as being unacceptable to the bulk of the electorate. No candidate would have provided a clearer contrast of brand and policies than Sanders would have. Sanders disruptive policies and the tax increases associated with them, as well as his own quirky personality might have made Trump's personal foibles more tolerable to some voters. A Sanders candidacy could have turned the election into a referendum on the country's future as either a capitalist or socialist one instead of the battle for the soul of the nation in which Trump was cast as the anti-American authoritarian versus the more traditional Democrat that the Biden campaign sold the public late in the campaign.

Once Joe Biden became the Democratic nominee, Trump's task became much more daunting. Biden sold in a wide variety of audiences and his campaign built an effective contrast between his personal decency and Trumps' more colorful behavior. Biden's team had the good sense to stay out of the way as Donald Trump failed to manage the COVID pandemic and the subsequent crises that it unleashed. He presented himself as a working-class guy just like Trump presented himself. Trump branded Biden as "Sleepy Joe" and argued that he was too old to be President. Even worse, Trump argued that Biden would just be a trojan horse for the far-left wing of the Democratic Party. One problem with this line of argument was that many Americans saw Biden's boringness as more of a feature than a bug. A second problem was that many Americans had moved in a leftward direction on economic policy. Trump had left many Americans scared, exhausted, angry, and wondering if there was any tangible way to improve the economic, COVID, and racial situations in the country. Trump's version of an economic message was not what a lot of the electorate was hoping to hear from its 2020 candidates. Biden's understated personality and limited visibility campaign offered reassurance in a time of crisis. Biden's socially distanced events and mask wearing underscored that he took the pandemic more seriously than did the Trump campaign.

Trump was no longer asking people to try something once, instead he was asking for repeat business something that is more difficult to attract, and he was doing so against a challenger who was emotionally branded in a separate way than Hillary Clinton had been. While the Clinton Campaign stressed social cohesion and economic policy with its "Stronger Together" branding, Biden stressed recovery from covid, normality in public life, and a brighter future with his "Build Back Better" branding. Trump found more votes in 2020 than he had in 2016 but his opponents found even more than did he. Contrast the outcome that Donald Trump got on election night 2020 with the results the Republican Party got at the Congressional and subnational levels and the weakness in Trump's strategy is clear. The limited appeal that Democrats not named Joe Biden and not running simply as an anti-Trump had with the voters is also clear. Trump lost big in 2020 but the GOP did not in part because the Democrats were so focused on Trump. Many Republicans were branded differently than Donald Trump. The Republicans shaped a public perception that the Democrat's agenda amounted to defunding the police and instituting socialism. This was like the contrast that which Donald Trump had hoped to use against Sanders but could not against Biden. Therefore, Joe Biden's perceived centrism was a more difficult challenge for Trump. It is why Biden's strategy of focusing on his own race while not publicly embracing the progressives in the Democratic caucus made sense. The progressive agenda did not sell with more moderate Americans. Instead of promoting an unpopular agenda by participating in a Democratic coordinated campaign, Joe Biden spent his energy running his own race and negatively branding Donald Trump.

The 2020 Trump and Biden campaigns show the importance that brand emotions and personality play in political marketing. That someone like Donald Trump found a market and won the Presidency should not come as a surprise given recent American history. The people who run many of the institutions of American governmental public life are drawn from similar social and cultural institutions. They are distinct from the average American in terms of education, income, and values. Since the turn of the century, the country had suffered a major terrorist attack, fought two wars, and lived through a major economic crisis. The people running the country seemed insulated from the fallout of all this compared to their impact on average Americans. Trump's assertions about his prowess to fix public problems are very much in keeping with the image of the Presidency that Americans have seen since the early twentieth century. He was the angry avenger out to put right the things that the elite had done wrong. Joe Biden became something of an anti-Trump by stressing decency and empathy, by not being omnipresent, and by focusing on the biggest issue people had on their minds in 2020: the pandemic. Had Trump been more understated, reached out to some other audiences, and more appropriate for the times, he well might have won on substantive issues as UK Prime Minster Boris Johnson's advisors noted in the aftermath of the election.[3]

Pursuing brand omnipresence meant that Trump had to be in the center of everything continuously, appear to have most of the power in the system, and have readymade solutions for any problem that presented itself. In this Trump argued for the unitary executive theory as did his fellow Republicans Richard Nixon and George W. Bush (Skowronek et al. 2021). While Trump pursued a different branding strategy than his recent predecessors had, he continued the modern tradition of Presidents claiming to be a policy and political superman who could solve all problems once in office.[4] As most Presidents have discovered, once in office, Trump learned that the American system did not work in quite the way that he believed it did, that his predecessors had done more smart things than he might have imagined, and that events could take on a life of their own. It is not unusual for Presidents to be unable to fully respond to an event but completely able to shape public perceptions of their response to an event. Trump's Presidency seemed to lurch from crisis to crisis throughout its entirety. He failed to get Congress to repeal Obamacare and struggled to get a tax cut enacted even with a Republican majority. He was confronted with a bureaucracy that was skeptical of him at best and hostile toward him at worst. Within weeks of his taking office, events beyond his control pushed toward a confrontation with North Korea. The biggest event beyond his control was the COVID crisis and the timing of that could not have been worse for his electoral prospects. The timing could not have been better for his general election opponent who was partly running on the idea that he was competent, and Trump was not. In some ways, Trump was unlucky in the scale and timing of the COVID crisis but in others his single-mindedly sticking to his sticky branding and omnipresence strategy created his problems.

The COVID crisis showed the limits to Presidential and federal substantive powers. It showed the risks and opportunities for political leaders attempting to narrate a crisis and presenting themselves as able to solve all problems as many recent Presidents have. Trump may have promised better management than Americans had gotten from their politicians for decades. He lacked the public sector experience to deliver better management. His task was made more difficult because of the way in which the American Government shares authority across federal branches and the state governments. His ability to deal with COVID was further complicated because hardly anything was known about it when it appeared in the United States in 2020. He did not have the authority that he and past Presidents claimed to have and that the leaders of other countries do possess. He seemed to focus on taking actions that his Administration could claim credit for taking, consistent with the omnipresent sticky branding strategy but ignored the more mundane but important work that the federal government often plays in crises of supporting the work of state and local governments. Instead, there were actions taken by the United States under the Trump Administration and various state governments that were sometimes competitive with each other and often contradictory. Trump's failure as a marketer was that he did not adjust to the way in which public sentiment had shifted in response to COVID instead he stuck with his brand. He did not use the symbolic power that the Presidency and White House offer for most of his term. With the notable exception of holding the 2020 GOP convention at the White House, Trump kept most of his marketing efforts focused on himself not the institution of the Presidency. Instead, his was a Presidency of one unresolved crisis and one ongoing confrontation after another.

Trump's confrontational strategy versus the unelected was only possible because of the rise of the unitary executive and the development of a permanent bureaucracy with its own interests, norms, and cultures as Skowronek et al. (2021) note. Like any good marketer, Trump played to his core audiences. He was not the first politician to market himself by pushing a particular vision of courts and the regulatory state. He made his effort to do so an integral part of his brand. Trump was not fighting bureaucrats; he was fighting the deep state. He was not just fighting liberal activist judges; he was fighting Obama and Clinton judges. Trump placed conservative fare into a sticky brand that emphasized confrontation and disruption. As with all things Trump, this mobilized both his supporters and opponents because of the authentic way in which he expressed his sentiments. While voters have often heard about controversial policies in confrontational terms, Trump made his argument in emotive, highly memorable ways.

Trump used the judiciary as a branding foil by railing against a stream of rulings against his Executive orders by "Obama Judges." He could explain away his substantive failures as a product of having to fight the unelected on their own terms. Trump pointed to the number of judges that he appointed as proof that the promises he had made in 2016 were kept in office. Trump used Republican notions about what the Judiciary should do and how it should do it. This led him to articulate standard Republican positions on these topics and a slew of social issues, but he did so by using sticky branding. His appeals were more resonant with his supporters and opponents. When Trump made a nomination, two ways to look at his choice were through the prisms of policymaking and marketing. Trump's nomination battles were about policy and personality but also about brand building and fundraising. Progressive groups talk about "women's reproductive rights" and "access to health care" or "choice" and argue "women will die" every time the Conservatives produced another judicial or agency head nominee who wants to make changes to abortion policy. On the other hand, the anti-abortion groups market themselves as being "pro-family" and "pro-life" rather than just saying that they are against abortion. Thus, Trump's emotive language was simply a social media optimization of a long-running partisan battle.

The Brett Kavanaugh confirmation hearings provide a case in point. They were a brand building exercise for many different entities. Trump and several Democratic Presidential hopefuls used it as part of their Presidential campaigns, the media used it to grab eyeballs, generate revenue, and interest groups seeking support for their organizations and policies. This was a multiplayer brand battle that happened to play out regarding a Supreme Court vacancy. This was a battle about a variety of policy questions that were aimed at specific highly attentive audiences. One of the highest profile issues in these hearings with that of reproductive rights. These rights were established by court decisions and have become fodder for endless marketing and branding campaigns. When Kavanaugh did not say he would overturn Roe and disqualify himself in the process, these hearings moved into other areas in which the Court has ruled before devolving into a fight about personal characteristics. This battle became a proxy battle over the need for equality of treatment and procedural fairness versus the rights of sexual assault survivors. This debate had been taking place for the last several years on college campuses and had become a cause Celebre among conservatives. It had become a big issue for Trump's opponents given his personal behavior. Trump wanted to "fight back in the press and on the Hill, especially after Kavanaugh showed White House counsel Don McGahn his decades-old calendars showing he had not attended a party where Ford alleged the assault had taken place." Trump realized the nomination might fail in the latest #MeToo frenzy, but if so wanted to go down fighting.[5] This juicy subtext produced hours of media coverage and attracted huge ratings and lots of clicks, but it changed no minds, and nobody considered what impact is all this behavior having on the political system or the citizen's attitudes toward it. The Kavanaugh hearings worked for Trump because it allowed him to again take credit for keeping a campaign promise. It worked for his opponents because they were able to witness against the devil. It worked for all of them as fundraising and brand building opportunities.

Trump's efforts to build a wall across the Southern border provide an example of how he branded a policy issue for the social media age and how a focus on marketing collided with the President's position in the contemporary American system. Much of the border is already fenced or is physically difficult to cross. Immigration is an issue that Trump and the Democrats have both built strong brands around. Trump pitched his wall as part of a clear, coherent narrative in which America was awash in people who should not be here, who engaged in criminal and socially destabilizing activities while driving down American wages, and who should be removed forthwith. Further, his story assumed that the sovereign state of Mexico would somehow fund the wall on request. While proposing a wall was an excellent branding choice, it was questionable as public policy given the cost, extensive public input, and environmental impact processes that are involved when the federal government undertakes a large construction project. National power is also limited in the American system meaning that the President's ability to keep brand promises is likewise limited.

Trump's vision that Mexico would pay for the wall or that Congress would authorize and fully fund its construction so long as the Senate filibuster remained in place was unrealistic. It made for an excellent brand story and Trump made mighty efforts to keep this promise. Like any good marketer, Trump pivoted from one activity to another to show that he was trying to keep this promise. Trump used the power of executive orders and reprogramming funds to build parts of the wall because those actions were within the authority the Presidency holds. Trump shut the government down and declared a national emergency to try to build the wall. The government shutdown was prolonged, visible, and focused public attention on unpaid federal workers and contractors. The matter came to a head when air traffic controllers began calling in sick to work and President Trump reopened the government without getting funding for his wall.

Shortly afterward, Trump tried again by declaring a national emergency to bypass the regular legislative process and build the wall. None of these behaviors got the desired policy result or helped Trump in the short term but they did show his audience that he would go to great lengths to keep his substantive promises while showing that his brand promise of disruption was real. While this did not help him in the short term, or with those outside his target audiences it showed those in his audiences a good faith effort to keep a promise and that Trump's brand promise of disruption was very real. This shutdown and the emergency declaration show how political marketers place a premium on showing that they have kept their promises or at least made a good faith effort to do so. Congressional Democrats, aware of this marketing imperative, would do anything to keep him from building the full wall for political, policy, and, for those members of Congress who represent border communities, constituency concerns. Regardless of if a wall would work or not, the fight over the wall became a brand battle in which Trump's disruptive, nationalistic, branding faced off against the Democrats multicultural, globalist branding. In this case, Trump made a highly visible effort that yielded some results and he highlighted those as they happened and in his 2020 campaign.

The Trump sticky brand, his upset win, and disruptive policies ran headlong into a Democratic coalition that thought its fortunes on the rise with the election of Barack Obama. Trump in person and in brand represented much of what Democrats sought to change about America. For many Democrats and independent voters, Trump's brand, personal traits, and policy choices were either directly threatening or distasteful. The Democrats' 2016 candidate, Hillary Clinton, was well prepared, had her own strong brand and the added element of being the first woman nominated for the Presidency by a major American political party and was well ahead in most polls for weeks prior to Election Day. The contrast between Donald Trump and Hillary Clinton in many ways could not have been any starker. Donald Trump seemed the antithesis of all that Clinton and Obama represented. His victory was stunning to many Democrats, Americans, and people globally.

Trump tried to disrupt elites in both parties and other areas of American life not just in the political realm. Trump also tried to change the GOP and, by doing so, challenged the policy and professional positions of the party's elite. His election was a direct threat to the way in which the American government and politics had evolved to operate thus it is not surprising that he generated significant bureaucratic resistance, negative media coverage, and interest group opposition. Many of the people in these institutions seemed to oppose Trump because he posed a threat to their policy and professional positions. Trump posed a threat to the culture of expertise and the idea of the meritocracy that helped them get into their positions. Instead of expertise, he offered populism as a public policy prescription and disrupted elite networks by bringing people into public life from places other than think tanks, universities, and the bureaucracy. Trump wanted to take their professional positions, wipe out their culture of expertise and elite degrees, and replace it with a populist philosophy and individuals who had either been loyalty to him or had been prominent in the business or media worlds. Not surprisingly, he encountered resistance from every element of the established occupants of these positions. Trump's attempted hostile takeover threatened to displace established politicians, think tanks, and interest groups. It also threatened a slew of policies popular with one or both political parties. If he had marketed a platform branded product line carrying the tag of "Trump versus Everybody," they would have sold well and not exaggerated the situation in Washington.

Trump experienced the same struggles that Bill Clinton and Richard Nixon experienced. Like these two predecessors, Trump won a close electoral victory and was trying to reposition his party. While one could argue that all these candidates won because they articulated positions closer to the positions and values that the voters held than were their opponents. One could argue that they won because Americans like to rotate partisan control of the Presidency. Their defeated opponents focused on more nefarious possibilities and learned that focusing on personal scandal and controversial policies could form the basis of lengthy investigations and marketing campaigns. Nixon resigned before he could be impeached while Clinton and Trump were impeached, tried, and the charges were dismissed. Like Clinton, Trump was the target of accusations and investigations from the moment he claimed victory. Nixon, Clinton, and Trump all won nominating contests against establishment candidates. All won general elections with less than 50% of the popular vote. All three were opposed for reasons of brand style, ideology, policies, and the class of which they presented themselves as being members of. Clinton presented himself as the archetype of a working-class Southern white guy (even appropriating the name Bubba for his marketing purposes), Trump played the role of a New York tycoon and Nixon was presented as an outsider standing up on behalf of the forgotten man to liberals, elites, and communists who hated him because of that. These three differed in brand personality and class presentation from the other recent popular vote loser: George W. Bush. Bush sold himself as someone who would unite the country in the wake of the divisiveness of the Clinton years. He was very much within the class boundaries of the Washington establishment and ran as a restorer of the elite consensus not its challenger to it. He did not question the virtue of elite domination of the country's political and cultural institutions as Mr. Nixon and Mr. Trump had; he took advantage of it. He met the cultural expectations of what the good President should be in ways that Nixon, Clinton, and Trump all failed to do thus attacks on Bush centered on the way in which he came to office at first then competence and personal traits as time moved on. Otherwise, attacks on the Bush Administration focused on Vice President Dick Cheney or Defense Secretary Donald Rumsfeld. Bush's position was strengthened by the onset of an immediate national emergency in the form of the attacks on September 11, 2001. Subsequent events like the failure to find weapons of mass destruction in Iraq (the pretext for the war), revelations about the ways in which the United States had conducted the war on terror were damaging to Bush. Nixon was saddled with an unpopular war that served to activate youthful opposition to it while Clinton and Trump served in office during periods when the United States was not confronted with an immediate national crisis meaning their opponents had no reason to restrain their attacks.

In the Nixon, Clinton, and Trump cases, show the way in which the Revelation, Investigation, Prosecution model that Ginsberg and Shefter (1999)[6] have written about has been used in recent decades. One of the reasons why these three candidates were vulnerable to such attacks is that they were proposing things and representing groups that were outside the political mainstream at the time. A second reason was because they were taking on an elite and policies that were themselves vulnerable. Nixon and Trump both came into office in the wake of social upheavals that had not yet been fully legitimated and institutionalized. Clinton entered office in the opposite situation. Given these environmental conditions fractiousness seems inevitable. The authenticity of Trump's brand and the actions he has taken to keep his promises have accentuated the conflict. Donald Trump sounded like he meant what he said, said things that some considered offensive or scary, and visually showed that he was trying to keep his brand promises. His brand authenticity and omnipresence galvanized his supporters and opponents. In addition to wiping out Obama's accomplishments, Trump seemed determined to wipe out the liberal domestic order that grew from the New Deal to the Reagan years. Internationally, he was arguing with Woodrow Wilson's ideas as much as he was with anyone in contemporary American politics' notions. Trump took on an elite that was vulnerable given its associations with a series of policy failures and environmental changes driven by social media and the internet. Its claims of expertise were being undermined thus it is not surprising that Trump succeeded or that his opponents saw him as an immediate danger.

Trump's audience skewed older, more religious, more rural, and more male. He made in roads with voters of color. Trump's messaging had populists, nationalist racial, and single cultural elements in it that had not been promoted since the 1992 Buchanan campaign. Trump's brand did not just scare the Democrats, it made a lot of Republicans nervous too. Donald Trump challenged the world the liberal Democrats and free trade Republicans built. He also challenged their right to dominate the nation's political life based on their elite credentials. There were large numbers of Americans who yearned for something other than what the elites were offering who were akin to the people who had voted for Ross Perot years ago.[7] Trump's genius as a marketer rested on his ability to identify an underserved market and then position himself as its champion. Donald Trump struggled in Washington because his brand persona represented the first serious threat to business as usual and the dominant political class in both parties since Ronald Reagan came to Washington. Some of the reaction to Trump was about class representation and values. Some of it was about policies. Some of it was about which social class should govern. Much like FDR's opponents seventy years ago, some of the complaints of Trump opponents can be summed up as unhappiness with him being in office. "These sentimens were clearly expressed in Hillary Clinton's statement during the 2016 campaign that half of Trump supporters belonged in a "basket of deplorables" because of their views on social issues. However crudely she was trying to segment the market because she noted that the other half were disappointed with the government and wanted change, but that part of the quote was lost to history once it hit the media just like Mitt Romney's amateur segmentation of the electorate in 2012. The Trump marketing machine lost no time in capitalizing on this mistake, sold t-shirts, and created a graphic entitled "les deplorables" for use at a subsequent rally.[8]

Trump generated a similar reaction to the one that George W. Bush's and Ronald Reagan's Presidencies did from their partisan opponents. Trump also faced an intramural challenge from traditional conservative and moderate Republicans. Trump's sticky branding and his social media optimization deepened the opposition to him, kept it mobilized, and made it willing to latch onto any negative information about him that came along. His opponents routinely complained that his Administration was threatening our democracy. The irony of this is that much of what is being defended as democratic in a policy sense was decided by courts and bureaucracy not Congress and the President. Donald Trump's nationalistic branding can be seen as a form of democratic corrective to the excesses of the administrative state and a narrow elite more than the rise of authoritarianism. It can also be seen as either advocating for enhanced patriotism in which all can share or as a nationalistic pitch reinforcing white supremacy depending on the audience of which one is a member. Trump took advantage of social sorting and microtargeting to build a coalition that was just big and well distributed enough to win in 2016 and barely loses in 2020. It was his sticky omnipresent emotional branding that made this outcome possible.

As Mason (2018) has noted, Americans seem ready to fight with each other over political questions that do not seem worthy of the effort. She argues that this disquiet is the result of sorting. While sorting is certainly part of the equation, it is the emotional branding that really drives it. Donald Trump's effort to achieve brand omnipresence placed our differences in front of us daily. He is the perfect political figure for a country whose politics have turned into the same emotional brand battle with which sports fans are familiar. In sports team branding, our team is good, the other team is bad, it does dirty things, and it cheats, it employs people with bad values, and thus we could never support it. Not surprisingly, the fans of the opposing team often say the same things about our favorite team. The difference between sports and politics is that in one there are always clear outcomes while in the other there hardly ever are. Both involve emotional engagement by a set of spectators based around a coherent narrative that says that athletes fight for team, city, or country and are like us. Trump and his opponents reflect a similar coherent emotional branding that as do sports teams and sporting events. He or they are good or evil and we must win at all costs meaning no compromise is possible. We can see this in the rhetoric that Mr. Trump and his opponents routinely used about each other and in the way in which both presented what could be legitimate causes for argument as either unprecedented or a direct threat to the Republic. Usually, these conflicts were simply the kinds of disputes that the separated American system encourages. Branding combined with effective positioning allows campaigns to stake out positions that could resonate with specific niche audiences even if nobody else supported them. Success in political branding does not assure of political tranquility and social harmony thereafter. The Trump era was a constant brand battle between Mr. Trump and his opponents. Both he and his opponents enjoyed staunch support from some segments of the electorate but neither of them has been able to break out into a dominant market position.

The mediating institutions in a society like media outlets, interest groups, and think tanks all have incentives to segment their audiences, develop emotional brands, and present those to their defined audiences. Many did so in response to the rise of Donald Trump. Trump as a candidate provided hours of must watch content for cable tv news outlets. Trump in the White House was ideal for the branding of interest groups, media outlets, and federal agencies (internally and externally). Instead of the Washington Post or New York Times simply being subscription-based media, they marketed themselves as guardians of democracy and argue that their members (not subscribers) are supporting their "mission." For the mainstream media, there are now lots of more ideologically based branded competitors who have lower costs than do they. While Democrats like to complain about the Fox News Channel with its "fair and balanced, we report you decide" branding, their complaints omit the host of other conservative media platforms that have appeared in recent years like Breitbart, the Daily Caller, Alex Jones' Infowars, and many others that attract focused but engaged audiences and all of which gave Donald Trump a shot to pitch niche audiences while a candidate and hold their loyalty as President.[9] Given the proliferation of media outlets and avalanche of content, it is not surprising that people see one version or another of the same event depending on what audience segments in which they reside. Nor is surprising that the marketers are so focused on keeping their market position by differentiating themselves from each other via the use of distinctive emotions and brand promises.

Trump's campaign and election spurred a great deal of interest in media products and a need for branded differentiation and segmentation of these entities. Donald Trump's election allowed news organizations to develop specific branding around their "mission" as the New York Times put it or to slogans on their mastheads like the Washington Post did when it added "Democracy Dies in the Darkness" to its masthead. Mr. Trump was subscription, ratings, and advertising rate gold. Especially for legacy media like newspapers, covering Trump was excellent for business but it was also good for cable news outlets seeking a way to keep people from cutting the cord and for MSNBC and CNN to develop a stronger position vis-a-vis their main competitor and long-running rating champion: Fox News. Not that Fox was upset. It continually played up its ties to the Trump Administration and frequently noted that the President himself was a regular viewer. Trump appeared regularly as a topic because people could not get enough stories about him. This was particularly true in the 2018 midterm election and the amount of free coverage Trump received was equal to about two billion dollars of paid media coverage according to the *New York Times*[10]. Because Trump publicly disdained the media and routinely pointed them out at his events, it is not surprising that he has received significantly more negative media coverage than have his opponents or most of his Presidential predecessors. This was not much of a problem for Mr. Trump or really for most Republicans because they extensively use the press as a straw man and complain about media bias against them.

Trump revived interest in the NBC weekly tv show "Saturday Night Live" and gave a host of late night comics material so much so that it became difficult to distinguish one from another. The audiences for these shows do not overlap with the Trump target audiences nor are they based in the same physical locations as those in which Trump voters live so these are further examples of segment reinforcing not society making media activities. Trump has energized opponents in the interest group universe especially the ACLU an organization that wanted to increase its emotional pitches to the public as its leader Anthony Romero made plain by saying "There's a lot we learned from the NRA," Romero said. "If we could be a little less legalistic and focus less on the brain and more on the heart and trying to change the culture, we thought we would have a bigger impact."[11] They pushed the Trump Administration in court at every turn and did the activist training that they never had previously.[12] This was good for business even if having Trump in the White House might not have been good for their policy preferences. Their activities could have been incorporated into Trump's branding and helped his reelection chances too. The group has pushed Democrats to take positions on controversial issues aspects of its agenda including voting rights for prisoners. Sure enough, some presented this was presented as arguing for voting rights for the Boston Marathon bomber and Donald Trump was all over that idea[13]. The themes and issues that the ACLU works with resonate with its customers but these and the ACLU's customers can bolster Donald Trump's brand too. Trump's election created a situation in which a variety of commercial entities have thought it important to signal their audiences through branding and advertising what their position on Mr. Trump's Presidency was and Mr. Trump showed those positions to his audiences in a big to show how awful the other folks are and how much under siege his voters and he are.

Donald Trump has shown that a sticky brand, an emotional brand that focuses on a series of niches and niche issues can achieve omnipresence and win an election. He has yet to show that a candidate or campaign that relies on these techniques can attract repeat business or build a durable political movement that consistently wins. The sticky branding strategy builds audience awareness of the brand and gets people to try the product. This is true for any kind of marketer that adopts it. The brand's promises must be kept, and the product must work as advertised to attract repeat customers. The way that Trump's campaign distributed and built awareness for its brand and then attracted first time business can be said to be a success because Trump won the election. The lingering question is does a brand have the capability to attract enough repeat business to build durable brand loyalty? Throughout his campaign and term in the White House, Trump built deep brand loyalty in his target audiences but also drove some traditional GOP audiences, like upper income college educated whites toward the Democratic Party. This shift cost Republicans their House majority in 2018 and put their Senate majority in jeopardy in 2020. The shift gave Trump a tougher road to gain reelection than might have been the case for a different President who had presided over such a similarly strong economy. The question of Trump's branding and the way it appealed to working-class voters raises a question about the costs of this as well as its benefits. If Trump had attracted more working-class voters of all races while holding a lot of moderate college educated whites, then the strategy could be said to have been a success. If the audience attracted is smaller than the audience repelled then, even if the brand has considerable potency with the smaller audience, building it in ways that only resonated with them would be shown to have been an error. The outcome of the 2020 election shows this point.

Trump's emphasis on showing that promises made have been kept was consistent with the way in which marketers use branding. COVID caused a huge marketing problem for him because it put his brand promise of excellent managerial skills to the test, and he came up short. While Trump's most loyal customers continued to support him, and some others voted against Joe Biden more than voted for him, his substantive and stylistic failures during the pandemic made Joe Biden into an attractive option for many who usually vote Republican. Branded politicians the world over have suffered this fate when they failed to keep their brand promises. This is a cautionary tale for anyone using a brand strategy: failure to keep promises means losing market share. This problem is particularly pronounced for American Presidents because the system's separation of powers makes failure more likely than success. It is difficult for branded Presidents to delivery on policy or promises of national unity. While Trump's class-based branding mitigated some of this strategic problem, the problem itself remained because even casual voters want reassurance and results in a crisis. Instead, they got a confrontation between Trump and the media, blame placed on foreign, state, and local governments, and an ever-shifting analysis for hours on end on live television by Trump of what was happening and why it was happening. While this helped Trump remains omnipresent during the COVID crisis, it did not assure that people liked what they saw or that more people would be attracted than driven away by Trump's performance during this time. if he was making the establishment uncomfortable in visible ways? He was delivering on his brand promises to his core audiences. Thus, continual conflict helped Mr. Trump keep his core supporters on board and his brand omnipresent.

Trump's success produced disquiet in the Republican Party but also put it into power. Winning the 2016 election papered over a fight regarding what the party's product should be. A similar fight is underway in the Democratic Party. Many on the left wing of the Democratic Party expect that their ideas and candidates will become dominant because of demography but this is not a consensus position in the party or the country. The moderate wing of the party tends to emphasize things like the ways in which House districts are drawn or the varying turnout levels in different social groups to explain why this is less likely than it might appear. They tend to emphasize that, without winning swing districts in 2018, there would be no Democratic House majority and that, just as prior to the 1972 election, a lurch to the left would be a road to electoral disaster. The Democratic Super Tuesday outcomes in which older voters participated at a much higher rate than did younger voters showed that Donald Trump was on to something in his targeting of older voters. The Democrats have struggled to attract much of the white working-class vote in recent elections as well. Despite their win in 2020, the Democrats are still faced with the prospect of a Trump campaign appealing to specific portions of the African American and Hispanic audiences all of which present the party with a series of policy, branding, and targeting dilemmas. Even worse, Mr. Trump's election presented an existential threat to some Democratic constituencies and many Democratic policy priorities. Thus, presenting him as the devil in Democratic marketing allowed the party to attempt to avoid defining its own ideological position. Presenting Trump as the devil postponed a series of battles over public policy that burst into the open in the 2020 primaries and continues as of this writing. The campaign to brand Trump as the devil was successful because most Democrats proclaimed that they would vote for whomever emerged victorious from their primary process in 2020 and have continued to respond to negative messaging about Donald Trump into the Biden Administration.

Some, like Trump advisor Steven Bannon, argued that one of Trump's goals was to encourage the Democrats to move further to the left because by doing so they would make the GOP candidates in general and, especially the Trumpian ones, look more moderate by comparison[14]. The Republican Party got this strategy to work down ticket in 2020. Trump, on the other hand was running as an incumbent against an opponent who was well known, perceived as a centrist, and who stressed his personal decency. A lot of progressive Democrats might not have been thrilled with their nominee, but he sold with other Democrats and swing voters If politics is a choice between competing products, it makes sense for a political marketer to try to position their offering as close to the bulk of the customers interests and ideology as possible. It likewise makes sense to as closer to where the bulk of the customers are and to try to encourage the other party to move away from the relative middle. Because Trump had driven away so many tradition Republicans and independents who often voted for Republicans and because Biden presented himself as a normal guy with moderate Democratic views, he was positioned closer to the center of the electorate than was Trump in 2020. Trump had gotten a warning in 2018 when his party lost control of the House of Representatives to a Democratic Party running on the notion that they would hold Donald Trump accountable and try to do something about healthcare and climate change, but he stuck to his brand despite the shellacking his party took. Democrats also targeted specific audiences with tales of Trump's bad personal behavior or the negative nature of his policies in areas of concern to them. This meant that the Democrats won elections partly because people voted against Trump not for their agenda. This meant that there were a variety of kinds of Democrats just as there are multiple kinds of Republicans. These splits appear in several ways. It took the Democrats a while to decide to impeach Donald Trump and while few Republicans supported the first impeachment, they took the opportunity to state their objections to Mr. Trump while it was occurring.

The visible contrast between the demographic, geographic, and psychographic composition of the Democratic and Republican caucuses in the House of Representatives strikingly shows how segmentation, emotional branding and lowered barriers to entry are reshaping American politics in a way that is moving the two parties further apart. They now have radically distinct issue positions, and this makes consensus difficult to achieve. Simply, the parties are not trying to appeal to the same audience segments. As a result, in many parts of the country, people are exposed to one type of candidate ideologically or another more than they are to competitive elections. Moving forward, a reasonable person might ask if it is possible to get the country back onto an even keel or if strife is our future at least in the shorter term. While much of the country and the Congress might agree about many things, the way in which brands are built, distributed, and stood by must be stood by makes it likely that strife will be the order of the day for some time to come. The same can be said of the way in which strong emotional and sticky brands generate strong public responses.

The Trump Presidency era shows that politics has become an all-out brand battle. Trump's opponents dug in for all-out confrontation from the moment he was elected just as Biden's did once Trump departed. Some of their activities even turned into brands of their own like the "resistance" and the Women's March (which had a logo in the form of a specific pink hat). Such engagement and merchandising can be great for business as conservative entrepreneurs have long shown but its impact on civility in American public life or on the system's ability to function is much more dubious. During the Trump years, the Democrats and their affiliated interest groups repeatedly launched lawsuits in friendly jurisdictions to block Trump's Executive Orders and to develop a pretext to remove him from office (the emoluments lawsuits). The Democrats vigorously fought back on against Trump a host of policy questions. Trump, ever brand conscious, fought back and often instigated confrontations instead of trying to build consensus. Each side accused the other of staking out positions purely for political gain not policy preference. Both could be right about that. Identifying an audience and serving its needs are key parts of branding. The rise of competing brands at the national political level, in a separated political system, has reduced the ability of the two parties to cooperate in controversial areas. Instead, they use controversial issues to run fundraising and mobilization campaigns. Political marketing gives the political producer the incentive to find problems to solve and new battles to fight. Political marketing, branding, and segmentation emphasize division over unity. Donald Trump was the embodiment of all these trends but so too were some of his opponents provides for emphasizing division over unity. Given his unique gifts as a marketer and communicator, it is not surprising that his opponents have mobilized En masse against him. This all-out brand battle that we have witnessed for the last several years raises the question of how this results in a new governing consensus or any at all in Washington. The Biden and Trump Administrations show one possibility in that they were elected along with a narrow Congressional majority, but both tried to govern like they had won a huge electoral mandate. Doing this is consistent with branded politics but it means that the political marketer can show delivery and that promises made have been kept. As Trump and Biden have learned the hard way, getting things done in a hotly contested, branded, environment is not easily accomplished.

A lot of Americans find the whole thing to be exhausting. Some might have voted for Biden because he promised an end to Trump's brand omnipresence and emotional sticky branding in the White House thus bringing back normality. Others might have consumed more partisan and infotainment media to deal with Trump's marketing. These Americans well could have arrived at the conclusion that Trump was either wonderful or anathema depending on which information bubble they were in. Still others, mostly in the political middle, might have felt their concerns were totally ignored as both parties catered to their hard-core audiences. We saw the politicization of everything from flags to sports to food during the Trump years. We saw incessant demands that people be on the red or blue team politically. It is hard to see how this situation resolves quickly or well. Like Ronald Reagan, Donald Trump is a uniquely talented political communicator but unlike Reagan it is not obvious that there is a real movement supporting him.[15] The techniques Trump used to win the election and the techniques his young progressive rivals are using show that the amount of ideological diversity represented in the country's political institutions might be broadening. This combined with the incentives provided by branding and marketing to speak in emotional terms to specific audiences often using niche issues is not a formula for building social consensus. On the other hand, when Americans are exposed to each other in person, they find more commonalities than what the brand world of politics indicates is the case.[16] The misperceptions about others that branding, and segmentation are causing seem to be worse given the more education one has and the more one pays attention to the news.[17] Trump and his opponents embodied the problem because they focus on structured emotional narratives and environments. All events are fitted into the brand and presented in a way that is aimed at keeping people engaged but the realities of life in America differ from the brand stories.[18] Americans assume more people in the other party hold extreme views than do. This is worsened by the fact that those who share political material on social media have more negative perceptions about the opposite party than those who do not share.[19] While this shows that segmentation is a key tool through which a brand can be built, it also shows that this tactic can cause more disquiet than exists as seems to be the case in the United States at present while this works for marketing the parties and candidates, it is causing people to perceive more disagreement in society than exists.[20]

The Trump years show that commercial marketing techniques have fully entered and reshaped American politics. As the Trump Administration shows, knowing how to use these techniques does not assure that the marketers using them will be good at dealing with Congress, leading the bureaucracy, or fulfilling the symbolic leadership aspect of being President. Branding incentivizes certain qualities like telling an emotional story and continually adding to it, scripting appropriate visuals and events, and keeping promises regardless of what other audiences think of them. This latter point is not a big deal for corporate marketing, but it is for politics because one of the conflict points between political and commercial branding is that eventually the successful political leader will have to compromise because of the structure of the American system or depend on Executive Orders to get things done and will struggle to fulfill the symbolic role that the Presidency occupies in American political life. Someone like Donald Trump or a Democrat equivalent who used a combination of sticky branding, built an omnipresent emotional brand, and focused on presenting it only to their key audiences might not be the key to long-term political and policy success or promote domestic tranquility even if it can sometimes win elections.

Trump focused on the Electoral College because it was possible for him to find enough support on a state-by-state basis for his offering that he could win. It narrowly worked in 2016 and narrowly failed in 2020. Trump's strategy was likely to produce close elections because his stick brand only appealed to a few audiences in specific places. That Americans were told prior to both elections that Trump had little chance of winning set the stage for the disquiet that happened in the aftermath both times. Many people felt his 2016 election was either illegitimate because he did not win the popular vote or because foreign interference had produced his victory. They tried to overturn the results through lawsuits, lobbying state legislators, trying to encourage faithless electors, and raising a challenge in Congress on the day that body met to certify the results. Donald Trump would replicate these efforts but take them to a higher level in 2020 using sticky, emotional branding, and the brand omnipresence strategy. Trump developed a platform brand for the effort "#stopthesteal" and organized a large rally just before the legislative session to certify the Electoral College results began.[21] He had marketed the idea that the election was stolen from him for two months by the time January 6th dawned and he encouraged people to attend the rally by saying that it would be "wild."[22] None of Trump's claims about electoral fraud were based on facts nor was it possible that the Vice President could have kept Trump in office by not certifying the state-level election results. Trump's rally drew supporters from across the country and his rhetoric during his speech that day was highly emotive. Trump's marketing campaign cast doubt on the incoming Administration's legitimacy, was partly responsible for the deadly events of January 6th but also raised a hefty sum of money that Trump presented as being used in his legal defense fund.[23] This too was a fiction because most of the money raised went to retire his campaign debt.[24] The entire episode shows how consumer marketing techniques can be used for unethical ends Trump raised a lot of money and kept himself in the public eye through this effort, but it generated a situation that turned both violent and lethal. It eventually led to Trump being banned from Twitter and Facebook meaning that they severely damaged his direct-to-consumer marketing operation.

In the end, more people voted against Trump than voted for him meaning he lost but the Republican Party did not lose at other levels of government. Trump's political demise reinvigorated the battle over the

Republican Party's brand, product, and core audiences. Trump brought new energy and audiences to the Republican Party but did so at the cost of driving away other audiences. One of the things that his omnipresence strategy did was to make all public issues about Donald Trump in some fashion. His departure from the White House and the onset of one of the most liberal policy administrations since the New Deal has the potential to make politics more about policy and ideology than about personality and brand omnipresence moving forward. The closeness of the 2020 election became the fodder for a Trump marketing campaign, set in motion a battle over the Republican Party's product, brand, and audiences, and a fight over the rules under which future elections will be conducted. Even after the election, with a chance to keep full Republican control of the Senate, Donald Trump could not stop focusing on his own circumstances and promoting his own brand. Trump's loyalty was, in the end, to Trump first, last, and always.

Once Joe Biden was able to be nominated because of his victory in the 2020 South Carolina primary, it was logical that the Democrats did so and that a lot of establishment Republicans rallied around him through vehicles like the Lincoln Project and the #NeverTrump movement.[25] Joe Biden promised a restoration of the old order culturally and stylistically even if he had to make policy concessions to the Democrats' progressive wing in the process. His election has had the effect of keeping established elites in their positions. It also had the effect of solidifying the direct-to-consumer marketing model that Trump pioneered. The Biden Administration has repeatedly argued that because its policies are popular with the American public at a national level, the Congress that represents Americans at the state and more local level should go along with his proposals. As it always has, political marketing and branding encourage people to think about politics in immediate, highly structured ways that might lead to outcomes that they might not support a few years later but that too can be used as part of a future political marketing campaign.

NOTES

1. Breitbart. "Mike Bloomberg Tells Fox News 'I'm Not Upset with Many Trump Policies, 'Just the Way, He's Doing It.' *Breitbart.* March 3, 2020 https://www.breitbart.com/2020-election/2020/03/03/mike-bloomb erg-tells-fox-news-im-not-upset-with-many-trump-policies-just-the-way-hes-doing-it/, accessed March 3, 2020.

2. Aaron Blake. "Donald Trump Says He Would Have Won a Popular-Vote Election. And He Could Be Right." Washington Post. November 15. 2016. https://www.washingtonpost.com/news/the-fix/wp/2016/11/14/trump-lost-the-popular-vote-that-doesnt-mean-he-would-have-lost-a-popular-vote-election/?utm_term=.ec4e279ec653, accessed August 1, 2019.
3. Charlie Cooper. "Boris Johnson's U.S. Election Lesson." *Politico.* November 9, 2020. https://www.politico.eu/article/boris-johnson-us-election-lesson/amp/?__twitter_impression=true.
4. For an in-depth discussion of the phenomenon see Jeremi Suri *the Impossible Presidency. (2017).*
5. Howard Kurtz. "Trump Team Held Back Dirt on Kavanaugh Accuser, New Book Says." *Fox News* July 8, 2019 (https://www.foxnews.com/politics/trump-team-held-back-dirt-on-kavanaugh-accuser-new-book-says, accessed July 15, 2019).
6. Ginsberg and Shefter (1999).
7. Zito and Todd (2018, pp. 49–72).
8. Debbie Encalada. "Donald Trump Is Now Selling 'Deplorable Shirts'." Complex. Com. September 20, 2019 (https://www.complex.com/style/2016/09/donald-trump-selling-deplorable-t-shirts, accessed July 9 2018.
9. For an in-depth examination of the role Breitbart in particular play in Trump's rise see Michael Kirk and Gabrielle Schonder" Interviews with Stephen K. Bannon." *PBS Frontline.* Zero Tolerance." Interviews conducted March 17 and September 19, 2019. https://www.pbs.org/wgbh/frontline/interview/steve-bannon-2/, accessed March 5, 2020.
10. Jim Tankersley and Ben Casselman. "Did a Tax Increase Tucked into Trump's Tax Cut Come Back to Bite Republicans?" *New York Times.* November 19, 2018. https://www.nytimes.com/2018/11/19/us/pol itics/trump-tax-cut-republican.html, accessed August 2, 2019.
11. Marin Cogan. "The Twilight of Free Speech Liberalism." *New Republic.* July 16, 2018, https://newrepublic.com/article/148873/free-speech-lib eralism-aclu, accessed July 9, 2019.
12. Ibid.
13. Christopher Cadelago. "How the ACLU Is Setting Up Trump for a Field Day in 2020. The Group Is Deploying Hundreds of People to Get Democratic Candidates on Video Taking Positions on Hot-Button Topics Like Felon Voting." *Politico.* May 5, 2019. (https://www.politico.com/story/2019/05/05/aclu-democrats-trump-2020-civil-liberties-1300563, accessed July 9, 2019.
14. Wolff (2018, p. 310).
15. Zito and Todd (2018, p. 10).

16. Amanda Ripley. "Democrats and Republicans Are Very Bad at Guessing Each Other's Beliefs." *Washington Post*, June 26. 2019 https://www.was hingtonpost.com/opinions/democrats-and-republicans-are-very-bad-at-guessing-each-others-beliefs/2019/06/21/bcd061b2-92c7-11e9-b58a-a6a9afaa0e3e_story.html?utm_term=.e5967af7936d, accessed July 9, 2019.
17. Ibid.
18. Daniel Yudkin, Stephen Hawkins and Tim Dixon. "The Perception Gap: How False Impressions Are Pulling Americans Apart." More in Common Hidden Tribes Project. June 2019. https://perceptiongap.us/.accessed. July 9, 2019.
19. Ibid.
20. Ibid.
21. Rebecca Ballhaus, Joe Palazzolo and Andrew Ristuccia. "Trump and His Allies Set the Stage for Riot Well Before January 6th." *Wall Street Journal*. January 8, 2021, https://www.wsj.com/articles/trump-and-his-allies-set-the-stage-for-riot-well-before-january-6-11610156283
22. Ibid.
23. Josh Dawsey and Michelle Ye, He Lee. "Trump Raises More Than $170 Million Appealing on False Election Claims." *Washington Post*. December 1, 2020. https://www.washingtonpost.com/politics/trump-raises-more-than-150-million-appealing-to-false-election-claims/2020/11/30/82e 922e6-3347-11eb-afe6-e4dbee9689f8_story.html.
24. Ibid.
25. For an in-depth discussion of the 2020 Trump and Biden brand battle see Cosgrove and Shrader in Moufahim, 2021.

REFERENCES

Bachner, Jennifer and Benjamin Ginsberg. *What Washington Gets Wrong: The Unelected Officials Who Actually Run the Government and Their Misconceptions About the American People*. Prometheus, 2016.

Ginsberg, Benjamin and Martin Shefter. *Politics by Other Means: Politicians, Prosecutors and the Press from Watergate to Whitewater*. W.W. Norton, 1999.

Mason, Liliana. *Uncivil Agreement: How Politics Became Our Identity*. University of Chicago Press, 2018.

Skowronek, Stephen, John A. Dearborn and Desmond King. *Phantoms of a Beleaguered Republic: The Deep State and the Unitary Executive*. Oxford University Press, 2021.

Wolff, Michael. *Fire and Fury: Inside the Trump White House*. Henry Holt and Company, 2018.

Zito, Salena and Brad Todd. *The Great Revolt Crown Forum*, 2018.

BIBLIOGRAPHY

Adams, Scott. *Win Bigly: Persuasion in a World Where Facts Don't Matter.* Penguin, 2017.
Bachner, Jennifer and Benjamin Ginsberg. *What Washington Gets Wrong: The Unelected Officials Who Actually Run the Government and Their Misconceptions about the American People.* Prometheus, 2016.
Barber, Benjamin. *Consumed.* W.W. Norton, 2008.
Bellah, Robert N. *Habits of the Heart.* Harper Collins, 1985.
Bendix, Rheinhard. *Kings or People: Power and the Mandate to Rule.* University of California Press, 1980
Bernays, Edward (Ed.). *The Engineering of Consent.* University of Oklahoma Press, 1955.
———. (Introduction by Mark Crispin Miller). *Propaganda.* Ig Publishing, 2004.
———. *Public Relations.* OU Press, 2013.
Bishop, Bill. *The Big Sort* Mariner Books, 2009.
Brooks, David. *Bobos in Paradise. The New Upper Class and How They Got There.* Simon and Schuster, 2001.
Carnes, Nicholas. *White Collar Government.* University of Chicago Press, 2013.
Cosgrove, Kenneth. *Branded Conservatives.* New York: Peter Lang, 2007.
———. "GOP Brand Refresh." In Jaime Gillies (ed.) *Political Marketing in the 2016 US Presidential Election.* Palgrave, (August, 2017)
———. "2016:The Emotional Brand Wins." In Darren Liliker, Daniel Jackson and Anastasia Veneti (eds.) *US Election Analysis 2016- Media, Voters and the Campaign.* The Center for the Study of Journalism, Culture and Community, the University of Bournemouth (United Kingdom). November 2016.

———. "Donald Trump, the Brand, the Disjunctive Leader and Brand Ethics." In Jaime Gilles (ed.). *Political Marketing in the 2020 U.S. Presidential Election*. Palgrave, 2020.

——— and Nathan Shrader. "Political Branding in the USA Election of 2020." In Mona Moufahim (ed.) *Political Branding in Turbulent Times*. Palgrave-Macmillan, 2021.

Coppins, Mackay. *The Wilderness*. Little, Brown, 2015.

Eatwell, Roger and Matthew Goodwin. *National Populism: The Revolt Against Liberal Democracy*. Pelican, 2018.

Edsall, Thomas and Mary Byrne Edsall. *Chain Reaction: The Impact of Race, Rights and Taxes on American Politcs*. W.W. Norton, 1991.

Fournier, Ron, Douglas Sosnik and Matthew Dowd. *Applebee's America: How Successful Politicial, Business and Religious Leaders Connect with the New American Community*. Simon and Schuster, 2006.

Ginsberg, Benjamin and Martin Shefter. *Politics by Other Means: Politicians, Prosecutors and the Press from Watergate to Whitewater*. W.W. Norton, 1999.

Green, Joshua. *Devil's Bargain: Steve Bannon, Donald Trump and the Storming of the US Presidency*. Penguin, 2017.

Greenberg, David. *Republic of Spin*. New York: Norton, 2016

Jardina, Ashley. *White Identity Politics*. Cambridge University Press, 2019.

Hall-Jamieson, Kathleen. *Packaging the Presidency: A History and Criticism of Presidential Campaign Advertising* (3rd Edition) Oxford University Press, 1996.

Hall-Jamieson. Kathleen. *Packaging The Presidency*. Oxford University Press, 2006.

Hitchcock William. *The Age of Eisenhower: America and the World in the 1950's*. New York. Simon and Schuster, 2018.

Issenberg, Sasha. *The Victory Lab: The Secret Science of Winning Campaigns*. Crown, 2013.

Pearlman, Jeff. *Football for a Buck: The Crazy Rise and Even Crazier Demise of the USFL*. Mariner Books, 2018.

Judis, John B. *The Populist Explosion* Columbia Global Reports, 2016.

———. *The Nationalist Revival: Trade, Immigration and the Revolt Against Globalization* Columbia Global Reports, 2018.

Lewandowski, Corey R. and David N. Bossie. *Let Trump Be Trump: The Inside Story of His Rise to the Presidency*. Center Street, 2017.

Liebovich, Mark. *This Town*. New York: Penguin, 2013.

Mark, Margaret and Carol Pearson. *The Hero and the Outlaw*. McGraw-Hill Education, 2001.

Manheim, Jarol B. *The Death of A Thousand Cuts*. Routledge, 2000.

Mason, Liliana. *Uncivil Agreement: How Politics Became Our Identity*. Chicago. University of Chicago Press, 2018.

Miller, Jeremy. *Sticky Branding: 12.5 Principles To Stand Out, Attract Customers and Grow an Incredible Brand*. Page Two Books, 2015.

Mills, C. Wright. *The Power Elite*. Oxford University Press (Reprint Edition), 1975.

Murray, Charles. *Coming Apart; The State of White America*. Crown Forum, 2012.

Neustadt, Richard. *The Presidential Power: The Politics of Leadership from Roosevelt to Reagan*. Free Press, 1991.

Norris, Pippa and Ronald Inglehart. *Cultural Backlash: Trump, Brexit and Authoritarian Populism*. Cambridge University Press, 2019.

O'Brien, Timothy L. *Trump Nation*. Open Road Media, 2015.

Pollack, Joel B. and Larry Schweikart. *How Trump Won: The Inside Story of A Revolution*. Regnery Publishing, 2017.

Postman, Neil. *Amusing Ourselves to Death: Public Discourse in the Age of Show Business*. Viking Penguin, 1985.

Reis, Al and Jack Trout. *Positioning: The Battle For Your Mind*. McGraw-Hill, 2001.

Schier, Steven E. and Todd E. Eberly. *The Trump Presidency: Outsider in the Oval Office*. Rowman and Littlefield, 2017.

Sims, Cliff. *Team of Vipers: My 500 Extrodinary Days in the Trump White House*. Thomas Dunne Books, 2019

Skocpol, Theda. *Diminished Democracy: From Membership to Management in American Civic Life* . University of Oklahoma Press, 2013.

Skowronek, Stephen. *The Politics Presidents Make*. Belknap Press, 1997.

———. *Presidential Leadership in Political Time: Reprise and Reappraisal* (2nd edition). University Press of Kansas, 2011.

Skowronek, Stephen, John Dearborn, and Desmond King *Phantoms of a Beleagured Republic*. Oxford University Press, 2021.

Sosnik, Douglass B., Matthew Dowd and Ron Fournier. *Applebees America: How Successful Political Business and Religious Leaders Connect with the New American Community*. Simon and Schuster, 2007.

Suri, Jermi. *The Impossible Presidency*. Hachette Book Group, 2017.

Turow, Joseph. *Breaking Up America*. Chicago: University of Chicago Press, 2007.

———. *Niche Envy*. MIT Press, 2008.

Trump, Donald J. and Tony Schwartz. *The Art of the Deal*. Ballantine Books, 2009.

———. *Great Again*. Threshold Editions, 2015.

Wolff, Michael. *Fire and Fury: Inside the Trump White House*. New York: Henry Holt and Company, 2018.

Woodward, Bob. *Fear: Trump in the White House*. New York: Simon and Schuester, 2018.

Zyman, Sergio. *The End of Marketing as We Know It*. Harper Business, 2000.
Zito, Salena and Brad Todd *The Great Revolt* Crown Forum, 2018.
Zyman, Sergio and Armin Brott. *The End of Advertising as we Know It* Wiley, 2002.

Index

Lightning Source UK Ltd.
Milton Keynes UK
UKHW042037021122
411532UK00002B/54